growing fruit & vegetables

growing fruit & vegetables

The complete practical guide to kitchen gardening, from planning and planting to care and maintenance

Richard Bird

HERMES HOUSE

This edition published by Hermes House in 2003

Hermes House
is an imprint of Anness Publishing Limited
Hermes House,
88–89 Blackfriars Road,
London SE1 8HA

A CIP catalogue record for this book is available from the British Library.

Publisher: Joanna Lorenz
Executive Editor: Caroline Davison
Designer: Ruth Hope
Production Controller: Ann Childers
Illustrator: Liz Pepperell

Previously published as *The Kitchen Garden Book*

2 3 4 5 6 7 8 9 10

Publishers' note: In the United States, the burning of plants or bulbs (if they are diseased, for example) is prohibited.

Page One **A bay tree clipped into a spiral.**
Page Two **Vegetable plots can be decorative as well as productive.**
Page Four **Brick paths divide up this large informal vegetable garden.**

contents

introduction

ABOVE **Retaining a kitchen garden with dwarf box hedging is the ideal way to keep the area neat and tidy. Here, sunflowers add the perfect decorative touch to the garden.**

BELOW **These terracotta forcers are used to hurry vegetables such as rhubarb into growth. They also serve an ornamental purpose, dressing up what can be a dull vegetable plot.**

At the beginning of the 21st century it may seem something of an anachronism that people in the so-called civilized world should be growing their own vegetables. Not only are they readily available from supermarkets, but there is also so much else to do with our time. But take a look at people who do grow their own produce and you will usually find healthy, happy souls who enjoy good food – there's more to it than saving a little money.

In the days when spending a few pennies on seed saved much more at the greengrocers, growing vegetables used to be the cheap option, but this is no longer necessarily true, particularly if you include your own time in the equation.

People's reasons for growing vegetables and fruit vary widely, but nearly all vegetable gardeners would say that the crops you grow yourself are far superior to those you buy. There is, of course, an element of one-upmanship about this, but this is far from the whole story.

Above all, vegetables from your own garden are fresh. They can be in the ground one minute and in the pot the next. Once you have tasted fresh vegetables you realize the vast difference between them and the glossy, but days-old ones in the supermarkets. Mass-produced vegetables have been bred to different criteria from those that we grow in the garden. Greengrocers and supermarkets want fruit that will arrive at the shops looking fresh and undamaged, and so the produce has tough skins, which also give them a long shelf life. Fruit and vegetables from the garden do not have to travel.

Farmers want to harvest a crop all at once, so it is important that all the peas, for example, are ready for picking on the same day. Gardeners, on the other hand, want the reverse – they want as long a season as possible. Supermarkets want all the vegetables they stock to be the same size and to look the same, but gardeners, provided they are not interested in exhibiting, are not so fussy.

At the bottom of the list of qualities that are demanded by shops and supermarkets, and frequently not on the list at all, is taste. Customers go back to buy carrots every week without any thought to what the last batch tasted like. Gardeners, however, have a wide choice of carrot seeds, many selected for flavour, and they can choose the variety with the taste they like best.

Another advantage, allied to taste, is that gardeners know what has been put on the food. Today, gardeners choose to use few chemical sprays and powders, but crops bought from supermarkets have been doused in an ever-increasing number of compounds to make sure that, among other things, they come to the shops in a totally unblemished state. Gardeners can know that their food is completely untainted by chemicals.

Garden vegetables are the ultimate in convenience food. Admittedly, you have to wash them, but they sit there just waiting to be harvested when you want them. You may need only one stalk of celery, so why go and buy a whole bunch, when you can quickly cut one stalk from the garden? This is much more economical and saves on time spent shopping. Excess produce can be frozen or stored, and used when you need it.

Kitchen gardens can be decorative, too. Even a simple garden with everything grown in rows or blocks is likely to be attractive, but when they are planted as part of a potager, vegetables can be arranged in even more decorative ways.

ABOVE **Here, pink-flowered chives, red lettuce and purple cabbage as well as fennel and parsley create an informal vegetable garden.**

Lastly, as well as having healthy food, the gardener gets plenty of exercise and fresh air. There is also a sense of closeness to nature. A cliché perhaps, but there is still something fundamental about getting your hands dirty and listening to the birds as you work.

That is the end of the philosophy of the kitchen garden. From this point the book becomes a practical one. It concentrates on describing the techniques required to produce an attractive and productive kitchen garden. With this book as a guide you will soon not only be growing your own produce but acquiring a whole set of skills, many of them traditional ones, handed down over the centuries, and others that are the result of modern experience.

designing a kitchen garden

Before you even contemplate putting a spade in the soil, it is a very useful exercise to sit down and think about what you are trying to achieve in your kitchen garden. Firstly, you need to consider whether you have the time, space and conditions to achieve what you want.

The design of a kitchen garden can then be approached in two ways. It can be either purely functional, in which case you simply have to ensure that the layout and planting of the garden will produce the largest possible volume of produce. Alternatively, you might like to adopt a more decorative approach, orchestrating the design so that the garden is pleasing to look at as well as productive.

There is also a variety of more technical considerations to take into account. For example, how you are going to get the best out of your plot? Will there be any limitations to your plans caused by lack of space, problem soils and difficult weather conditions, and how can the overall layout help to prevent the influx of pests and diseases? Once you have thought through questions such as these, you can start having fun and planning your garden in greater detail.

RIGHT **This is a traditional kitchen garden, with vegetables neatly lined up in rows. Although it is autumn, there will be plenty of vegetables in season over the next few months.**

There are several factors to consider when planning the overall design of a kitchen garden. Many of these relate to more specific issues and are dealt with later in more detail but are mentioned here in a general context.

What do you want?

The first priority is to work out what you want. Do you want a productive garden that will provide food for a large family or for selling or giving away? If so, you will probably be planting varieties of vegetables in bulk, which reduces the possibility of using intricate patterns. If, however, you are thinking in terms of a decorative feature, with the vegetable crops as a secondary consideration, you are going to need a different approach to laying out the kitchen garden. What do you want to include? Are you hoping to grow fruit and herbs as well as vegetables? This kind of decision will influence how much space you need and how you use it.

Do you want a greenhouse? If so, is it going to be within your kitchen garden or will it be tucked away, out of sight in a corner of the garden? What are you going to do with items such as sheds, cold frames and compost bins? Someone with a working kitchen garden is likely to position these where they are convenient. If you want a decorative kitchen garden, you may well consider that these structures are eyesores and better located in a separate area, perhaps screened by a hedge.

LEFT **This is a highly decorative kitchen garden, in which a selection of flowering plants grows among the vegetables.**

How much time?

If you are going to do it properly, a kitchen garden takes up a tremendous amount of time. If you have help in the garden this may not be a problem, but if you do it all yourself, at weekends for example, you may find that time runs short during a critical period if there are two wet weekends followed by one when you are away from home. In other words, design the garden to suit the amount of time available. A large kitchen garden that has been neglected is a sad sight.

ABOVE **A well-ordered garden is attractive in its own way. Many gardeners take great pride in keeping everything neat and tidy, which not only looks good, but also increases productivity.**

How much space?

It may not be a question of deciding how much space you want to devote to vegetables; this may already be decided by the amount of space actually available. Do not try and squeeze too much into a small space. Remember that there may be a call on the space for other purposes – children playing, for example.

Suitability of the space

An important point to consider is whether the space you want to use is suitable for vegetables or whether you will have to modify the design to allow for problem areas. For example, there is no point in trying to grow vegetables under trees. Nor can they be grown on swamp-like ground. Removing the trees or, at least, reducing the shade they cast is possible, but it may be undesirable or too expensive. Wet ground can be drained, of course, but this, again, may be too expensive, and it may be better to turn that part of the garden into a pond.

What's the weather like?

Although it is not a serious problem for the design of the garden, the weather does play a part in your plans. A vegetable garden should have plenty of sunshine, so if you want to reserve the sunny part of the garden for relaxation and sunbathing, there may well be nowhere to grow vegetables. If the bottom of the garden is a frost hollow, growth will be delayed there, and this may upset the overall decorative balance of your garden even if it does not affect its productivity. Prevailing dry, wet, cold or warm climates may affect what you can grow and therefore limit the productive or decorative qualities of your intended garden.

The Vegetable Plot

In the working vegetable garden, the overall visual design may not be important. Vegetables are, of course, decorative in their own right, and even the most regimented plot, where everything is grown in rows, usually has some visual appeal. With this type of garden, however, the design is subordinate to convenience and output, with rectangular blocks composed of rows or blocks of crops.

ABOVE **Lack of space is not a problem if you want to grow your own vegetables. Even this small border functions as a working vegetable garden.**

Permanent structures

The first consideration is the position of more permanent items, such as greenhouses, cold frames, sheds and compost bins. The greenhouse needs plenty of light and should be away from cold winds. It should also be near the house because it often needs attention in the winter and at night. This also applies to cold frames. The shed and the compost bins can be more or less anywhere, although not too far away. If the compost bin is a long way away, you may be tempted to leave rotting vegetation lying around rather than clearing up.

All these structures need access paths, which again will dictate their position. A compost bin on the far side of a bed may fill a space, but it will be of little use if you have to walk over the bed to get to it. Putting in a path to it, however, will take up valuable growing space.

Bed design

The positioning of the beds should have prime consideration. Practice varies considerably on the shape and method employed. Most gardeners prefer to have large rectangular plots, 3.6m/12ft wide and as long as the garden allows. Typically, there are two such plots, one each side of a central path. Within these plots rows of vegetables are set out across the beds, with temporary narrow paths between each row.

Recent years have seen the reintroduction of a different method, which had fallen out of favour. This is the use of deep beds, only 1.2m/4ft wide. Such beds, can, in fact, be easily superimposed on the old system by dividing up the long plot into any number of 1.2 x 3.6m/4 x 12ft beds. The significance of the 1.2m/4ft width is that the whole bed can be reached from either side. These smaller beds have permanent paths on each side, which can be paved or left as bare earth.

Permanent planting

Most planting in the kitchen garden is done on an annual basis and changes every year, but there are some plants that stay in the same position for several, if not many, years. Vegetables such as rhubarb, globe artichokes and asparagus need a permanent base. Most fruit is permanent or is moved only every few years. Tree fruit, in particular, must be considered as a long-term addition to the garden. These types of plants are usually kept together, partly for convenience and partly because they can all be protected against birds by being included in one fruit cage.

Paths

Paths in a productive kitchen garden tend to be for access purposes and not seen as part of a decorative pattern.

RIGHT **This large traditional vegetable garden contains a great variety of foliage, which can be highly decorative.**

A Walled Vegetable Garden

A vegetable garden is basically a utilitarian space for growing vegetables, but it frequently becomes much more than that. Vegetables are decorative in their own right and a well-planned vegetable plot can usually become a very attractive part of the garden.

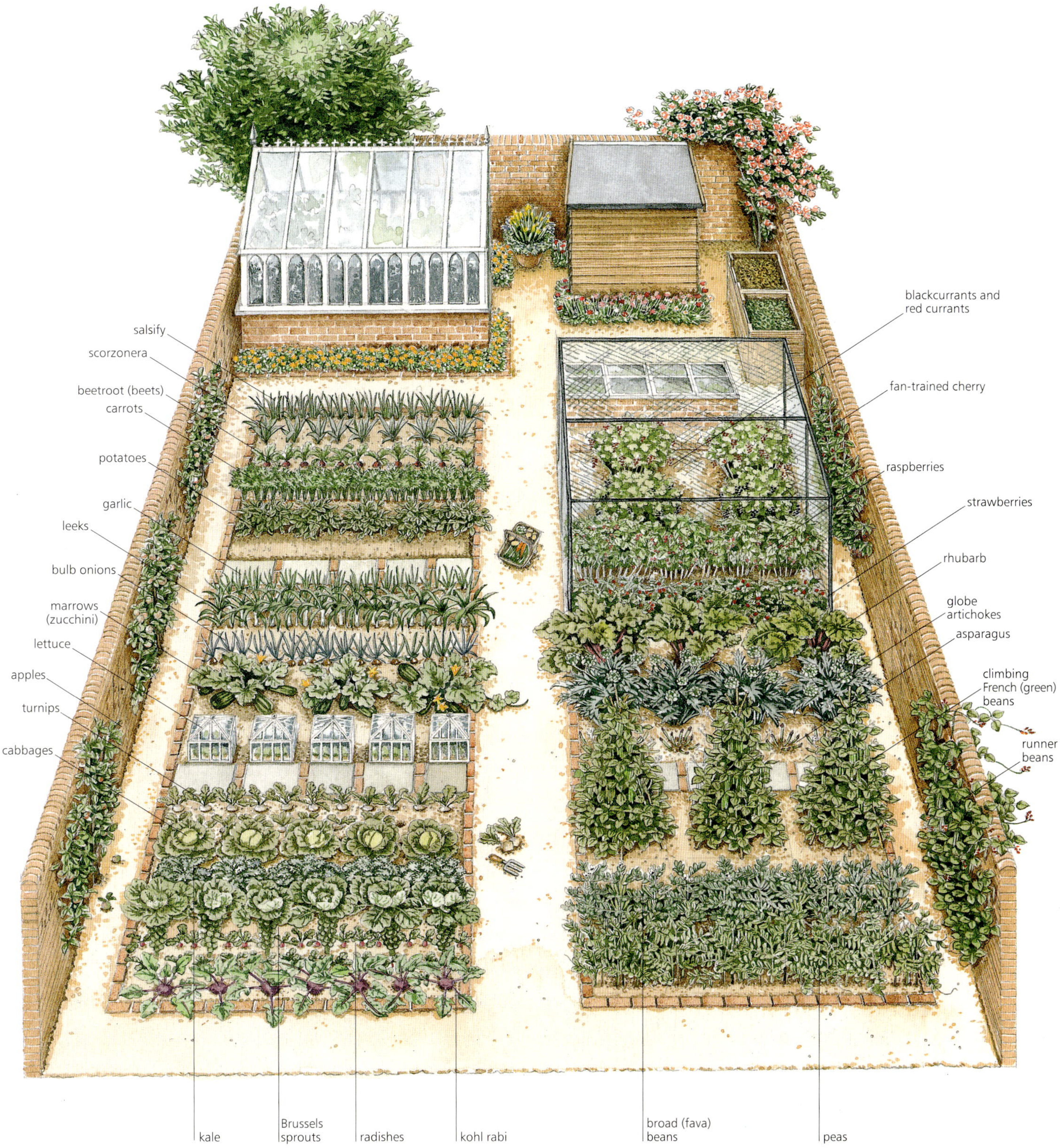

Decorative Fruit and Vegetables

ABOVE **Many vegetables are decorative in their own right. Both the flowers and foliage of these climbing beans are purple.**

One tends to think of vegetables and fruit as being grown either in special gardens or in beds within gardens that are devoted solely to them. There is, however, no reason why they should not be mixed with plants that are grown for decorative purposes. Most gardens have flowering and foliage plants, so why not mix a few vegetables in with them?

Decorative vegetables

Some vegetables seem to have been created for inclusion in decorative schemes. Ruby chard, also known as red-stemmed Swiss chard or rhubarb chard, is a perfect example. Although it is good to eat, its vivid red stems and deep purple foliage make it an ideal border plant, particularly in a position where a touch of bright colour is required. Beetroot (beets), while perhaps not quite as colourful, can be used in the same way.

Colour is not all. The foliage of carrots may not be particularly unusual in colour, but it has a wonderful filigree shape and soft texture. These qualities can be used to soften or link two neighbouring colours, or to break up an area of rather solid foliage.

Climbing plants, such as beans, peas, marrows (zucchini) and squashes, can be used to cover arbours and pergolas. Colourful squashes and marrows hanging down in a walkway can be an attractive, if unexpected, sight.

Decorative fruit

Fruit is even more adaptable than vegetables. Apple or plum trees create a dappled shade that is perfect for sitting under or for creating beds in which to grow shade-loving plants. They can be grown against walls as cordons, espaliers or fans, where they create beautiful two-dimensional patterns that can be even more attractive than conventional climbers. In addition to the shape, there are the blossom and the fruit to enjoy, and the leaves of some varieties of pears have wonderful autumn colours.

Walls are not the only way to display trained fruit trees. They can be used to decorate arbours, pergolas and arches. Grapes can also be used in this type of position, rather than training them in a regimented way against wirework in a fruit garden.

Some bush fruit, red currants and gooseberries in particular, can be grown as tree-form standards – that is, they have a thin, unbranched trunk with the "bush" sitting on top. These can look extremely attractive in borders and beds, especially

LEFT **Many vegetables, such as these purple-leaved Brussels sprouts, have dramatic leaves that make a vegetable plot look very striking.**

An Ornamental Fruit Garden

Fruit gardens should be laid out in the most productive way possible, ensuring that each plant has sufficient space to grow and develop as well as plenty of air and light. However, this does not prevent a fruit garden from being designed in an attractive way that makes the most of the natural beauty of the fruit trees and bushes.

if they are the centrepiece. Naturally, they look best when they are in full fruit.

Even strawberries can be used in a decorative manner. Alpine strawberries make good edging plants for borders. A single line between the border and a path, for example, can be extremely effective, especially as they have a long flowering season. They work really well around the edge of herb gardens but can be used in any type of border.

Decorative herbs

Although herbs can be kept together in a separate garden, they do lend themselves particularly well to being spread around the garden in the decorative borders. Shrubby plants, such as rosemary, sage and thyme, have an obvious decorative function, but so do many of the herbaceous varieties. The thin, grass-like leaves of chives, for example, contrast well with the bolder shapes of hostas, and they are also particularly good for edging paths. The frothy leaves of parsley can be used in much the same way.

Many herbs can be grown in decorative borders for their flowers rather than their leaves. The leaves of bergamot (*Monarda*), for example, are used as a herb, but the flowers, which are a bright bold red, are exceptionally decorative, making this a superb border plant.

Potagers

Strictly speaking, a potager is simply a kitchen garden, but it has taken on romantic overtones and is now taken to mean those kitchen gardens that have a decorative as well as productive function.

ABOVE **Flowers are often mixed in with the vegetables in a potager. Sweet peas are one of the most popular choices among gardeners.**

Overall design

The simplest design for a potager is a square or circle, and in many ways these take a lot of beating. Many gardeners, however, enjoy having much more complicated patterns than this, going on to divide the basic shape like the spokes of a wheel or creating four squares, perhaps. Much more intricate patterns can be created, with circles within squares or squares within circles. And so the list of design ideas expands.

The patterns do not have to be geometric. Some gardeners prefer more free-flowing plots, divided with swirls and curved lines. Although these can be extremely attractive, they can be difficult to plant effectively.

Sources of inspiration for such gardens may be visits to actual gardens or pictures in magazines or books. Other useful sources which are often overlooked are arts and crafts that use similar patterns. A book on patchwork, for example, can highlight all kinds of design ideas that can be mixed and matched with further ideas from other gardens.

Structural elements

The shapes of the beds are usually delineated by paths, which are both decorative in their own right and also useful in that they provide access to the beds. These can be paved with brick or stone, or covered with gravel. Although properly laid paths are ultimately best, it is possible to lay them in a temporary fashion until you are certain that you like the layout, or if you want to change the overall plan every few years. Simply lay paving stones, for example, directly onto the levelled soil.

A further way to delineate the beds is to surround them with low box hedging. This creates a permanent structure but it increases its attraction. The box plants will take a few years to become established but the effort and wait are worth it.

Other structural elements are more three-dimensional. Arches, for example, can be used, particularly in the centre of the garden, perhaps covered with fruit. Small trees and standard fruit bushes can be used as centrepieces for individual beds. All add to the shape and texture of the garden.

Designing with plants

The vegetables are the least permanent part of the garden. Just planting them out in lines or blocks will produce an attractive effect, but more interest can be generated by consciously

LEFT **Here, the flowers are situated close enough to the fruit and vegetables to become an integrated part of the potager.**

A Potager Garden

A potager is simply a kitchen garden, but it is used, increasingly, to mean a kitchen garden that has been laid out in a decorative manner. Instead of plants filling more or less random rows, a more complex and involved plan is drawn up, and the garden takes on a new dimension.

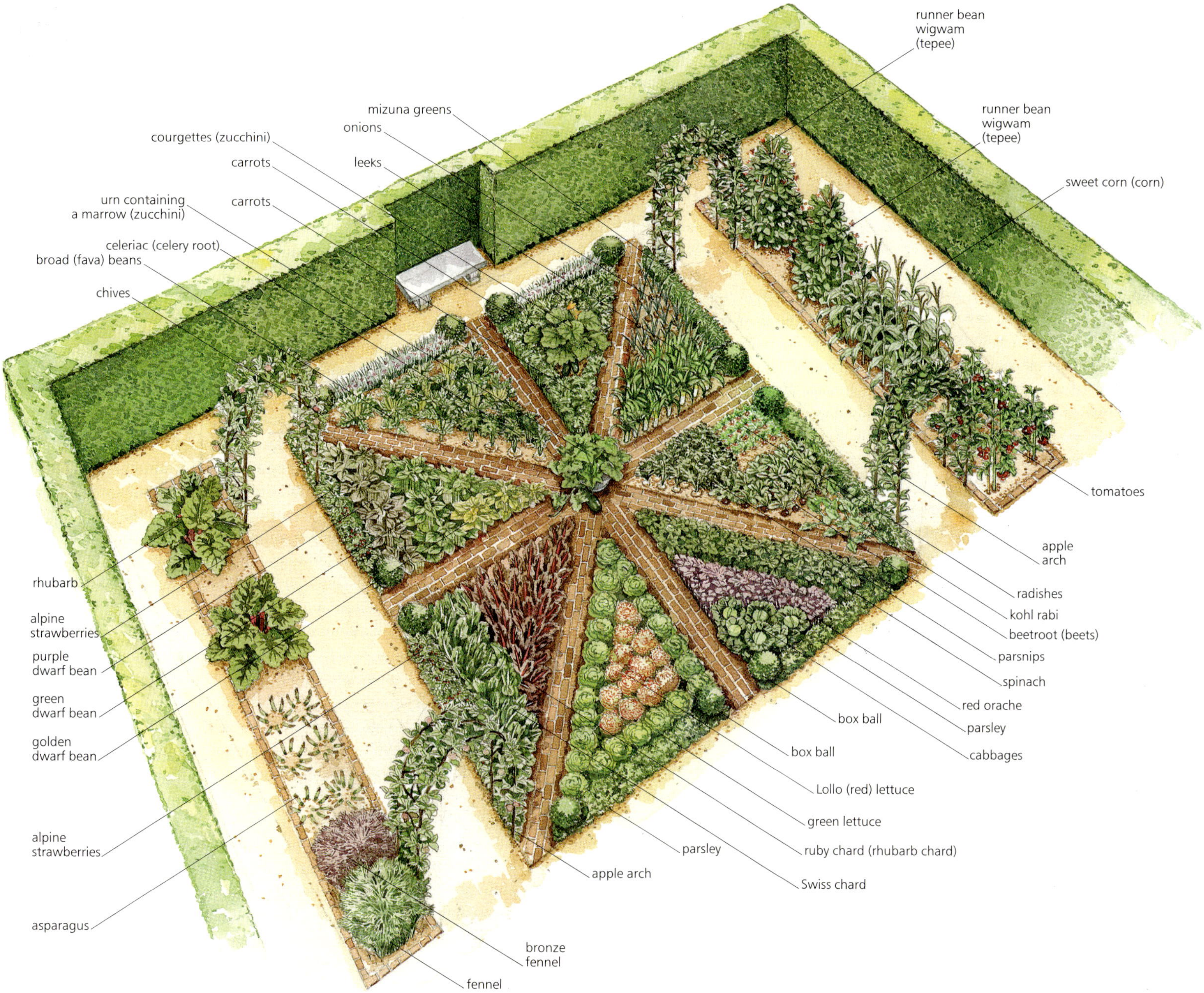

planning each bed, thinking about the plants' colours and textures. Red-leaved lettuces, for example, can be used as winding threads through green vegetables. Parsley can be used as edging, or as a boundary between groups of vegetables. Rows of beans growing up canes can divide beds into sections or they can be grown over archways. Plants need not be planted in blocks, they can be laid out in circles with other plants growing in the middle or around the outside.

However, there is a serious problem with such designs and that is whether to eat the vegetables or not! A meticulous design with every plant in its place is utterly ruined if one is taken off for use in the kitchen. This is something that you must plan for and a less formal style may be the answer.

Another factor to be borne in mind is that it is bad gardening practice to grow the same plants on the same ground each year. Because crops should be rotated, it is not possible to use the same pattern each year unless you create it using different plants.

Herb Gardens

Herb gardens tend to fulfil two functions. The first, and obvious one, is to provide herbs. The second arises from the fact that herbs can be highly decorative, making an attractive garden on their own.

ABOVE **Coriander (cilantro) is a popular herb with a pungent taste. Its delicate flowers and leaves are also decorative.**

Herbs as herbs

Although we grow almost as many herbs as our ancestors, they are primarily included in our gardens for romantic reasons. The number of herbs that most gardeners use in the kitchen is relatively small. But small as this number is, those we do use regularly are important. When you are designing a herb garden, make certain that these herbs are readily accessible from the path, and put those that are never or rarely used in the more inaccessible parts of the border.

The most frequently used herbs should be placed as near to the kitchen door as possible so that the cook can grab a handful when necessary. This means that either the herb garden should be located here or the important herbs should be mixed in with other plants in a decorative border. Another solution is to grow these particular herbs in a container or containers, which can then be placed near the kitchen door for easy access.

Herbs for atmosphere

Although many people regularly use a large number of herbs, most of the gardeners who maintain herb gardens do so because of their romantic associations. And there is no doubt that herbs are romantic. This is partly their history and partly the atmosphere they create in the garden. Herbs tend to be gentle plants, and only occasionally do we come across brash ones. The colours are muted and soft, the atmosphere they create is hazy. On sunny days the garden is perfumed by their scents and is drowsy with the sound of bees. This is the perfect garden in which to sit and relax, so you should remember to include a seat in your design.

Herbs by design

The layout of a herb garden depends largely on the space available, of course, but also on the time you can spend in it. Remember that a large one will take a lot of looking after.

It is possible to create quite small herb gardens, and the herb wheel is one of the most popular plans. An old cartwheel is laid out on prepared ground and the spaces between the spokes are filled with different herbs. When real wheels are not available, the same design can be created from

Important culinary herbs	
Basil	Marjoram
Bay	Mint
Chives	Parsley
Dill	Rosemary
French tarragon	Sage
Lovage	Thyme

LEFT **Box hedges associate well with herb gardens. They add order to what, at times, can be an untidy collection of herbs.**

A Formal Herb Garden

Herb gardens need to be carefully planned if they are to be attractive. Primarily a herb garden is a place for growing herbs for the kitchen, but it should also be a peaceful haven where the scents and colours of the plants can be enjoyed. However, it is worth remembering that a well maintained herb garden needs more attention than a vegetable plot.

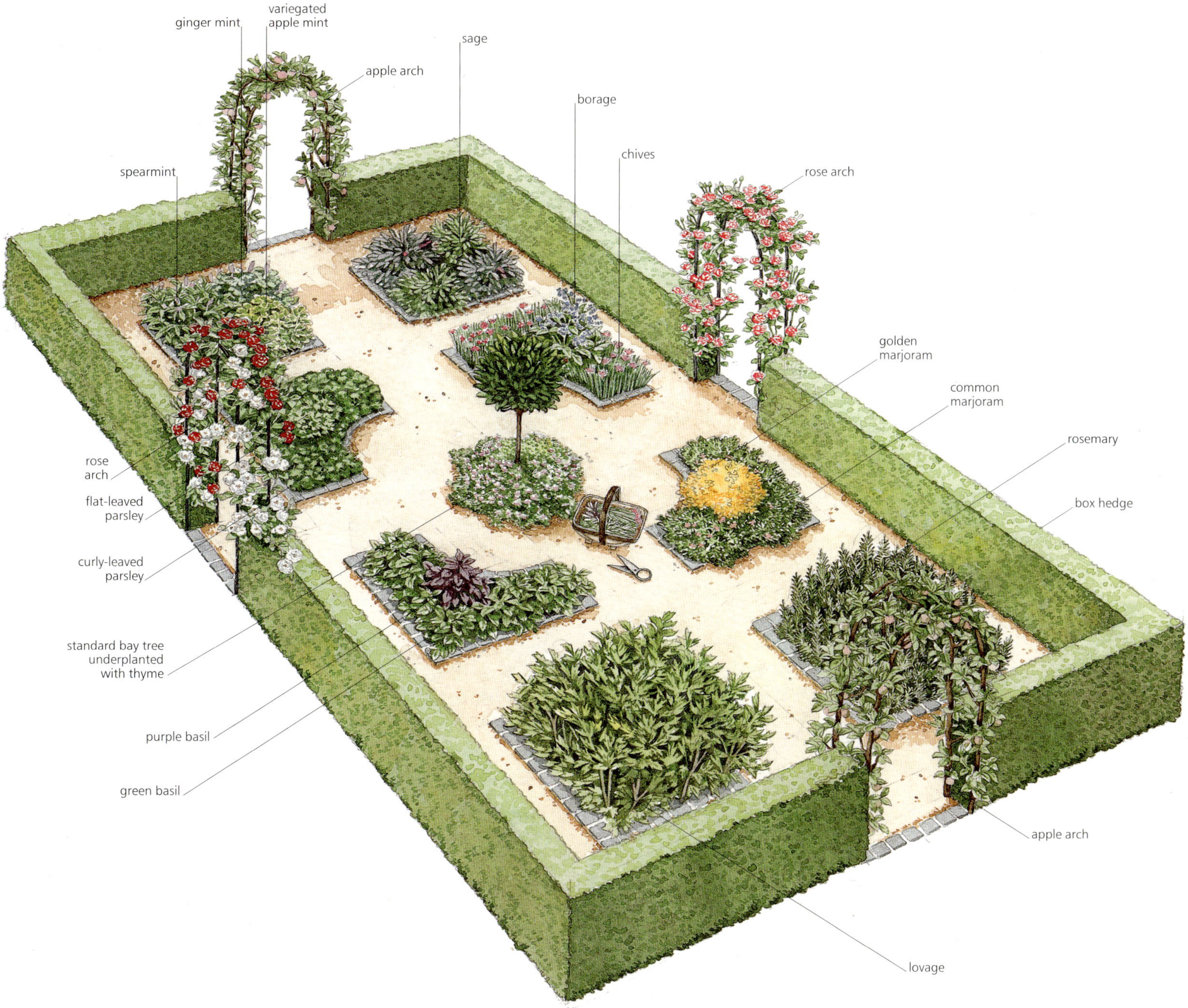

bricks. Remember not to use herbs that are too rampant – a sage bush, for example, will soon become big enough to cover the whole area of the wheel. If you want to use the more vigorous plants in a small area, regularly dig them out and replace them.

If you are working on a larger scale, almost any of the patterns mentioned as suitable for potagers can be used. It is worth mentioning that the only time of year when the internal divisions of the garden will be clearly seen is in the winter when the vegetation has died back. During the growing seasons, the lush growth will be such that the outlines of the beds are not easily seen. If you want to see the demarcations, edge the beds with low box hedges, which will also give good definition to the overall design.

Containers

Increasing interest is being shown in containers as a method of growing a few vegetables in a small space, perhaps on the patio or possibly even on a balcony or roof garden. This interest is fuelled by the range of beautiful containers that is now available from garden centres and nurseries.

ABOVE **A surprising amount can be grown in a relatively small space, as can be seen from this collection of herbs and vegetables in pots.**

The containers

Virtually any container can be used to grow vegetables, but success is more likely if it is reasonably large – the bigger the better, in fact. Most vegetables do not like to dry out and the greater the volume of compost (soil mix) that is available, the less chance there is of this occurring. A larger amount of space also allows you to grow several different plants in the same container, which is much more decorative than using just one type.

Terracotta pots are extremely attractive, but the porous nature of the material allows water to evaporate more quickly through the sides of the pot than through, say, a glazed one. Most pots are heavy even without compost (soil mix), so make sure you position them before you fill them. Large, black plastic buckets are practical and can be used successfully, although they are not as attractive as ceramic pots.

ABOVE LEFT **More than just a taste of peas can be grown in a container. However, it is important not to let the tub dry out.**

LEFT **Cabbage may not be the first planting idea that springs to mind when thinking of containers, but here four good specimens are growing happily in a plastic tub.**

Growing bags

If you do not mind their utilitarian appearance, growing bags – plastic sacks filled with a formulated growing medium – are an inexpensive way of growing vegetables. They are particularly useful for tomatoes, but they can be used for many other vegetables as well. They were originally developed for use in the greenhouse (where their appearance does not matter), but they can be used outside just as well. A warm corner, against a wall, is the ideal location.

Hanging baskets

Hanging baskets are not ideal for growing vegetables, mainly because they are too small, but a basket of decorative lettuces, perhaps a mixture of green and bronze varieties, can be eye-catching. Some varieties of tomato are trailing, producing tiny, bite-sized fruit, and these are ideal for baskets. A little imagination should allow you to create something productive as well as attractive.

The position

Containers of vegetables can be placed together with purely decorative containers, although they should not be grown in shade. Although plants such as aubergines (eggplants) and peppers are better grown in a warm situation, most other vegetables prefer not to get too hot, and you should bear in mind that plants grown in pots do not have the solid mass of earth around their roots to keep them cool during the day and it is possible that the roots can become too hot.

A Courtyard Kitchen Garden

You do not need a garden in order to grow vegetables. A patio, courtyard or even a balcony is sufficient to produce a few crops. With care, an attractive arrangement can be made which makes an original alternative to most container plantings. There is less weeding involved than in a conventional plot, but a container garden requires a great deal of watering.

Another problem with siting the containers in a warm place is that they will need watering several times a day.

You should, therefore, choose a warm but not hot place, preferably one where there is plenty of air circulating, but not causing a draught (draft).

From a decorative point of view, vegetables can be grown wherever they will fit in. A group of containers can make an attractive feature. You could include a tripod of beans and a tub of golden courgettes (zucchini) and tomatoes, with yellow as well as red ones to vary the scheme. Other pots might contain sweet or bell peppers or aubergines (eggplants), both of which are decorative. It is a question of using your imagination as well as checking growing times and choosing your favourite tastes that should determine what you do. If you do not like the results, you can always try something different next year.

planning
the crops

For most vegetable growers, the ultimate goal is their produce: they want to grow the best possible vegetables. In order to achieve this, the gardener needs to plan his or her crops very carefully, especially if lack of time and the size of garden are possible limitations. It is rather wasteful to take on a large kitchen garden if you cannot maintain it and, similarly, it is inadvisable to expect large harvests from a small plot of ground.

However, with planning and a careful use of space and time, a surprising amount can be grown. Some parts of the planning stage are largely aesthetic, but others will influence the quantity and quality of your crops. Techniques such as crop rotation, successional cropping and intercropping are particularly important in this context.

One of the first decisions to be made is whether to grow the vegetables in rows or in blocks. There are advantages and disadvantages to both systems, and in the end it is really a question of personal choice.

The consideration of all these factors will eventually become second nature to you. The experienced gardener does not have to think twice about them, but if you are approaching kitchen gardening for the first time, it is important to think about them carefully.

RIGHT **This kitchen garden has been packed with vegetables. No rows are left unfilled and the spaces between them have been mulched with grass clippings to keep the weeds at bay and to prevent the evaporation of water.**

While it is important to get pleasure out of a vegetable garden by arranging it in a pleasing and attractive style, it is equally important to remember that there is a range of practical considerations to be borne in mind when you are planning how to group your crops.

What do you want to grow?

The first factor is, of course, deciding what crops you want to grow. If no one in the family likes beetroot (beets), do you really want to grow them, even if they do look attractive? If space is short should you be growing something else that will be eaten? Potatoes are comparatively inexpensive from greengrocers and farm shops, and, since they take up a lot of space, is it worth your while growing them? If you really want to grow potatoes, perhaps you could compromise and grow a few earlies for that wonderful flavour that only potatoes cooked straight from the soil have, but buy in your maincrop, which will probably not taste all that different from those you would grow yourself.

It is also worth thinking carefully about how much of each crop you need to grow. Go by what you need and not by the quantity of seed in the packet. It is easy, for example, to plant out all the runner bean seeds you have bought only to find that the plants that result will produce far more beans than you could ever eat. Balance the space available against what you want to grow and the quantities that you will require of each. This leads on to the fact that you

BELOW **Rows of spring onions (scallions) have been alternated here with rows of carrots. This is a traditional way of deterring carrot root fly and is effective because the strong smell of the onions masks that of the carrots.**

should sow only to meet your immediate requirements. There really is no point in sowing a whole row of lettuce if you get round to eating only a few of them before they have bolted (run to seed). It is better to sow a third of a row now and another third in a couple of week's time and so on, in order to get a succession of vegetables rather than a glut which you probably won't be able to consume.

Designing the beds

Once you have decided what to grow, there is the layout to consider. Most gardeners use the traditional way of growing their plants in rows, but blocks are becoming more popular. One of the advantages of this method is that more plants can be grown in a single area, and it is thus ideal for a garden where space is limited.

Crop rotation is another important consideration. Gardeners have long known that it is not a good idea to grow the same crop on the same ground in successive years, and so the crops are "rotated". This is not difficult to achieve, but it does mean that if you are designing a decorative garden you cannot use the same design for two consecutive years unless you use different plants.

ABOVE **This small raised bed is not only decorative but very productive, and demonstrates just how much can be grown in a small garden.**

Allowing for more permanent plants

A point to consider when planning the layout is that some crops will remain in the ground over winter. It is rare to start off with a completely bare plot each spring. Sprouting broccoli, for example, will still be growing until late spring, while plants such as garlic and broad (fava) beans, planted in late autumn or early winter, will be there until summer. Remember to allow for these crops when you draw up your plan. Fruit trees and bushes also need a permanent position, as do some vegetables such as rhubarb that are not moved for years.

Crop Rotation

Crop rotation has been practised by farmers and gardeners for generations as a simple and effective precaution against pests and diseases. The basic idea is that if you grow the same type of plant on the same patch of ground every year, the soil will harbour pests and diseases from one season to the next. If you move the crop to another piece of ground, the pests and diseases will lose their host and will die out.

ABOVE **In a four-year rotation, courgettes (zucchini) would be grown in plot three. Alternatively, they can be grown on a compost heap.**

The practical side of this philosophy is the division of the vegetable garden into four or five areas. The different types of crops – brassicas, beans and so on – are moved from one plot to another so that they return to the same piece of ground only every fourth year.

For four-year crop rotation, the crops are divided into four groups – the fifth bed is used for the permanent plants, which obviously do not move. Look at the list of vegetables that you wish to grow for the coming year and divide them into their various groups. Allocate planting areas to each. Do the same for the following year, but move all the crops to another plot. If space is limited, a three-year rotation is better than nothing.

BELOW **Globe artichokes stay in the ground for several years, so they are grown in a permanent plot and do not form part of the rotation plan**

Four-Year Crop Rotation

Plot 1
Peas
Broad (fava) beans
French (green) beans
Runner beans

Plot 2
Cabbages
Brussels sprouts
Calabrese (Italian sprouting broccoli)
Broccoli
Kale
Radishes
Swedes (rutabaga or yellow turnips)
Turnips
Kohl rabi

Plot 3
Bulb onions
Spring onions (scallions)
Shallots
Leeks
Garlic
Sweet corn (corn)
Marrows (zucchini), squashes and pumpkins
Lettuce

Plot 4
Potatoes
Parsnips
Beetroot (beets)
Carrots
Salsify
Scorzonera
Celery
Celeriac (celery root)
Tomatoes

Plot 5 (permanent)
Rhubarb
Asparagus
Perennial herbs
Globe artichokes
Jerusalem artichokes
Seakale

Four-Year Crop Rotation

In many gardens, the differentiation between the plots is hardly discernible, but it makes life easier to split the garden into individual plots.

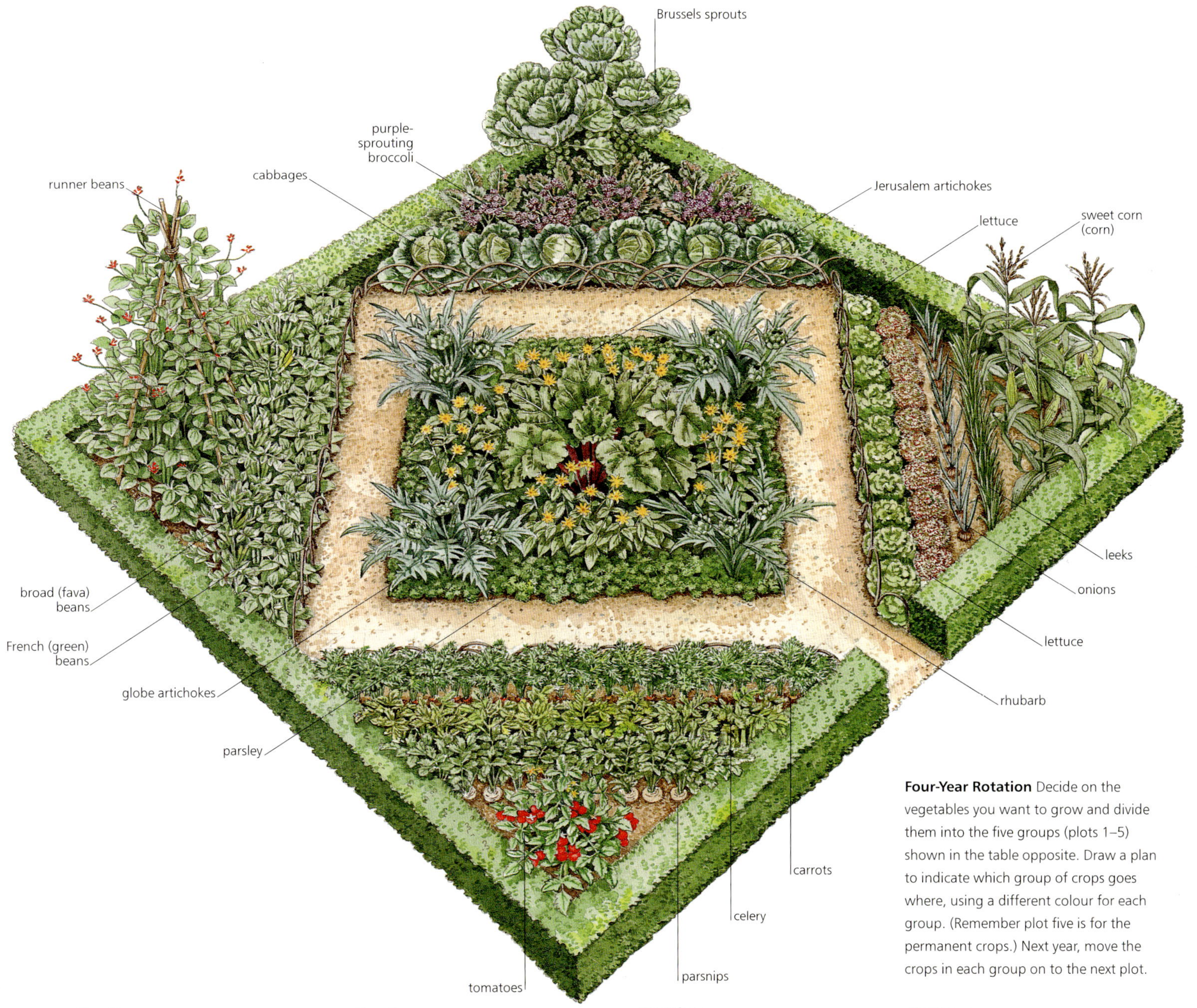

Four-Year Rotation Decide on the vegetables you want to grow and divide them into the five groups (plots 1–5) shown in the table opposite. Draw a plan to indicate which group of crops goes where, using a different colour for each group. (Remember plot five is for the permanent crops.) Next year, move the crops in each group on to the next plot.

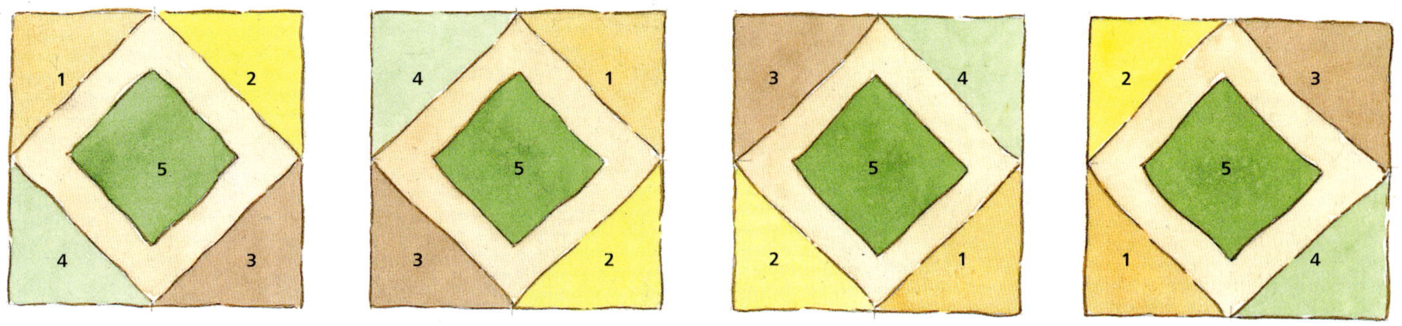

Three-Year Crop Rotation

This is a more conventional method of dividing up the garden into separate plots, keeping each group of plants together for rotating.

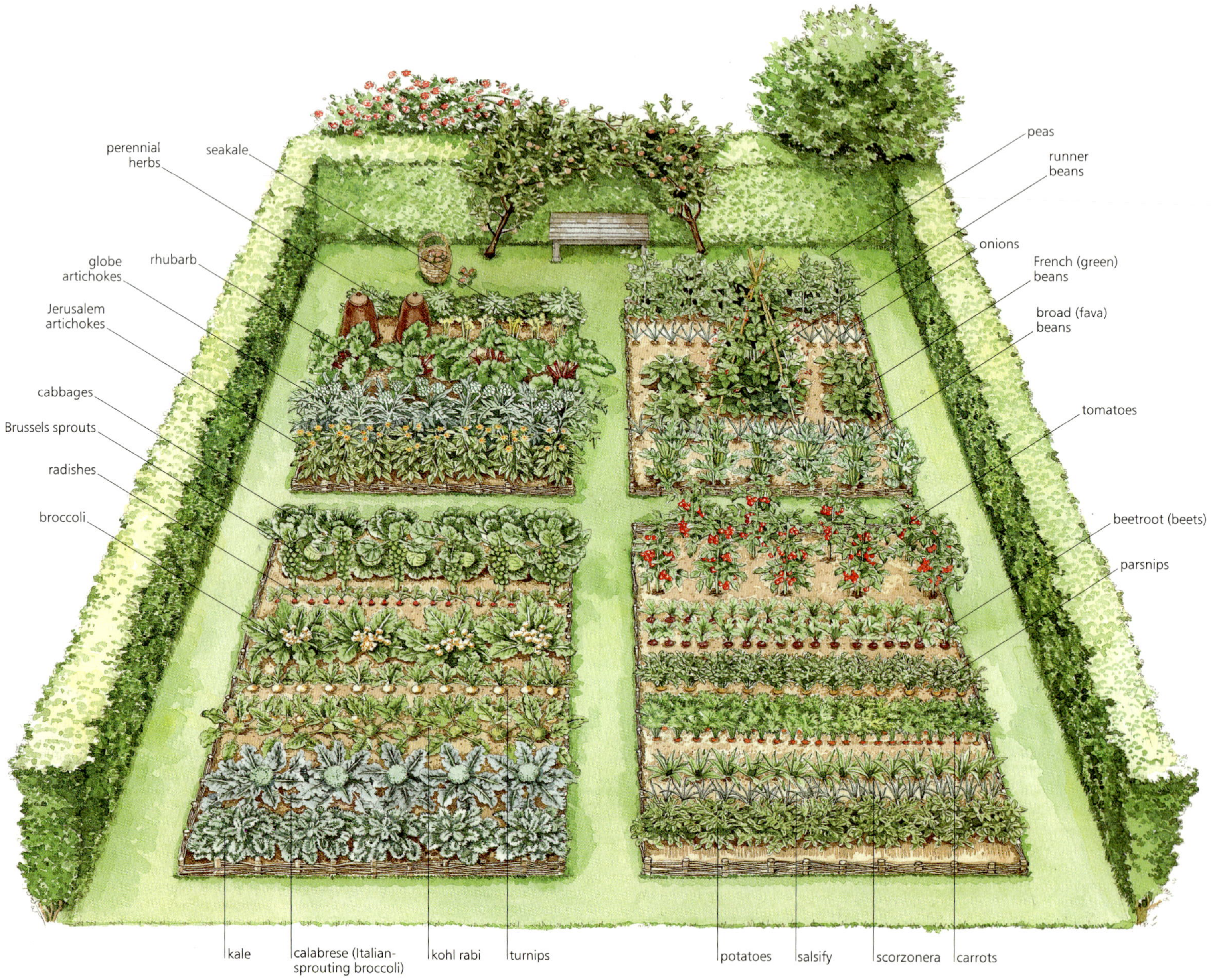

Three-Year Rotation

Decide on the vegetables you want to grow and divide into the four groups (plots 1–4) shown in the table opposite. Draw a plan to indicate which group of crops goes where, using a different colour for each group. (Remember plot four is for permanent crops.) Move the crops in each group to the next plot the following year.

Year One

Year Two

Year Three

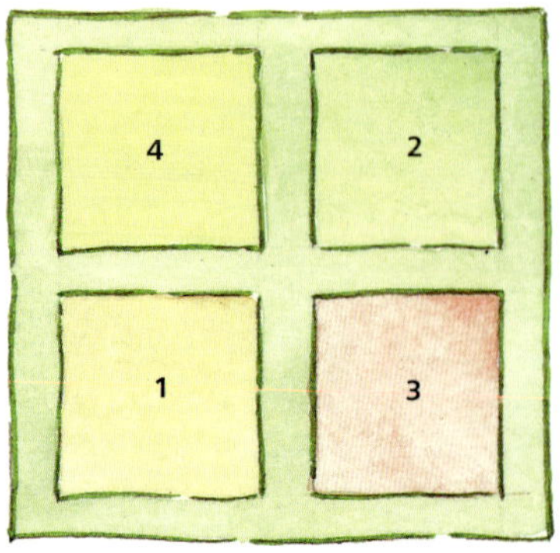

Three-Year Crop Rotation

Plot 1
Peas
Broad (fava) beans
French (green) beans
Runner beans
Bulb onions
Leeks
Sweet corn (corn)
Marrows (zucchini), squashes and pumpkins
Lettuce

Plot 2
Potatoes
Parsnips
Beetroot (beets)
Carrots
Salsify
Scorzonera
Tomatoes

Plot 3
Cabbages
Brussels sprouts
Calabrese (Italian sprouting broccoli)
Broccoli
Kale
Swede (rutabaga or yellow turnips)
Turnips
Kohl rabi
Radishes

Plot 4 (permanent)
Rhubarb
Asparagus
Perennial herbs
Globe artichokes
Jerusalem artichokes
Seakale

ABOVE **In a three-year crop rotation, tomatoes are grown in plot two, along with root crops such as parsnips and carrots.**

ABOVE **Rhubarb is planted in the permanent bed when crops are rotated, and can stay in the same position for up to 25 years.**

As well as having advantages in terms of pests and diseases, there are other reasons for moving crops around. Some crops will tolerate newly manured ground while others cannot. Thus, one plot can be heavily manured when it is dug in the autumn during the first year and cabbages and related plants can be planted in it in spring. In the following year the plot is simply dug, and the root crops, which do not like the soil too rich, are planted there.

Strict crop rotation is not the easiest of things to maintain. Many gardeners start off with good intentions and manage it for a few years, but gradually things begin to slip. Some brassicas that have been left in the ground over winter may block the space that is required for some other plants, or perhaps a few plants have been slipped in to fill a gap. Leaving plants in the ground until the following year so that you can collect your own seeds also plays havoc with rotation if you have only a small amount of space. If you find this happening, there is no need to worry.

In a small kitchen garden, crop rotation, although it is admirable in theory, is not that important in practice. One of the main difficulties is the amount of space required to put strict rotation into effect. In agricultural situations the crops are fields apart; even in a large garden, the distances involved can be quite large. In a small garden, however, it is often impossible to get the plots far enough apart for the pests or diseases not to be able to find their host plant. The other problem is that, in practice, four years is not always long enough to kill off all the diseases anyway.

This does not mean that crop rotation is unimportant, however, because it still has some effect. Yet it does mean that you should not lose any sleep if you are not able to follow the sequence to the exact letter. Most gardeners do not grow the same crop on the same ground for two years running in any case – with the exception of plants such as runner beans – but they do not follow strict crop rotation.

Rows

Vegetables have traditionally been grown in rows. Although some gardeners challenge the claims made for this method, suggesting that blocks and deep beds are better, rows are probably still the most widely used system.

The basic idea is simple: the vegetables are grown in a single line, with some crops, such as beans and peas, being grown in a double line. The lines or rows are separated by a distance somewhat wider than the breadth of the plants, so that there is bare earth between the rows. This bare earth acts as a path, allowing access for maintenance, such as weeding and watering, as well as for harvesting.

Growing vegetables in rows is an attractive way of producing them. The varying heights, shapes, textures and colours all show up well, with the rows looking like decorative ribbons stretched across the garden. Their appearance is not, however, the principal reason for growing vegetables in this way. There are practical considerations, too.

Access is one of the important benefits provided by individual rows. The paths between the rows allow the gardener to move freely among the plants without having to stretch. Each plant can be examined for condition as well as for pests and diseases. Pests have less chance of being overlooked if the plant can be clearly seen from at least two sides, and individual plants can be tended to if necessary. The bases of the plants can be easily seen for inspection, weeding and watering.

Another advantage is that there is plenty of air circulating among the plants, which helps considerably to reduce mildew-type diseases. The plants generally have plenty of space in which to develop, and the leaves are able to open out to receive the maximum amount of light. Finally, rows are easy to cover with the majority of cloches available.

Needless to say there are also disadvantages. The use of so many "paths" means that a lot of space is unproductive when you look at the plot as a whole, an important factor in a small garden, where space is limited. Another disadvantage is that the paths allow light to reach the soil, so increasing the number of weeds that germinate, although this is offset to some extent by the ease with which it is possible to hoe. With constant use, the paths become compacted, which does not help the soil structure. Although the whole bed will be dug each year, because it is so large it is necessary to walk over it

LEFT **Traditional rows of vegetables, filling all the available space, can be very decorative.**

while the ground is being prepared, again adding a certain degree of compaction. Constant hoeing will help overcome this by breaking up the soil and keeping it aerated. However, in dry weather, hoeing should be avoided as it encourages water loss. An alternative is to lay planks of wood between the rows. This not only helps to prevent soil compaction but also acts as a mulch which will help retain the moisture in the soil as well as keep weeds down.

ABOVE **The decorative quality of vegetables can be clearly seen in these rows. All the leaves are green and yet the variety of greens and the shapes of the leaves form a very attractive picture over a long season.**

LEFT **It is important to leave plenty of space for young plants to fill out. Rows with plenty of space between them also allow for access and easy weeding.**

Blocks and Deep Beds

Growing vegetables in blocks as opposed to rows is an old method that more or less dropped out of use in many countries but that has been reintroduced in recent years. The basic idea is to grow the plants in a square or rectangle, say five plants wide by five plants deep, rather than in a single row.

The vegetable plot is divided into smaller plots, each about 1.2m/4ft across and spanning the width of the main plot. These smaller beds are permanent, unlike rows, and between each is a path, either trodden earth or more substantial paving slabs or bricks. The width of the smaller beds is determined by the gardener's reach – 1.2m/4ft should allow access of about 60cm/24in from each side so that the entire bed can be reached without compacting the soil. Keeping off the beds means that the soil structure is always kept in top condition.

Some gardeners simply dig the soil in the existing plot, adding organic material to it as they go. Others prefer to create a deep bed system, either by digging deeper, using a double digging method, or by raising the height of the bed with boards or a low wall and then adding a mixture of good loam and organic material. The bed is worked from the path so that the soil is never compacted.

The advantage of a rich soil in good condition is that it will support more plants, and so most gardeners plant much more closely than in the conventional rows. This means that productivity is improved considerably, and many more plants can be raised from the same area of ground. As well as being productive, close planting also means that weed seeds have little chance of germinating.

A solid block of plants, however, makes it more difficult to get at any weeds, as well as making it harder to see if there are any pests and diseases lurking below the leaves. Because the plants are close together, there is likely to be less air circulating than around vegetables grown in rows, and this increases the possibility of diseases that like damp conditions with stagnant air. It is also not as easy to water the base of individual plants. Watering can, in fact, become erratic, with some areas ending up drier than others as water runs off the leaves. Another disadvantage is that it is not as easy to cover the vegetables with cloches, and although it is, of course, possible to construct a cover, this will not be as mobile as individual cloches.

You can take advantage of both methods by using deep beds, with their rich soil conditions, and planting short rows across the beds instead of blocks. This method works well for those gardeners who feel that digging destroys the structure of the soil. They dig the soil initially, adding plenty of organic material, but thereafter only top-dress the surface with more organic material, perhaps hoeing it in or allowing the worms to move it below the surface. Although this benefits the soil, most gardeners prefer the more traditional method of digging at least once a year because this has other advantages.

ABOVE **These blocks of contrasting lettuces have been planted in deep beds that are almost flush with the ground. The beds have been dug deeply rather than built up.**

RIGHT **Each of these blocks of vegetables and herbs is about 1.2m/4ft wide, which allows access from the paths running across the plot.**

LEFT **Boards create a greater depth of fertile soil, so vegetables can be planted much closer together.**

Intercropping

There can be few gardeners who have enough space to grow everything they wish, and this is particularly true of those with small gardens. One way partly to overcome the problem is to make sure that every available piece of land is in use and to avoid letting ground lie idle.

There are two main ways to ensure that the land is used efficiently. The first is to plant quick-growing crops among slower ones so that the former have been harvested before the latter have grown sufficiently to fill the space. Brussels sprouts, for example, are planted at anything up to 75cm/30in apart, depending on the size of the variety. For several weeks after they have been planted there is a lot of empty space around each plant. This can be filled with a crop such as lettuce or radishes that takes only a short while to come to maturity.

Some plants, however, cannot be planted out in the early part of the season, and rather than leave the ground empty, it can be filled with a temporary crop. For example, a bed of lettuces can be planted and the first ones to be harvested can be replaced by young sweet corn (corn), the rest of the lettuces being harvested as the corn develops.

A similar idea can be used with station-sown seeds. For example, parsnip seeds can be sown in groups of three at, say, 23cm/9in intervals. In between each group a few radishes can be sown. This method has advantages in that not only will the quick-growing radishes make use of the ground before the parsnips need it, but, because parsnips are slow to germinate, the radishes will actually mark the row, making it easier to hoe off any weeds without disturbing the parsnips, which are still below ground.

Another aspect of intercropping is purely decorative. A simple example is to intercrop red-leaved lettuces with green ones. To create these effects, it is best to raise the plants in trays or modules and plant them out in a pattern when they are large enough.

When you are intercropping for visual effects, take care in the choice of neighbours. There is little point in planting decorative lettuces next to potatoes, which will eventually flop over and smother them. However, from the productive point of view it is a good idea to plant lettuces between rows of potatoes before the latter have emerged or have reached any height, because the lettuces will be cropped before the ground is smothered by the potato leaves.

BELOW **Intercropping carrots with lettuces – here a tinted variety known as 'Nelson' – makes for a very decorative effect.**

ABOVE **Here, a short row of radishes is being sown between individual cabbages. They will crop long before the cabbages have grown large enough to cover them.**

ABOVE **As an alternative to sowing, individual lettuces can be planted between slow-growing plants such as cabbages.**

Successional Crops

Closely related to the question of intercropping is that of successional sowing and planting. The idea behind this is to phase the crops so that your plot provides a continuous stream of produce and not a series of sudden gluts. In other words, this is another method of ensuring that you get the most out of your ground.

Many gardeners have a tendency to sow a complete row right across their plot, whether they need that amount of produce or not, simply because a whole row looks better than a short one. This can be wasteful, because two-thirds of the row may bolt before you have consumed it and then you are left with nothing. It is far better to sow a third of a row of, say, spinach, wait two or three weeks and then sow another third and finally the last section two or three weeks later still. This means that the crops will reach maturity at two- to three-week intervals, spreading out so that you have spinach for two months or more rather than for the two to three weeks that would have been the case if you had sown the whole row at once.

Another way of securing a succession of crops is to choose varieties that mature at different times. Peas, for example, are classified into first earlies and maincrop types, and within these groups some varieties produce peas sooner than others. Choosing several different varieties rather than just one will provide a much longer harvesting season.

The same principle is true of fruit. Choosing different varieties of raspberries, for example, will enable you to harvest fruit from early summer right through to late autumn. This also applies to strawberries, apples and many other types of fruit.

There may, of course, be times when you do not want to spread the harvesting. For example, if you like to freeze vegetables for winter use it is easier if, for example, all your peas mature at once so that you can quickly freeze them and replant the ground with another crop of something else – late turnips perhaps. Vegetables that all crop at once are usually marked in the seed catalogues as being suitable for freezing.

If you are creating a vegetable garden as a decorative feature as well as a productive one, successional sowing and planting becomes doubly important. Any crop removed, whether it is a single lettuce or a row or a wigwam (tepee) of peas will leave a gap and the sooner it is filled the better the garden will look.

Both from the productive and the visual point of view it is always worthwhile having a few plants coming along in pots ready to plant out. Lettuce, Swiss chard and parsley, for example, can be sown at two-week intervals in modules to provide a good supply of plants to fill the gaps.

Another aspect of successional cropping is replacing one crop with another as soon as it is finished. Thus, replant the ground occupied by broad (fava) beans with a late crop of leeks as the beans are finished or plant out spring cabbage in the space that becomes available when the onions are harvested. Keep the ground producing for you even if you only sow green manure, which is dug back into the soil later in the year.

RIGHT **Some crops are better planted at intervals so that they do not all mature at the same time. To facilitate this, it is often easier to fill long rows with several different types of vegetables rather than leave gaps to be sown later.**

greenhouses

sheds and equipment

Considering the large number of tools and equipment that is now available from the average garden centre, the gardener can actually get by with buying surprisingly few of them, as long as they are chosen carefully and with a view to what is actually needed. Starting a vegetable garden need not be a costly business. You do not, for example, have to invest in a large greenhouse or in cold frames, although a shed will prove useful if you do not want to perform unhygienic gardening tasks in the kitchen. A wheelbarrow is the only mechanical device that most gardeners will require although many may use a rotavator (rototiller) for digging larger plots. There are also many excellent second-hand tools to be had, very often at a fraction of the price of new ones that may be of an inferior quality, so it is worth spending a little time on finding the best tools.

ABOVE **Greenhouses are available in a variety of shapes and sizes, which means that you should be able to find one to suit your garden.**

In many ways gardening is a very personal hobby and no more so than in the choice of tools and other equipment. Everybody has their favourite selection of tools and feels lost if, for example, they are working in someone else's garden without these items.

What do you really need?

Life is much easier in the garden if you have items such as a wheelbarrow, but bear in mind that, in a small garden, you can grow an extra couple of plants in the space needed to store it. Indeed, most things, such as weeds and compost, can be carried in a bucket in small-scale gardening.

One of the problems with owning a lot of tools and equipment is that you need somewhere to keep them, and that means there is even less garden for growing once you have erected the requisite shed. The advantage of having just a few hand tools is that they will usually fit into the back of the garage or even under the stairs in the house. Once you own a large rotavator (rototiller), no one will be pleased when it is trundled across the carpet to put it away or its sharp tines scratch the side of the car as you try to manoeuvre it into and out of a tightly packed garage.

Once you start to use a rotavator (rototiller) your gardening will be on a scale that usually means having a shed devoted to tools, and you may want to consider having a combined tool and potting shed – it should be a simple matter to put a bench down one side of a tool shed. Having a potting shed may seem to be rather an old-fashioned idea, but once you have had one you will find it difficult to manage without. However, it is not essential, and many successful gardeners manage quite well without one.

Do you need a greenhouse or cold frame?

Just as a handful of tools are all that you need to get started, it is also not essential to have a greenhouse and cold frames. There is no doubt that such structures are useful and will make your life much easier in many ways, but they are expensive in terms of both cost and space – and also in terms of the

time you will spend in them if you have only a limited number of hours available for gardening. In any case, most of the things that you will do in a greenhouse can be carried out elsewhere. Any propagation, for example, that is necessary can be done on the kitchen windowsill (as long as the cook is sympathetic), while tomatoes and cucumbers, which are the most common greenhouse crops, can be grown in the open, even if it means they crop later.

If, however, you intend to garden on a large scale and do wish to invest in a greenhouse, then bear in mind that the design is very much a matter of personal preference. Often your choice of greenhouse will be dictated by what you can comfortably fit into the available space in your garden as much as by its aesthetic appeal. In spite of the wide variety of greenhouses now on the market, there is still ample scope for the keen amateur to design and build a greenhouse suited to his or her own specifications and requirements. If you are not that practically minded, however, and do not want to go to the expense of buying a greenhouse, you might like to consider using polythene (plastic) tunnels instead. Although not very attractive, these tunnels are a cheap and practical alternative to the traditional greenhouse.

ABOVE **A small vegetable and herb garden such as this does not require a large battery of tools.**

BELOW **Terracotta pots, which are used for blanching seakale and other vegetables, such as endives, make striking ornaments in the garden.**

Greenhouses

The ultimate goal of most gardeners is to have a greenhouse, for it extends the possibilities of the garden tremendously. Such a structure can be used for propagation, for growing tender or winter crops and for overwintering plants that cannot be safely left outside. There is a fourth, often unspoken, use and that is to keep the gardener dry and warm in winter.

ABOVE **The marigolds planted with a row of tomatoes in this greenhouse will ward off potential pests, a technique known as companion planting.**

Most of the horticultural operations that are done in a greenhouse can be achieved perfectly satisfactorily in cold frames. Most gardeners, however, prefer to carry them out in the warmth and comfort of the greenhouse, rather than bending over a cold frame in a cold or wet wind.

Choosing a greenhouse

As with any equipment, the first thing to consider are your reasons for making the purchase. Why do you want a greenhouse? What are you going to do with it? This is an important stage, because answering these questions will help to determine the size. Cost and the available space will also obviously influence the size, but if possible, make use the prime consideration. Most gardeners, slightly tongue in cheek, will tell you to work out the size and then double it. There is some truth in this old saw, and many, if not most, gardeners wish that they had bought a larger greenhouse than the one they did. So buy larger rather than smaller if you possibly can.

BELOW **This standard straight-sided greenhouse is made of aluminium, but it has been painted green, rather than being left silver, so that it blends in better with the colours of the garden.**

Material

These days the choice is mainly between wood and aluminium, although it is still possible to find old iron-frame greenhouses, and some more expensive ones are a combination of materials, such as brick and wood. For most gardeners the choice is simply an aluminium frame, because it is the cheapest style available, but there are other factors to be taken into consideration. For example, wooden greenhouses are far more attractive than aluminium ones. However, although they usually fit more sympathetically into the garden, they are more expensive and the upkeep is more time-consuming. Wooden greenhouses are slightly warmer in winter. It is possible to make your own, working to your own design and dimensions.

Aluminium greenhouses are cheap and easy to maintain. The cheaper ones may, however, be rather flimsy, and in exposed positions the sides may flex and the glass fall out! They normally come in standard sizes, but because they are modular, there is a choice of the number of windows and their position. Some companies will build to your specifications, but this is obviously a more expensive option. It is now possible to buy aluminium greenhouses where the frame is painted, which partially disguises the aluminium.

Glass can now be replaced with plastic. Most gardeners prefer the traditional material, but if there are children around it is often more sensible to go for plastic on safety grounds.

RIGHT **An unusually shaped greenhouse with a steeply pitched roof that not only looks different from conventional greenhouses, but has the added advantage that the steep sides absorb the low winter sun more easily.**

IMPERIAL GREENHOUSE
ROBINSONS

LEFT It is vital not to let greenhouses over-heat. Opening the windows at the right time is not always possible if you are not at home during the hottest part of the day, but automatic window-openers will do the job for you.

Digging in

The old-fashioned idea of sinking the greenhouse into the ground is a good one as long as you can overcome any drainage problems. Steps lead down to the door, and on to a central aisle, dug out of the soil. The side benches are laid on the natural soil level and the roof springs from a low wall on the ground. The advantage of this system, apart from the fact that it is relatively cheap, is that the soil acts as a vast storage heater. Gardeners using such a greenhouse find that as long as they provide some form of insulation, no heat is required to overwinter tender plants. Traditionally, a wooden framework would have been used for the roof, but aluminium would do just as well.

Shape

The shape of the greenhouse is a matter of personal preference. Traditional styles have vertical sides, but some new ones have sloping sides, which allow in more light – especially useful during winter when the sun is low or if you have trays of seedlings on the floor.

Octagonal greenhouses are suitable for small sites, and many people find them more decorative than the traditional shapes. Because they are almost round, the "aisle" is just a central standing area, thus saving a lot of wasted space. However, the amount of useful space is still quite small.

Lean-to greenhouses can be built against walls, which not only saves space but also makes use of the warmth that is usually found in the wall, especially house walls. These are obviously much cheaper than a full greenhouse, but the amount of useful space within them is limited because the light does not come from all directions and plants can get drawn. Painting the wall white helps because more light is reflected back onto the plants.

Ventilation

When you buy a greenhouse, make sure that it has as many opening windows as you can afford because the free passage of air through the structure is of the utmost

ABOVE Insulating the greenhouse is important during the cold winter months, helping to keep heating costs down as well as preventing any violent fluctuations in temperature. Polythene (plastic) bubble insulation is cheap and efficient.

LEFT Some plants, such as peppers, grow better in a greenhouse than they do outside in the open air. In a greenhouse, they are assured of a constant temperature and humidity.

LEFT **It is important to keep the sun out of the greenhouse during the hottest part of the year. Shading helps to keep the temperature down and also protects the plants from the scorching effects of the sun.**

importance. Stagnant air in a greenhouse is a killer, as all kinds of fungal diseases are likely to develop very quickly. Openings can either be covered with conventional windows or with louvres. If you are away during daylight hours in summer, the time when windows need to be opened on hot days, automatic openers can be used. The mechanism opens the windows as soon as a specified pre-set temperature is reached. Having a door at each end helps on larger houses. In winter, windows should be left open as much as possible, and, when it is necessary to close them, use a fan to keep the air circulating.

Heating

There are various methods of heating a greenhouse, but one of the most versatile is with electricity. Although the cost per unit of heat may be greater, the control of its output through the use of thermostats is such that no heat (or money) is wasted, because the appliance comes on only when the temperature drops below a certain point. Thermostatically controlled gas heaters are also now becoming available. Paraffin heaters are cheap, but they need to be regularly filled and maintained and they produce large amounts of water vapour, which encourages disease unless the greenhouse is ventilated.

Heating bills can be reduced by insulating the greenhouse. Double glazing is the ultimate but is expensive. A cheaper alternative is to line the house with sheets of clear polythene (plastic), preferably containing air bubbles. If you have only a few plants that need protecting, it is cheaper to close off one end of the greenhouse with polythene and heat just this area. If the number of plants is small enough, a heated propagator or a cloche over a heated bench may be sufficient.

Shading

Greenhouses need to be as light as possible, especially during the winter, but at the same time bright sunshine should be kept out as this will raise the temperature too much. It is possible to buy shade netting, which can be draped over the outside or clipped to the inside of the glass. This is easy to remove in overcast periods. An opaque wash applied to the glass reduces the effect of the sun considerably, but it is time-consuming to keep removing it during dull weather, so it is usually left in place from early summer to mid-autumn. There is one form of wash that becomes transparent when it rains, thus letting in more light.

Fittings

The full height of the greenhouse is needed for tomatoes and cucumbers, which can be grown in growing bags on the floor. Benching or staging is a useful addition, at least down one side, and can be made of wood or longer-lasting aluminium.

If the staging has raised sides it can be filled with sand. This is useful for sinking pots in to help keep them warm and moist. Heating cables can also be used to keep the bench warm, and building a polythene (plastic) or glass cabinet or lid on top will turn it into an effective propagating bench.

Polytunnels

Polythene (plastic) tunnels are a cheap alternative to greenhouses. They are ideal for growing winter and early spring vegetables and for housing and propagating plants until they are ready to plant out. They are, however, rather ugly and can get very cold, and the polythene will need replacing every three years or so.

RIGHT **Electric fan heaters are very efficient. When equipped with thermostats, they only come on when extra heat is required. They can also be used to circulate the air on still, damp days.**

Tools and Equipment

To look in the average garden centre you would imagine that you need a tremendous battery of tools and equipment before you could ever consider gardening, but in fact you can start (and continue) gardening with relatively few tools and no equipment at all.

Tools are personal things, so one gardener may always use a spade for digging, no matter how soft the ground, whereas another would always use a fork as long as the ground was not too heavy. The type of hoe for certain jobs is another subject on which gardeners hold widely different opinions.

Buying tools

It is not necessary to buy a vast armoury of tools when you first start gardening. Most of the jobs can be done with a small basic kit. When you are buying, always choose the best you can afford. Many of the cheaper tools are made of pressed steel, which soon becomes blunt, will often bend and may even break. Stainless steel is undoubtedly the best, but tools made of this tend to be expensive. Ordinary steel implements can be almost as good, especially if you keep them clean. Avoid tools that are made of aluminium. Trowels and hand forks especially are often made of aluminium, but they wear down and blunt quickly and are not good value for money.

Soil Testers

The chemical composition of the soil can be tested by the gardener by using one of a range of soil testers. The most commonly used checks the acidity/alkalinity of the soil. It is chemical based and involves mixing soil samples with water and checking the colour against a chart. More complicated tests indicate whether there is a shortage of minerals or trace elements. The balance can then be adjusted by adding lime or fertilizers to the soil.

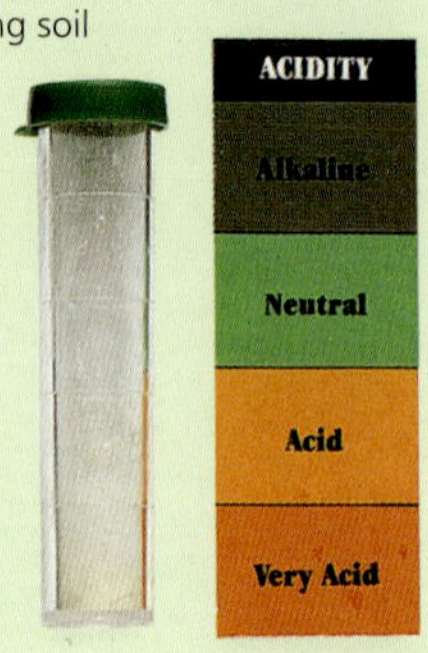

Second-hand

A good way to acquire a collection of tools is to buy them second-hand. There are advantages to this. One is that they are usually much cheaper than new ones. Frequently, too, they are made of much better steel than cheap, modern ones and still retain a keen edge, even after many years' use. In the past gardening tools were made with a much greater variation in design and size. If you go to buy a modern spade, for example, you will probably find that the sizes in the shop are all the same – designed for the "average" gardener. Old tools come in all shapes and

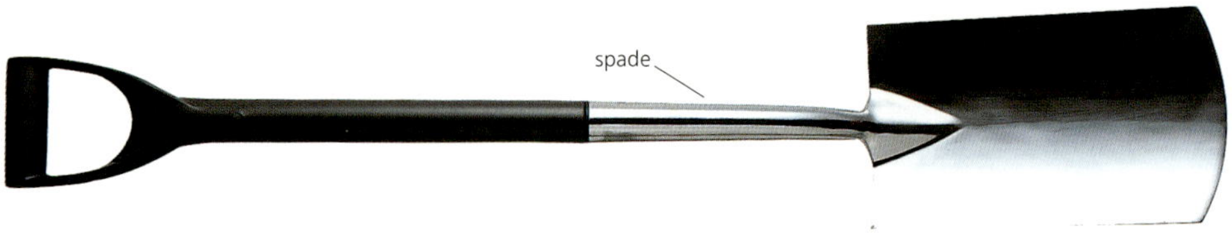

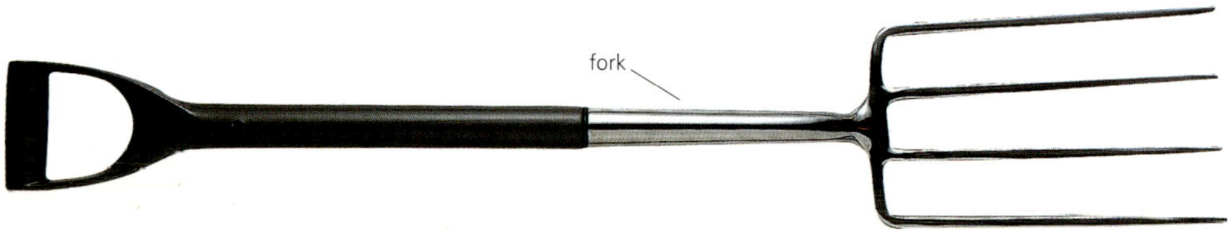

Labelling and Tying

When working in the garden, it is useful to have a tray of odds and ends, such as string, raffia, plant ties and labels. You never know when you might need them. For example, it is always difficult to remember what has been planted or sown where – it may be weeks before seed you have sown is visible above ground.

sizes, and if you find modern tools uncomfortable to use you are more likely to find an old one that is made just for you.

Not all old tools are good by any means, of course, but by keeping an eye out and buying only good quality ones you will end up with tools that will more than see you through your gardening career and at a relatively modest price. Car boot fairs (garage sales) and rural junk shops (second-hand stores) are the places to look out for them. Avoid antique shops where such tools are sold at inflated prices to be hung as decorations on the wall rather than to be used.

Care and maintenance

Look after your tools. If you do this they will not only always be in tip-top working condition but will last a lifetime. Scrape all the mud and any vegetation off the tools as soon as you have used them. Once they are clean, run an oily rag lightly over the metal parts. The thin film of oil will stop the metal from corroding. This not only makes the tools last longer but also makes them easier to use because less effort is needed to use a clean spade than one with a rough surface of rust.

In addition, keep the wooden parts clean, wiping them over with linseed oil if the wood becomes too dry.

Keep all blades sharp. Hang tools up if possible. Standing spades and hoes on the ground, especially if it is concrete, will blunt them over time. Keep them away from children.

Equipment

It is possible to run a vegetable and fruit garden with no mechanical aids at all. However, if you have grass paths, a lawn mower will, obviously, be more than useful – it will be essential. Hedge cutters, too, are useful, although hedges can be cut by hand much more easily than grass paths.

In the vegetable garden itself the only mechanical device that you may require is a rotavator (rototiller), which can be used for digging and breaking up the soil. Unless you have a large garden, however, this is not absolutely necessary, although it does make life easier if you want to break down a heavy soil into a fine tilth.

Keep all your equipment maintained. There is nothing worse than wanting a piece of machinery to use in a hurry only to find that it will not start. After the weather, machinery is the most stressful part of gardening.

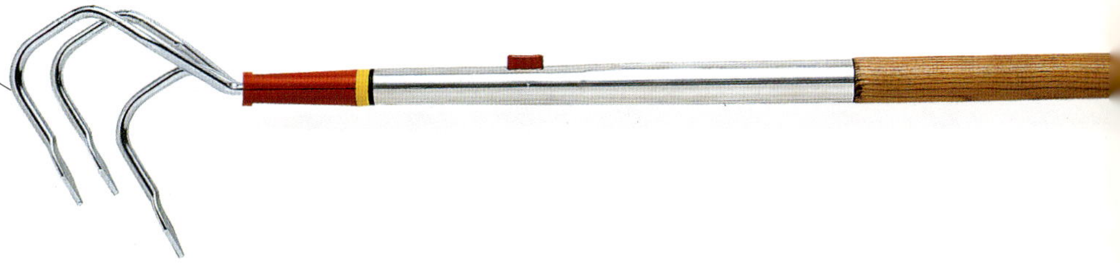

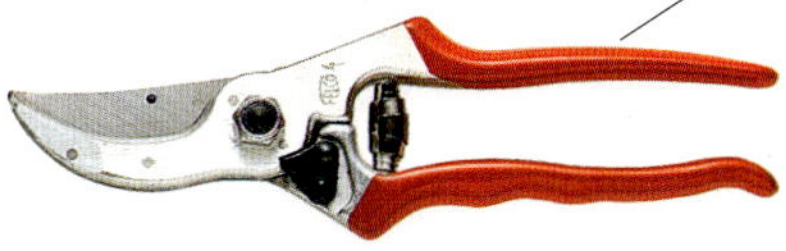

Tool Sheds

The larger the garden and the more tools you have, the bigger the problem you will have in storing them. It is possible to keep a handful of items in a cupboard in the house or hanging on the garage wall. Gradually, however, more and more space is required.

When gardening, you will accumulate bags of compost (soil mix) to be stored as well as a multitude of pots, and, depending on where you live, the wheelbarrow might be best stored under cover. The ultimate solution to these problems is to get a tool shed.

Buying

As with a greenhouse, whenever you buy a shed it always seems to be too small soon after you get it, so think carefully before you buy. What do you need it for? If it is just to store tools, then it is possible to buy a small shed that is no more than a cupboard. This might have just enough space to hang tools and stand a couple of sacks of compost (soil mix) and some pots on the floor, but there will not be enough room to walk into it.

If you want to keep non-gardening things in there as well – a couple of bicycles, perhaps, as well as the garden furniture – you are obviously going to need far more space.

BELOW **Although it is not absolutely essential, a potting shed is a useful place to work, especially on a wet day.**

It is worth considering whether you want to use it as a combined tool and potting shed, and this would obviously require yet more space. Ultimately, the decision is likely to depend on how much money you want to spend and the amount of room available.

Materials

Most tool sheds are made out of wood, and they are usually purchased in prefabricated sections that are bolted together on site. The cheaper softwoods will last for years if they are treated with preservatives at regular intervals. The more expensive cedar sheds will last much longer, although they, too, benefit from treatment with preservatives. Cheap plastic and sheet metal sheds are also available, but they generally look cheap and do not last long. If that is all you can afford, tuck it out of sight – behind a hedge or screen, for example.

There is no reason why you should not make your own shed. This would not necessarily work out cheaper than buying one, but at least it can be tailor-made to the site and to your requirements. Wooden structures can be dismantled and moved elsewhere, but for a more robust and warmer building, it could be made from brick. Remember to check local planning laws before you begin work on it.

Cheaper sheds are supplied without floors and are simply set on the ground – but it is preferable to have a concrete base. Concrete is cold and unyielding to feet if you have to stand on it for any length of time – while potting, for example. A wooden floor, set above the earth or concrete, is warmer, but unless it is well supported from below, it flexes as you walk on it and in some cases the whole shed may rock. Windows take up valuable wall space, but if your shed is a reasonable size or if you are using it for potting, they are essential to let in light.

ABOVE **As well as being the ideal place to store your tools, equipment and other gardening materials, a tool shed can be attractive in its own dusty way.**

Organization

Most hand tools can be hung on the walls using ready-made racks or by using wooden dowel pegs set into a strip of wood. If there is space it is a good idea to build a potting bench along one wall, preferably under a window. Equipment or bags of compost (soil mix) can be stored below the bench, while shelves above it can carry pots or smaller tools. An old bathroom cabinet or a similar small cupboard with a child-proof lock is useful for keeping chemicals in if you use them. Open bags of compost tend to get spilt, so it is a good idea to store them in plastic dustbins (containers) that fit under the bench.

RIGHT **This selection of tools is still in working order, even after many years' work. Clean and well oiled, they should give many more years' good service.**

Cold Frames

Cold frames are rather underrated by many gardeners. They are not only useful in their own right but they can also be used for most of the jobs that are undertaken in the greenhouse. They are less expensive than greenhouses, take up less space and are cheaper to keep warm. Their main disadvantage is that the gardener works outside and not inside in the warm and dry as with a greenhouse.

Uses

In the vegetable garden, cold frames are frequently used for producing winter or early crops of such vegetables as carrots. The frame can be in a permanent position in the garden or moved, rather like a large cloche, onto the vegetable bed itself. The vegetables can be grown either directly in the soil or in growing bags. Later in the year, the cold frame can be used for growing cucumbers or melons.

Another basic use is to afford protection and warmth to trays of seeds or seedlings. Once the plants are ready to go out, the lights can be opened over a period of a week or two to harden off the plants before they are planted out.

Materials

As with greenhouses, the cheaper cold frames are made from aluminium. Their advantage is that they are light enough to move around, but they are not good at retaining heat. Wooden ones are better at this, and cold frames with solid walls made from brick, concrete or even old railway sleepers (ties) provide much better protection during the winter.

Aluminium-framed cold frames can be designed to include glass in the sides, which allows in more light. Solid-sided ones are much warmer but light can enter only through the glass above. It is a good idea to paint the inside of the walls white to reflect some of the light.

Lights (lids) that are glazed with glass are generally preferable, but plastic can be used where there is danger of accidents – if children or elderly people are in the garden, for example.

Heating

Most cold frames, as their name suggests, are not heated. However, it is easier and cheaper to provide some warmth than in a greenhouse, and if you want to propagate or overwinter tender plants it may be possible to supply some form of heat. Electric heating cables installed in the sand below the pots and around the walls of the frame is the easiest method. It is also the most efficient if the cables are connected to a thermostat that switches the electricity on only when heat is required.

Hotbeds

A traditional way to heat cold frames is to set them on a pile of farmyard manure, usually horse dung. As the dung breaks down it releases more than enough heat to keep the frames warm. Soil can be laid on top of the manure and a wide range of vegetables grown in it during the winter. The manure should be fresh, and once it has rotted down and no longer generates heat, it can be spread on the garden and dug in.

Insulation

It is easy to insulate cold frames because they are small. The simplest way is to throw an old carpet over the frame on cold nights.

LEFT **When the seedlings are fully acclimatized and ready to be planted out, the lights (lids) can be left off altogether.**

This may be sufficient to hold in the residual heat, so no extra heating is required to keep the frame above freezing. More efficient methods would be to cover the frames with bubble polythene (plastic) or even to line the inside of the lights with it.

Ventilation

When it is not necessary to keep the frames tightly shut to avoid heat loss, it is sensible to open them slightly, even if it is just a crack, to let air circulate among the plants. This helps prevent various fungal diseases, especially botrytis, which cause seedlings to die through rotting.

RIGHT **A cold frame with a partially opened light (lid) so that the greenhouse-grown seedlings gradually become acclimatized to the outside conditions.**

BELOW **A brick cold frame with a soil bed for growing winter and early spring vegetables.**

Cloches

Cloches are portable forms of protection, rather like miniature cold frames. They are mainly employed during the winter and early spring, but they can be used at any time of year to bring on a crop or to protect it.

ABOVE **A rigid plastic cloche is easy to use. The sections butt up against each other and can be pegged into the soil. Endpieces are also available.**

Uses

There are frequently times when you want to cosset a few plants. They may need protection from the cold or it may be that they are not particularly worried by the cold but need a little warmth to make them grow faster. One row of strawberries, for example, can be covered with cloches to make them fruit one or even two weeks earlier than they would if uncovered. During the winter, broad (fava) beans will come on better if they are protected not only from the cold but also the extremes of rain and wind. Cloches can also be used to protect plants from predators.

In wet and cold areas cloches can be used to cover the ground so that it both dries out and warms up ready for sowing. This will often enable the gardener to sow several weeks earlier than the weather would otherwise allow in the unprotected garden.

In autumn, cloches can be used to cover ripening or harvested vegetables. For example, cordon tomatoes can be lowered to the ground onto straw and allowed to ripen under cloches, while onions that have been harvested in a wet summer can be placed under cloches to "harden off" before storing.

Materials

Some of the earliest cloches were glass bell jars – like upside-down glass vases – which were placed over individual plants. Other traditional cloches were made from sheets of glass, and the earliest types were held in iron frameworks, and resembled miniature greenhouses. Later, cloches became simpler, and the glass was held together by metal or, more recently, plastic or rubber clips. These were known as barn or tent cloches because of their shapes, and could cover a single plant or a whole row when arranged in a line.

Glass is still used, but most cloches are made of polythene (sheet vinyl or plastic) or rigid plastic. There are two main types. One is made up of individual units, which link up in some way, and the other is like a miniature polytunnel, with a single sheet of polythene stretched along the length of the row.

All cloches will do the job they are designed to do. Glass should last the longest, unless you are careless. Although plastics and polythene (sheet vinyl) have a more limited lifespan, they are generally cheaper to replace and are usually lighter and easier to store.

Making your own

Bought cloches may not fit the length or width of the rows in your garden, especially if you are growing in deep beds or blocks. It is relatively simple to make your own. For smaller rows, several hoops of galvanized wire are pushed into the earth at intervals of 60cm/24in and a sheet of polythene (plastic) is laid over them. Place more wire hoops over the first, so that the polythene is trapped between them and held securely. For real security the sides and the two ends of the polythene can be buried in the earth.

For larger beds hoops can be made from lengths of plastic water pipe. Place a stick or iron stake in the ground on each side of the block or row and place the end of the pipe over the stake, forming a hoop. Proceed as before, using more hoops to hold the polythene (plastic) in place, or use strings stretched over the polythene next to the hoops and attached to wire hooks sunk into the ground.

LEFT **Glass bell jars are simple cloches for covering one plant. They are expensive, but plastic sweet jars make a good, if not as attractive, alternative.**

RIGHT **Old-fashioned cloches are particularly good for decorative vegetable gardens. However, they are also very expensive.**

soil

The soil in your garden is your most valuable asset, and it should be cared for accordingly. Some gardeners are lucky and inherit soil in good condition, others find that their soil was once good but is now a little tired and in need of attention. Unlucky gardeners start with virgin soil, often a heavy clay and filled with builder's rubble. Even good soil needs care, while the other two types of soil, especially the heavy soil, need plenty of attention. However, given time and energy even a heavy soil will become fertile and workable, and produce good vegetables.

The main tool in the gardener's armoury is organic material: farmyard manure, garden compost and many other well-rotted forms of humus. It is never possible to have too much of this if you want good soil. Gravel and sharp sand can also be used in the battle against heavy soil. When added to clay, these fine crushed stones separate the particles of clay and allow water to drain through.

Once you have improved your soil, you will find that there is nothing more satisfying than turning a barren soil into a fertile one.

RIGHT A soil that is well worked is ideal for growing vegetables as long as its structure and fertility are maintained by the addition of well-rotted organic material.

Know your soil

All soils are different, and even in a single garden the soil may vary from place to place. Look at your soil: notice how it absorbs water, how well plants grow, what does well and what does not. Check several sites around the garden with a soil test kit – small kits are available from garden centres. The more you study and get to know your soil, the better gardener you will become and the better crops you will grow. The two main aspects to consider are its structure and its fertility. If you can get these right, the rest of your gardening should be easy.

Working the soil

Some people are lucky: they take over a garden that has been well worked. Others are not so fortunate: they inherit a new site that is little more than pure clay. However, although the people who have a well-worked garden may think they can relax, it is important that they keep on treating the ground with respect. If they neglect to feed the soil, it will become tired and infertile; if they stomp around on it after heavy rain, the soil will become compacted and the beautiful structure that has been built up over the years will be lost.

Those with a new garden will have to work hard, especially if it is heavy clay, but gradually, season by season, the soil will improve until eventually it will be unrecognizable. I remember my father moving to a garden in which the soil was nothing but solid yellow clay; by the time he hung up his boots for the last time, it was possible to dig the ground with a fork in midwinter, such was the extent to which its condition had been improved. It does not take a lifetime to improve the soil, however, and even a few seasons will make a real difference.

There are few soils that the average householder will encounter in which it is impossible to grow vegetables. Simply digging and sowing will produce results – not necessarily good results, especially if you do just that every year, but nonetheless, it will produce results. However, if it is fed with organic material the soil will soon not only be easier to work but will also produce better crops.

BELOW Using raised beds is one method of creating a controlled medium, away from the influence of the native soil. For example, a fertile loam can be imported and used in a bed on top of a heavy clay, thus providing an "instant" garden.

Better crops

By better crops we mean bigger and tastier vegetables. Vegetables that are half-starved or that grow in dry soils are often tough and bitter tasting. Compost and similar materials help to retain moisture in the soil, releasing it to the plants over a long period, thus reducing the risk of drought and dry soil. Quantity is also improved, because a richer soil will support more plants. It is worth remembering, too, that undernourished, struggling plants are more susceptible to pests and diseases, and providing good soil is, therefore, a way of protecting your plants and reducing the need for chemicals.

There's nothing like muck

The greatest soil improver of them all is well-rotted organic material of some sort. This is relatively cheap, especially if bought in quantity, and in some areas stables give horse manure away free to anyone prepared to collect it – a bargain that should never be overlooked. There is also a great deal of garden and kitchen waste that can be recycled.

BELOW **Working from wooden planks is a useful way of avoiding walking directly on the soil, which can cause it to compact. This precaution is especially important when the soil is wet.**

Types of Soil

Vegetables can, within reason, be grown on most soils, but, as one would expect, there is an optimum soil in which the best vegetables can be grown. Most soils can be persuaded, with varying degrees of effort, to move towards that optimum, but the starting point is often different.

ABOVE **The better the soil, the better the crops will be. Keeping the soil in good condition is the key to successful kitchen gardening.**

Clay

When they work well clay soils can be fertile, but their structure is the despair of most gardeners. Clay is heavy and the particles cling together, making the soil sticky. Clay soil compacts easily, forming a solid lump that roots find hard to penetrate and that is difficult to dig. Try not to walk on clay soils when they are wet. This tendency to become compacted and sticky means that clay soils are slow to drain, but, once drained, they "set" like concrete, becoming a hard mass. They also tend to be cold and slow to warm up, making them unsuitable for early crops.

Clay soil is not, one would think, a good basis for growing vegetables, yet many of the best gardens are on clay. Clay soils are usually rich, and all the hard effort needed in the initial stages to improve the soil will pay off in the long term.

Sandy soils

Soils that are made up of sand and silts are quite different. They have few of the sticky clay particles but are made up of individual grains that allow the water to pass through quickly. This quick passage of water through the soil tends to leach (wash) out nutrients, so the soils are often poor. But they also tend to be much warmer in winter and are quicker to warm in spring, thus making it easier to get early crops. Silts contain particles that are a bit more clay-like in texture than those found in sandy soils, and they hold more moisture and nutrients.

Both types of soil are easy to improve and are not difficult to work. Sand does not compact like clay does (although it is still not good practice to walk on beds), but silty soils are more susceptible to the impact of feet and wheelbarrows. Adding organic material can temper their insatiable thirst.

Loams

The soil of most gardeners' dreams is loam. This is a combination of clay and sandy soils, with the best elements of both. They tend to be free draining, but at the same time

BELOW **Soil that has been well worked, as the soil in this garden clearly has, is essential to the production of good crops of vegetables.**

COMMON TYPES OF SOIL

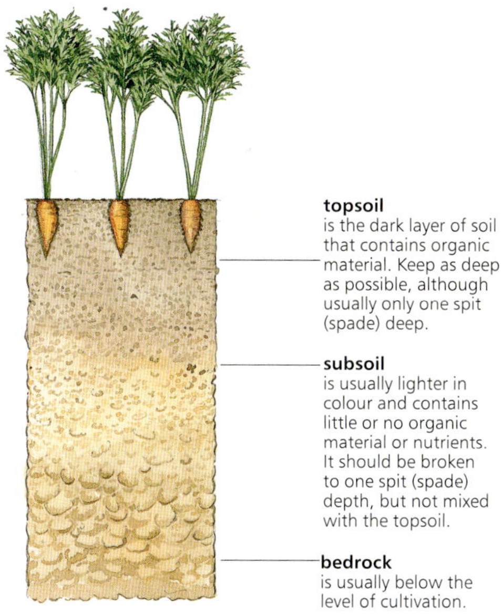

Soil profile A typical soil profile usually consists of three main elements: an upper layer of dark, fertile topsoil; a middle layer of lighter, infertile subsoil; and a lower layer of bedrock, which ranges from a few to hundreds of metres (yards) deep.

moisture retentive. This description – free draining and moisture retentive – is often used of soils and potting mixes and it may seem a contradiction. It means that the soil is sufficiently free draining to allow excess moisture to drain away, but enough moisture is retained for the plant without it standing in stagnant water. Such soils are easy to work at any time of the year, and they warm up well in spring and are thus good for early crops.

Acid and alkaline soils

Another way of classifying soils is by their acidity or alkalinity. Those that are based on peat (peat moss) are acid; those that include chalk or limestone are alkaline. Gardeners use a scale of pH levels to indicate the degree of acidity or alkalinity. Very acid is 1, neutral is 7 and very alkaline is 14, although soils rarely have values at the extremes of the scale. Although they can be grown on a wider range of soils, vegetables are usually grown in soils with a pH of 5.5–7.5, with the optimum conditions being around 6.5. So, the best pH for growing vegetables is slightly on the acid side of neutral. A test with a soil kit will show the rating in your own garden. You can adjust the acid soils of a garden, but it is more difficult to alter alkaline ones.

pH values

1.0	extremely acid
4.0	maximum acidity tolerated by most plants
5.5	maximum acidity for reasonable vegetables
6.0	maximum acidity for good vegetables
6.5	optimum for the best vegetables
7.0	neutral, maximum alkalinity for good vegetables
7.5	maximum alkalinity for reasonable vegetables
8.0	maximum tolerated by most plants
14.0	extremely alkaline

TESTING THE SOIL FOR NUTRIENTS

1 Collect the soil sample 5–8cm/2–3in below the surface. Take a number of samples, but test each one separately.

2 With this kit, mix one part of soil with five parts of water. Shake well in a jar, then allow the water to settle.

3 Draw off some of the settled liquid from the top few centimetres (about an inch) for your test.

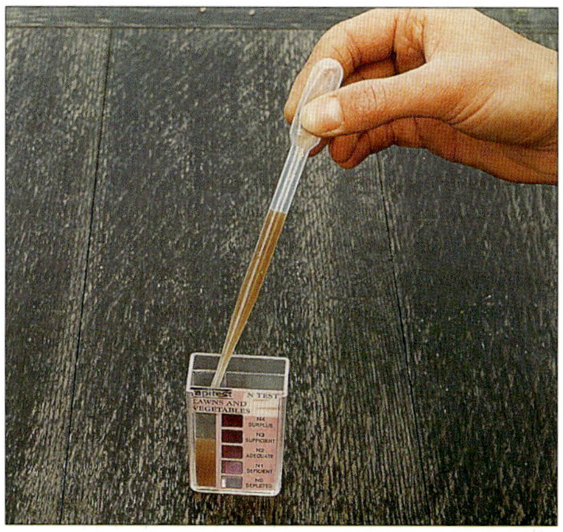

4 Carefully transfer the solution to the test chamber in the plastic container, using the pipette.

5 Select a colour-coded capsule (one for each nutrient). Put the powder in the chamber, replace the cap and shake well.

6 After a few minutes, compare the colour of the liquid with the shade panel of the container.

Improving Drainage

Few garden plants, and certainly no vegetables, like to sit in stagnant water – watercress, of course, likes water, but it must be running. A free-draining soil is of the utmost importance if you want to grow decent crops. In the majority of gardens this simply means improving the soil, but in a few gardens, where the problem is serious, it will mean installing a drainage system first.

Section through a land drain This cross-section of a typical land drain shows the various layers of materials from which it is constructed, including the topsoil, an inverted turf or perforated plastic membrane, gravel, peabeach or crushed stone, and the land-drain pipe.

Working the soil

In many gardens wet soil can be improved simply by improving the soil itself so that the water drains away. One way to achieve this is to add organic material to improve the soil's fertility. The fibrous material contained in the organic matter helps to break up the clay particles, allowing water to pass through. This material eventually breaks down and so it should be added every time the soil is dug.

The other method is to add gravel or grit to the soil. The best material for this is what used to be known as horticultural grit – that is, grit up to about 5mm/¼in in diameter. Flint grit that has been crushed is best because the angular faces allow water to drain away better than the rounded surfaces of the uncrushed grits, such as peabeach. It may seem sacrilege to add stones to soil, but these fine gravels will make all the difference.

Drainage systems

Of course, it is no good improving the soil if the water still does not have anywhere to go. In fact, the situation could become worse because the well-drained soil in the bed could become a sump, with water running off adjacent paths and lawns into it. If water lies in the garden, then there is nothing for it but to install proper drainage. This can be a big undertaking, and many gardeners may prefer to get professional help.

The basic idea is to channel the water away from the garden. It may be possible to send it into a ditch, but under no circumstances should you connect it to the main drainage system from the house because this is bound to be breaking all kinds of local laws and regulations. If you do not have a ditch, there are two possible solutions. The first is to dig a soakaway. This is a deep hole, usually at least 2m/6ft deep, filled with clean rubble. Water runs out of the drainage pipes into the hole from which it slowly soaks away into the surrounding soil, well below the level of the beds. Alternatively, if the lay of the land allows it, excess water can be piped into a decorative pond, along with other surface water – such as that from the roof of the house, for example.

The drainage system that removes the water from the land is constructed by digging a series of trenches about 60cm/24in deep. There is one main trench, and the others join it at an angle. The trenches should slope towards the soakaway if the

LEFT **Good drainage ensures that this garden is able to support a diverse array of flowers and vegetables, including cabbages and sunflowers.**

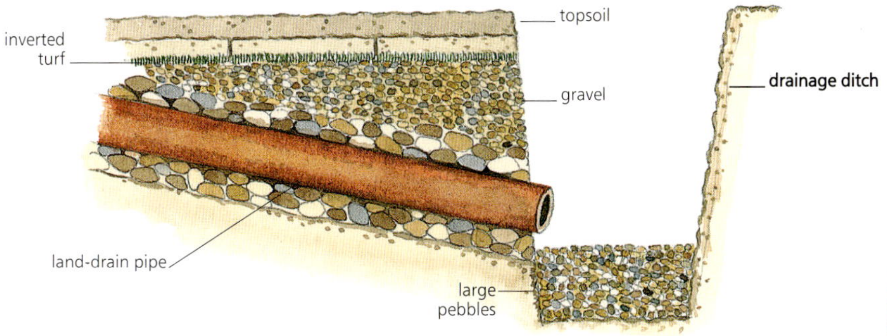

Land drain on a flat site This is a section through a land drain on a flat site, showing the fall of the pipe – in this case the angle is exaggerated – which slopes down into a drainage ditch. The water percolates through the soil and pebbles and into the pipe, which then delivers it to the drainage ditch.

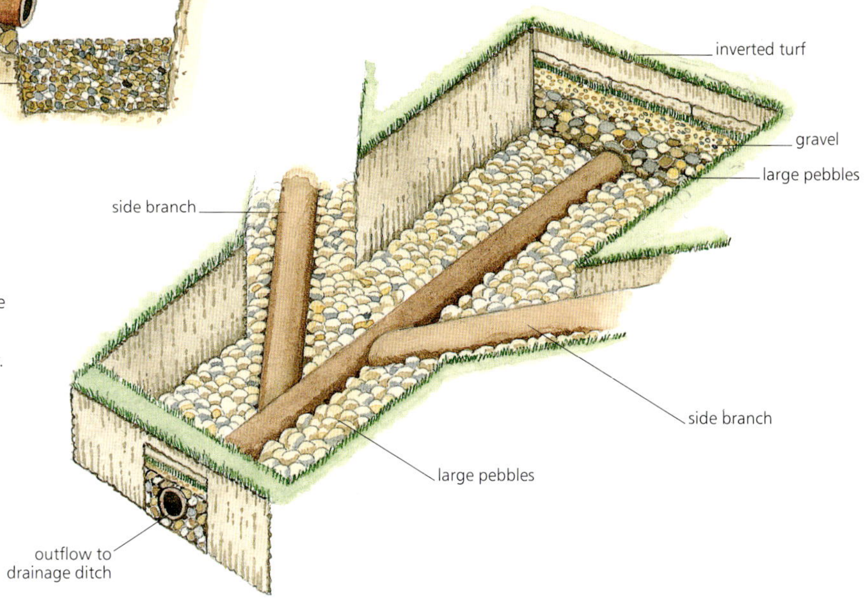

Land drain on a sloping site An aerial view of the drainage system, showing the side branches, which are constructed in the same way as the main pipe. When the ground slopes, the pipes are laid parallel to the ground, so that the water can drain away.

Laying a soakaway If there is no ditch or drain available, then the water must be directed into a soakaway. This is a large hole filled with clean rubble or large stones. In lighter soils, it should be lined with bricks to prevent it filling with soil.

ground is flat, but should run parallel to the surface if the ground slopes. Perforated plastic tubing that comes in a continuous reel is the cheapest form of piping. This is laid on gravel with more gravel laid on top. Upturned turves are then laid on the top of the gravel (to prevent soil from washing into the gravel and blocking the drainage) and the topsoil is replaced. If turf is not available, a pervious plastic membrane can be used.

As an alternative to plastic piping, traditional tile drains can be used. These are short lengths of ceramic pipe laid with a small gap between each. A less efficient, but traditional, method is to use French drains – fill a trench with rubble and top it off with upturned turves and topsoil.

WORKING IN ORGANIC MATTER

1 Soil that has been dug in the autumn can have more organic matter worked into the top layer in the spring. Spread the organic matter over the surface.

2 Lightly work the organic material into the top layer of soil with a fork. There is no need for full-scale digging.

Soil Structure

Perhaps the most important task in any garden is to improve and maintain the quality of the soil. Good-quality soil should be the aim of any gardener who wants to grow vegetables or fruit. To ignore the soil is to ignore one of the garden's most important assets.

ABOVE **Green manure helps to improve both the structure and fertility of the soil. Sow it when the ground is not being used for anything else and then dig it in before it flowers and seeds.**

Organic material

The key to improving the soil in your garden is organic material. This is an all-embracing term that covers any vegetable matter that has been broken down into an odourless, fibrous compost. It includes such things as rotted garden waste, kitchen vegetable waste, farmyard manures (which are plant materials that have passed through animals) and other plant waste material.

It is important that any such material should be well-rotted. If it is still in the process of breaking down, it will need nitrogen to complete the process and will extract it from the soil. This, of course, is the reverse of what the gardener wants – the gardener's aim is, in fact, to add nitrogen to the soil. If you are unsure, a good indicator that the material has broken down sufficiently is that it becomes odourless. Even horse manure is free from odour once it has rotted down, and manuring a garden should not be the smelly occupation it is often depicted as being.

Some substances contain undesirable chemicals, but these will be removed if the material is stacked and allowed to weather. Bark and other shredded woody materials may contain resins, for example, while animal and bird manures may contain ammonia from urea. These chemicals will evaporate or be converted by weathering.

Digging in

The best way to apply organic material to the vegetable garden is to dig it in. In this way it becomes incorporated into the soil. If possible, double dig the bed, adding material all the way to the bottom of both spits. This will help to retain moisture and supply nutrients where they are needed, which is down by the roots. It will also encourage roots to delve deeply rather than remaining on the surface where easy water can be obtained from the odd rain shower or watering can. The deeper the roots go the more stable will be the plant's water supply and the plant will grow at a regular pace rather than in unproductive fits and starts. This will produce much better plants.

Top-dressing

Once the ground has been planted, especially with permanent vegetables and fruit, it is impossible to dig in organic material to anything more than a couple of inches. The damage done by disturbing roots makes it pointless to attempt to go any deeper. The answer here is to top-dress with well-rotted matter. A 10cm/4in layer of, say farmyard manure, will be slowly worked into the soil by the earthworms. As well as being taken into the soil, such a dressing will also act as a mulch, protecting the ground from drying out as well as preventing any weed seeds from germinating.

The top-dressing should also be free from any weed seeds or you will be creating problems rather than solving them. Properly made compost and the other types of material that can be used should always be weed free and suitable for use in this way.

Fruit and permanent plantings

For any type of plant that will be in position for several if not many years, it is important that the soil is in the best possible condition before planting begins. Once planted it will be impossible to dig in more material, and

IMPROVING SOIL FERTILITY

The fertility of the soil is much improved by the addition of organic material, but a quick boost can also be achieved by adding an organic fertilizer, spreading it over the surface and then raking it in.

REDUCING SOIL ACIDITY

The acidity of the soil can be reduced by adding lime some weeks before planting and working it in with a rake. Check the soil with a soil testing kit to see how much lime is required.

LEFT **A garden in which the soil is well cared for will reward the gardener with a plentiful harvest. In this large walled kitchen garden, rows of brassicas and espaliered fruit bushes nestle between beds planted with cosmos and marigolds.**

you will have to depend on top-dressing. Although this is a good supplement, it is not an alternative to proper preparation in the first place. The ground should be double dug if possible, and you should add as much organic matter as you can get, especially in the lower layers of soil.

Improving the soil's pH

The other aspect of improving soil is to improve the pH level. For vegetables, as we have noted, the level to aim at is pH6.5, but anything between 6 and 7 is still good, while 5.5–7.5 is acceptable.

If the soil is too acid, the pH can be adjusted somewhat by adding lime to the soil. Three types of lime can be used for reducing soil acidity. Ordinary lime (calcium carbonate) is the safest to use. Quicklime (calcium oxide) is the strongest and most caustic, but it may cause damage. Slaked lime (calcium hydroxide) is quicklime with water added; it is not as strong as quicklime and is therefore less dangerous. Always take safety precautions when you are applying lime and follow the quantities recommended by the manufacturer on the packet. Do not add lime at the same time as manure, because this will release ammonia, which can damage the plants. Spread the lime over the soil at the rate prescribed on the packet and rake it in. Do not sow or plant in the ground for at least a month. Do not over-lime.

It is not as easy to reduce the alkalinity of soil. Peat (peat moss) used to be recommended for this purpose, but not only is collecting peat environmentally unsound, it breaks down quickly and needs to be constantly replaced. Most organic manures are on the acid side and help to bring down the levels. Leafmould, especially that from pine trees, is also acid.

Spent mushroom compost contains lime and is useful for reducing acidity, but it should not be used on chalky (alkaline) soils.

When not to add manure

Not all crops like to be grown in soil that has been freshly manured. Root crops, such as parsnips, for example, tend to "fork" when the soil is too rich. This means that, instead of the single, long, tapering roots, they have short stubby roots with several branches. The parsnip may taste the same, but it is not so convenient to clean and peel.

The way to prevent this happening is to avoid manuring before planting. Either use soil that has been manured from a previous crop – follow the brassicas, for example – or add the organic material during the previous autumn so that it has had a chance to break down before the root crops germinate and start to grow.

IMPROVING SOIL STRUCTURE

1 One of the best ways to improve the structure of the soil is to add as much organic material as you can, preferably when the soil is dug. For heavy soils, this is best done in the autumn.

2 If the soil has already been dug, then well-rotted organic material can be worked into the surface of the soil with a fork. The worms will complete the task of working it into the soil.

WORKING ON WET SOIL

It is best to avoid working on wet soil, but sometimes it is necessary. To ensure that the soil is not compacted and its structure destroyed, it is advisable to work from a plank of wood.

Soil Conditioners

Quite a range of organic conditioners is available to the gardener. Some are free – if you do not count the time taken in working and carting them. Others are relatively cheap, and some, usually those bought by the bag, can be quite expensive. However, not everyone has a stable nearby or enough space to store large quantities of material, and these gardeners will therefore need to buy it as required.

ABOVE **Farmyard manure should be left stacked in a heap until it has lost its smell and has finished rotting down.**

Farmyard manure

A traditional material and still much used by many country gardeners, farmyard manure has the advantage of adding bulk to the soil as well as supplying valuable nutrients. The manure can come from any form of livestock, although the most commonly available is horse manure. It can be obtained from most stables, and many are so glad to get rid of it that they will supply it free if you fetch it yourself. There are often stables situated around the edge of towns, so manure is usually available to town gardeners as well as to those in the country.

Some gardeners do not like the manure when it is mixed with wood shavings rather than with straw, but it is worth bearing in mind that the former is often less likely to contain weed seeds, and as long as it is stacked and allowed to rot down it is excellent for adding to the soil as well as for use as a top-dressing.

All manures should be stacked for a period of at least six months before they are used. When it is ready, it will have lost its dungy smell.

Garden compost

All gardeners should try to recycle as much of their garden and kitchen vegetable waste as possible. In essence, this is simply following nature's pattern, where leaves and stems are formed in the spring and die back in the autumn, falling to the ground and eventually rotting and returning to the plants as nutrients. In the garden some things are removed from the cycle, notably vegetables and fruit, but as much as possible should be recirculated.

Compost is not difficult to make, and, of course, it is absolutely free. If you have the space, use several bins so there is always some available for use.

Unless weeds that are in seed or diseased plants have been used, compost should be safe to use as a soil conditioner and as a mulch.

Leafmould

Leafmould is a natural soil conditioner. It is easy to make and should not cost anything. Only use leafmould made by yourself; never go down to the local woods and help yourself because this will disturb the wood's own cycle and will impoverish the soil there.

SOME ORGANIC MATERIALS

Four stakes knocked into the ground with a piece of wire-netting stretched around them will make the perfect compound for making leafmould. Simply add the leaves as they fall from the trees. It will take a couple of years for them to break down and what was a huge heap will shrink to a small layer by the time the process is complete.

Add leafmould to the soil or use it as a top-dressing. It is usually acid and can be used to reduce the pH of alkaline soil. Leafmould from pine needles is particularly acid.

Peat (peat moss)

This is expensive and does little for the soil because it breaks down too quickly and has little nutritive content. It is also ecologically unsound to use it.

Spent mushroom compost

Often available locally from mushroom farms, the spent compost is relatively cheap, especially if purchased in bulk. It is mainly used in the ornamental part of the garden, but it is still useful in the vegetable garden if it is allowed to rot down. It is particularly useful if the soil is on the acid side because it contains chalk.

Vegetable industrial waste

Several industries produce organic waste material that can be useful in the garden. Spent hop waste from the brewing industry has always been a favourite among those who can obtain it. Coco shells are now imported, although these are better used as a mulch than as a soil conditioner. Several other products are locally available. Allow them to rot well before using.

Green manure

Some crops can be grown simply to be dug back into the ground to improve the soil condition and to add nutrients. They are particularly useful on light soils that are left vacant for any length of time, such as over winter.

Green manures
Broad (fava) beans nitrogen fixing
Italian ryegrass quick growing
Lupins nitrogen fixing
Mustard quick growing
Phacelia quick growing
Red clover nitrogen fixing
Winter tare nitrogen fixing

Green manures can be sown in early autumn and dug in during spring. Alternatively, if you plant fast-growing varieties, you can use them whenever land becomes available during the growing season.

Avoid letting the green manure flower and seed, otherwise it will self-seed. Most of the foliage and stems can be used in the compost bin.

BELOW **Green manure can be grown as a separate crop or it can be grown between existing crops. Here, clover is grown amongst cabbages, where it not only fixes nitrogen in the soil, but also provides a ground cover, keeping the weeds down.**

Making Compost

Compost is a valuable material for any garden, but it is especially useful in the vegetable garden. It is free, apart from any capital required in installing compost bins, but these should last a lifetime and the overall cost should be negligible. A little bit of effort is required, but this is a small price to pay for the resulting gold-dust.

ABOVE **A range of organic materials can be used, but avoid cooked kitchen waste or any weeds that have seed in them. *Clockwise from top left:* kitchen waste, weeds, shreddings and grass clippings.**

The principle

The idea behind compost-making is to emulate the process in which a plant takes nutrients from the soil, dies and then rots, putting the nutrients back into the ground. In the garden, waste plant material is collected, piled in a heap and allowed to rot down before being returned to the soil as crumbly, sweet-smelling, fibrous material.

Because it is in a heap the rotting material generates heat, which encourages it to break down even more quickly. The heat also helps to kill pests and diseases as well as any weed seed in the compost. If the rotting material is to break down properly, a certain amount of moisture is needed, as well as air. If there is too much water, however, the process is slowed down; if there is insufficient air, the heap will go slimy and smell bad.

The process should take up to about three months, but many old fashioned gardeners like to retain the heap for much longer than that, growing marrows and courgettes (zucchini) on it before they break it up for use in the garden.

The compost bin

Gardeners always seem to generate more garden waste than they ever thought possible and never to have enough compost space, so when planning your bins, make sure you have enough. The overall aim is to have three: one to hold new waste, one that is in the process of breaking down, and the third that is ready for use.

The bins are traditionally made from wood (often scrap wood), and because these can be hand-made to fit your space and the amount of material available, this is still the best option. Sheet materials, such as corrugated iron, can also be used. Most ready-made bins are made of plastic, and although these work perfectly well, they may be a bit on the small side in a busy garden.

A bin should contain at least a cubic metre/3.5 cubic feet of compost for it to heat up adequately. If you have a large garden, a bin double this size would be even more efficient. The simplest bin can be made by nailing together four wooden pallets to form a box. If the front is made so that the slats are

RIGHT **Only a small proportion of the vegetables and flowers for cutting in this plot will be used. This means that most of the foliage and stems can be put in the compost bin.**

slotted in to form the wall, they can be removed as the bin is emptied, making the job of removing the compost easier. This is a refinement, however, and not essential.

Materials

Any plant garden waste can be used for composting as long as it does not contain weed seeds. (In fact, it is useful to have a separate bin for anything that contains seeds, because the compost can be used for permanent plantings such as trees. Compost used for this purpose will never come to the surface, and any seeds will be prevented from germinating.) You should also avoid including perennial weeds. Woody material, such as hedge clippings, can be used, but shred it first.

Kitchen vegetable waste, such as peelings and cores, can be used but avoid cooked vegetables, and do not include meat, which will attract rats and other vermin.

Technique

Placing a few branches or twiggy material in the bottom of the bin will help to keep the contents aerated. Put in the material as it becomes available but avoid building up deep layers of any one material, especially grass cuttings. Mix them with other materials.

To help keep the heap warm, cover it with an old carpet or sheet of polythene (plastic). This also prevents excess water from chilling the contents as well as swamping all the air spaces. The lid should be kept on until the compost is required.

Every so often, add a layer of farmyard manure if you can get it because it will provide extra nitrogen to speed things up. Failing this, you can buy special compost accelerators. It is not essential to add manure or an accelerator, however – it just means waiting a couple of weeks longer for your compost.

Air is important, and this usually percolates through the side of the bin, so leave a few gaps between the timbers. If you use old pallets, these are usually crudely made, with plenty of gaps. The colder material around the edges takes longer to break down than that in the centre of the heap, so turn the compost around every so often. This also loosens the pile and allows air to circulate.

MAKING COMPOST

1 A simple compost bin, which should be about 1m/3ft square, can be made by nailing four flat pallets together. These bins are usually roughly made, which means that there will be plenty of air holes between the slats.

2 Pile the waste into the compost bin, making certain that there are no thick layers of the same material. Grass clippings, for example, will not rot down if the layer is too thick because the air cannot penetrate.

3 It is important to keep the compost bin covered with an old mat or a sheet of polythene (sheet vinyl or plastic). This will help to keep in the heat generated by the rotting process and it will also prevent the compost bin from getting too wet in bad weather.

4 Every so often turn the contents of the bin with a fork, partly to let in air and partly to move the outside material, which is slow to rot, into the centre so that the rotting process speeds up. It is easier if you have several bins and turn the compost from one bin into another.

5 When the bin is full, cover the surface with a layer of soil and use it to grow marrows (zucchini), pumpkins or cucumbers. If you want to use the contents as soon as possible, omit the soil and keep covered with polythene. The finished product *(inset, below)* is dark brown, crumbly and has a sweet, earthy smell, not a rotting one. It can be used straight away or left covered until required.

Fertilizers

You cannot go on taking things out of the soil without putting anything back. In nature plants return the nutrients they have taken from the soil when they die. In the garden the vegetables are removed and eaten, and the chain is broken. Compost and other organic materials help to redress the balance, but there may not be enough available to do the job properly and then fertilizers are needed.

ABOVE **The most natural way of adding nutrients to the soil is to rot down old plant material in a compost bin, and then return it to the soil.**

What plants require

The main foods required by plants are nitrogen (N), phosphorus (P) and potassium (K), with smaller quantities of magnesium (Mg), calcium (Ca) and sulphur (S). They also require small amounts of what are known as trace elements, including iron (Fe) and manganese (Mn).

Each of the main nutrients tends to be used by the plant for one specific function. Thus nitrogen is concerned with plant growth and is used for promoting the rapid growth of the green parts of the plant. You should, therefore, add nitrogen to help leafy plants such as cabbage but cut back on it with plants such as runner beans, because you do not want to promote lush leaves at the expense of flowers and beans. Phosphorus, usually in the form of phosphates, is used to create good root growth as well as helping with the ripening of fruits, while potassium, in the form of potash, which is used to promote flowering and formation of good fruit, is, for example, the main ingredient in tomato feed.

The natural way

The most natural way to add nutrients to the soil is to use compost and other organic matter. As we have already seen, such materials are important to the general structure of the soil, but they also feed it. Well-rotted farmyard manure and garden compost have been the main way that gardeners have traditionally fed their gardens. However, some of today's gardeners are unhappy with this method because they claim that you cannot know which fertilizer you are adding and in what quantity, because the quality of organic materials varies so much. Although they concede that organic material is useful for adding bulk, they prefer to use bought fertilizers to feed the soil.

Organic material normally contains less of the main nutrients than concentrated fertilizers, but it is often strong in trace elements, and although they may not contain such a strong concentration of nitrogen, they do release it over a longer period which is of great benefit. Because of its other benefits, farmyard manure and garden compost are still the best way of treating the soil.

Organic fertilizers

Synthetic, concentrated fertilizers are broken down into two groups: organic and inorganic. Organic fertilizers are made up of chemicals derived from naturally occurring organic materials. So bonemeal (ground-up bones) is quite strong in nitrogen and phosphates,

INORGANIC FERTILIZERS

making it a good fertilizer to promote growth, especially at the start of a plant's life. Bonemeal also has the advantage in that it breaks down slowly, gradually releasing the fertilizer over a long period. When you apply bonemeal, you may want to wear gloves. Other organic fertilizers include fish, blood and bone; hoof and horn; and seaweed meal.

Because they are derived from natural products without any modification, they are deemed "safe" by organic growers.

Inorganic fertilizers

These are fertilizers that have been made artificially, although they are frequently derived from natural rocks and minerals and the process may just involve crushing. They are concentrated and are usually soluble in water. This means that they are instantly available for the plant and are useful for giving a plant a push when it is required. They do, however, tend to wash out of the soil quickly and need to be replaced.

Some are general fertilizers, and might contain equal proportions of nitrogen, phosphorus and potassium, for example. Others are much more specific. Superphosphate, for example, is entirely used for supplying phosphorus, while potassium sulphate is added to the soil when potassium is required.

ORGANIC FERTILIZERS

Increasing numbers of gardeners are turning against inorganic fertilizers, unaware that they are not as artificial as is generally believed. Many are not classified as organic simply because they are not derived from living things. Nevertheless, it is their concentrated form and the fact that they can be readily washed from the soil that lead many gardeners to object to their use.

Slow-release fertilizers

A modern trend is to coat the fertilizers so that they are released slowly into the soil. These are expensive in the short term, but because they do not leach away and do not need to be replaced as frequently, they can be considered more economic in the longer term. They are particularly useful for container planting, where constant watering is necessary (with its attendant rapid nutrient leaching).

LEFT **This kitchen garden is planted with a delightful mixture of herbs, vegetables and flowers, growing in well-fed beds.**

Digging and Breaking Down

Although it is a technique that is now being questioned by some gardeners, digging is still one of the main garden activities. It breaks up the soil, allowing the ingress of water and air, which are both important for plant growth. In addition, it also allows organic material to be incorporated deep down in the soil, right where the roots need it.

All weeds and their roots can be removed during digging, which also brings pests to the surface so that they can be destroyed. Also and importantly, it allows the gardener to keep an eye on the condition of the soil.

Single digging

The most frequently carried out method is single digging, of which there are two ways, one informal and the other formal. In the informal method the ground is usually already quite loose, and the gardener simply forks it over, turning it over and replacing it in the same position, hardly using any trench at all. This process is more frequently carried out on light or sandy soils.

Formal single digging is necessary on heavier soils and when there is organic material to be incorporated. First, a trench is dug across the width of the plot, and the earth taken from the trench is taken – in a wheelbarrow – to the other end of the bed. Compost or farmyard manure is put into the bottom of the trench and then another trench is dug. This time, the earth removed from the trench is put into the first trench to cover the organic material. This procedure is repeated down the length of the plot. When the final trench has been dug and organic material placed in it, it is refilled with the pile of soil taken from the first trench.

Further refinements can be applied. For example, the first trench can be dug so that it is two trenches wide. Dung is put in the bottom as usual, and then the next trench is dug but the soil is spread over the bottom of the previous two trenches, only half-filling them. This is then covered with another layer of dung and then the fourth trench dug, filling up the first. Trenches three and four are treated in the same way, being filled first with the soil from trench five and then from trench six. This method makes a better distribution of the organic material through the soil.

ABOVE **After a winter exposed to the weather, most soils will readily break down into a fine tilth by using a rake. More recently turned soil, may need to be broken down with a heavier hoe first.**

Double digging

Double digging is the method that is employed to break up the subsoil, and it is useful on any new plot of ground as well as when deep beds are being prepared.

Dig the trench as before, taking the earth to the end of the plot. Then dig the soil in the bottom of the trench to the depth of a fork or spade, adding in organic material. Add more organic material on top and then dig the next trench, placing the soil into the first. Repeat until the end of the plot is reached. Take care that you do not bring any subsoil up to the top.

SINGLE DIGGING

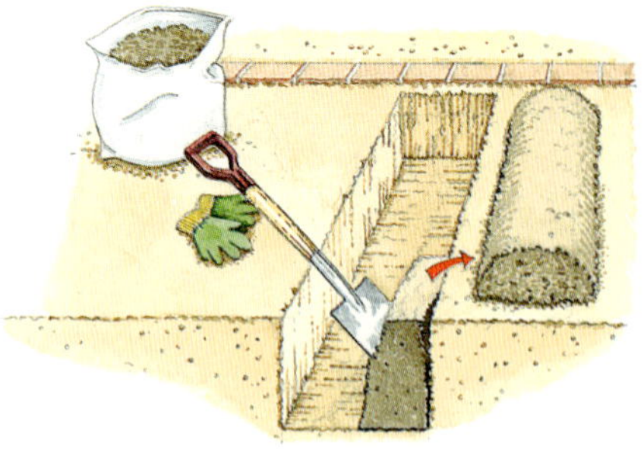

1 Start by digging a trench across the plot, putting the soil from the first trench to one side to be used later in the final trench.

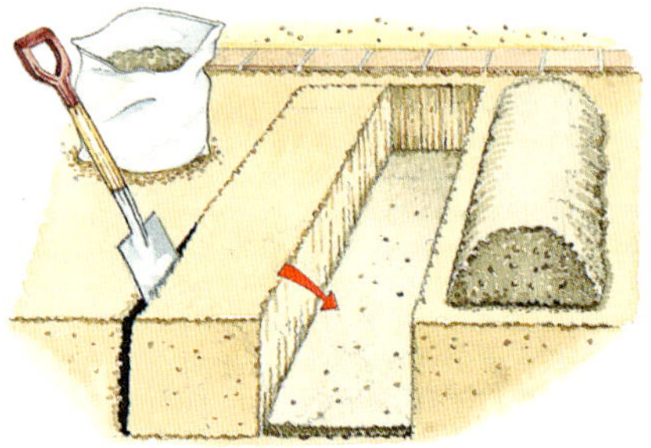

2 Put a layer of manure in the bottom of the trench. Dig out the next trench and cover over the manure in the first trench with earth taken from the second trench.

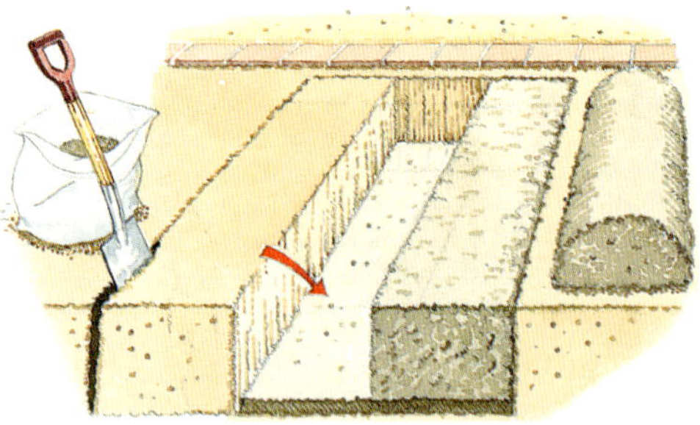

3 Repeat this process of adding manure to each trench and filling in with earth from the next, breaking up the soil as you go and keeping the surface as even as possible.

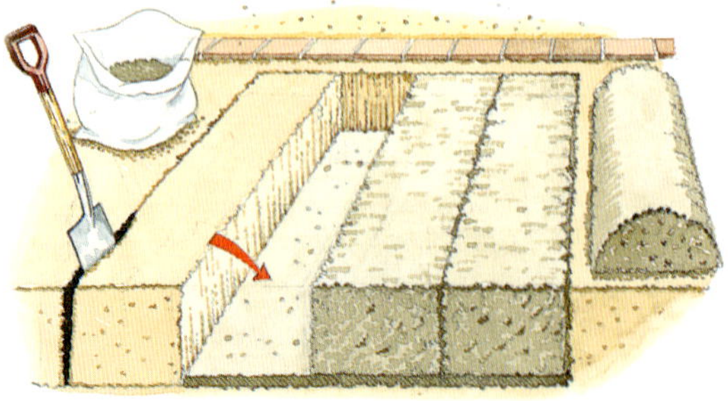

4 Continue down the length of the plot until you reach the final trench. This should be filled in with the earth taken from the first trench, which was set to one side.

DOUBLE DIGGING, METHOD ONE

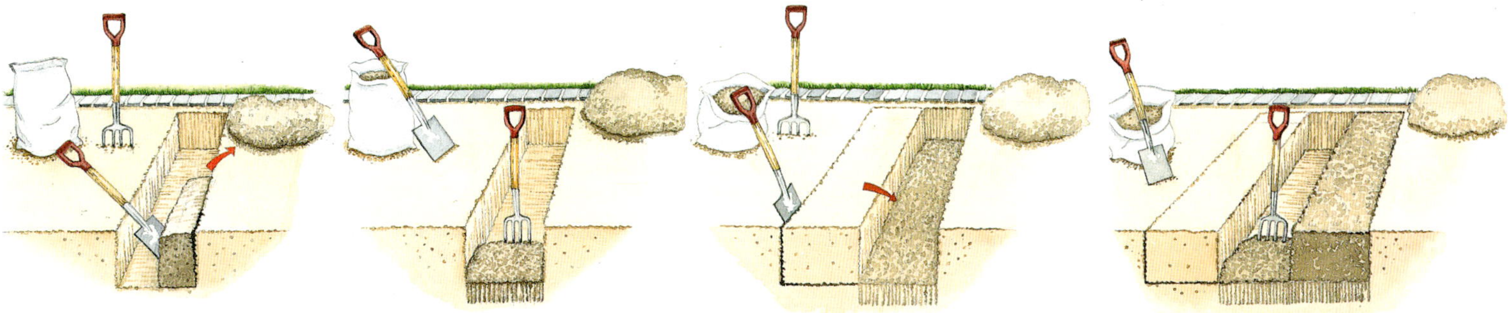

1 Dig a wide trench, placing the soil to one side to be used later when filling in the final trench.

2 Break up the soil at the bottom of the trench, adding manure to the soil as you proceed.

3 Dig the next trench, turning the soil over on top of the broken soil in the first trench.

4 Continue down the plot, ensuring that subsoil from the lower trench is not mixed with topsoil of the upper.

A method requiring more energy but giving better results is to dig out the first trench and then dig another below it, keeping the two soils separate. Dig out the top spit of the next trench and also put this to one side. Add organic material to the first double trench and dig the bottom spit of the second trench into it. Add more dung and then take the top spit of the third trench and place this on top of the new soil in the bottom of the first trench. Repeat down the plot and then fill in the remaining trenches with the reserved soil from the first ones.

Mechanical digging

It is possible to dig the soil using a mechanical rotavator (rototiller). These are, however, best used on large plots. One disadvantage of using a mechanical digger is that it cuts up weed roots into small pieces, and they are more difficult to remove by hand than with conventional digging.

Breaking down into a fine tilth

The best time to dig a heavy soil is in the autumn, then the winter frosts and rain will break it down for you. If clay soils are dug in the spring and allowed to dry out too much, they are difficult to break down because the clods set like concrete. A mechanical rotavator makes breaking the soil down easier, especially if the plot is large. For smaller plots, work on the soil when it is neither too wet nor too dry (experience will show you when), breaking it down, first with a large hoe and then with a rake. Shuffling along the surface with your feet will also help considerably, but do not do this if the ground is wet.

It is better to leave sandy soils until the spring because these do not need much breaking down. Raking the surface is usually all that is required.

Occasionally, the soil becomes too hard to break down. If this happens, water the soil with a sprinkler, leave it to dry slightly – so that it is no longer muddy – and then break it down. Alternatively, draw out a deep sowing row in the rough soil and fill it with potting compost (soil mix) and dig this in.

ABOVE **For larger gardens with heavy soil, a rotavator (rototiller) will break down the soil into a fine tilth. Even a small one saves a lot of time, especially if the soil is too dry to break down with a rake.**

DOUBLE DIGGING, METHOD TWO

1 Keeping soil from each level separate, dig first trench two spits deep. Fork over trench. Dig second trench one spit deep.

2 Add organic material to the first double trench and dig the lower spit of the second trench into it.

3 Dig an upper third trench one spit deep, and place the soil on top of that already placed in the first trench.

4 Continue, ensuring topsoil and subsoil do not mix. Fill in remaining trenches with soil taken from first ones.

techniques

There are almost as many different ways of doing things in the garden as there are gardeners. In truth, no one way is better than any other – it depends very much on who is doing what and where it is being done. Something that works for you may not help a gardener just a few doors away down the road.

Having said that, there is a certain amount of common ground in most of the techniques used in the vegetable garden, and the procedures we discuss here should stand you in good stead, even if you eventually develop your own methods. In this section you will find helpful advice on general kitchen gardening techniques, including sowing seed, both outdoors and under glass; thinning and transplanting seedlings; and harvesting and storing. There is also guidance on the cultivation of herbs, from initial planting to final drying as well as on growing, supporting and pruning fruit trees and bushes. Detailed advice on the techniques to master for individual crops are covered in the later chapters on specific vegetables, herbs and fruit.

Timing

There is an optimum time for most of the activities that are carried out in the garden, but precise timing is rarely crucial, and it does not matter if you cannot do something one week and have put it off to the next – or even later. Clay soils, for example, are best dug in autumn, but many gardeners never get around to it until spring.

Apart from social and business pressures that might upset your schedule, the weather and general garden conditions are likely to vary from year to year. When it comes to digging, for instance, a wet autumn may make it impossible for you to get onto the ground to dig it, and so you will have to wait until spring. When spring comes, you may want to get on with it and sow your carrots, but there is little point in doing this if the ground is still too cold, because carrots will not germinate until it has warmed up and any attempt to do so will end with wasted seeds.

It is, of course, wise to stick to the best timing if possible, particularly as there often comes a point when it is too late to do something. For example, there is little point in sowing most seeds after midsummer because they will not come to anything before autumn and winter set in.

Remember, though, that there is always another year. If things do go awry one year, there is always the next to look forward to.

ABOVE **Greenhouses need more care and attention than the open garden. Factors such as good hygiene and the control of pests and diseases must be borne in mind.**

Effort

Gardening can be strenuous, especially if you are elderly or not particularly fit. Do not overdo things, especially heavy tasks such as digging. Build up gradually, particularly after an idle winter. Many techniques and tools can be adapted for the disabled and elderly, but if things do become difficult, there is no shame in getting help of one sort or another.

Keeping tidy

When you are working in the garden, try to keep things tidy. Thinnings and weeds should always be removed from the beds to prevent the waste material promoting or harbouring disease. When you are harvesting produce, cut off and discard any fruit or vegetables that are rotten or diseased and do not leave them there to spread their problems. Many difficulties in the garden can be avoided by adopting techniques that result in a neat and tidy garden.

RIGHT **Most techniques involve working with nature, but a few are inevitably artificial. Terracotta rhubarb forcers, for example, are used to bring rhubarb crops to maturity faster than they would normally.**

Sowing in the Open

Most vegetables and herbs can be sown directly into the open ground. The two main advantages of doing this are that no indoor facilities are required and the plants' growth is not delayed when they are planted out. Some plants also resent their roots being disturbed.

ABOVE **Some seed, beetroot (beets) in particular, benefits from an hour's soaking in tepid water before sowing.**

Soil requirements

The main requirement is that the soil should be broken down into a fine tilth – in other words, the soil crumbs should be small. The soil should be neither too wet nor too dry. If it is wet, cover it with cloches or polythene (plastic) to prevent it being further wetted and wait until it dries out a little before sowing. If the soil is too dry, then water the ground a short time before sowing; there should be sufficient water to soak in but not leave a sticky surface. The ground should also be warm. Seeds sown in cold ground will frequently just sit there until they rot. Ideally, the soil should be at a temperature of at least 7°C/45°F.

LEFT **Vegetables that are usually planted out, rather than sown where they are to grow, such as these cabbages, can still be sown in the open and then transplanted when they are large enough.**

Seed requirements

Most of the seed that is available these days is of a high quality, especially when it comes from the major suppliers. The germination rate is usually good, although occasionally one gets an unsatisfactory batch. Non-germination, however, is usually due to some other factor, such as cold conditions. It is possible to keep your own seed, but only do this for non-F1 hybrids because F1s will not come true to type. Most seed is sold loose in packets, but seeds can be bought in other forms, and one of the most common is pelleted, when the seeds are coated with clay. The coating makes the seeds easier to handle and to sow. Increasingly, pre-germinated seeds and young seedlings are also becoming available. For most purposes, however, ordinary seeds will be suitable and certainly the cheapest.

Sowing in rows

The conventional way of sowing seeds is to do so in rows. Using a garden line for guidance, draw out a shallow drill in the fine soil with the corner of a hoe. If the ground is dry, water along the drill with a fine-rose watering can. Sow the seeds thinly. Mark the ends of the row with a label and a stick and draw the soil back over the drill with a rake. The

SOWING SEED

1 Draw out a shallow drill with the corner of a draw hoe, using a garden line to ensure that it is straight.

2 If the soil is dry, water along the length of the drill and allow it to drain before sowing seed.

3 Sow the seed along the drill, sowing it as thinly as possible to reduce the amount of thinning necessary.

4 Put a label at the end of the row clearly showing what is in the row. Put a stick or another label at the far end. Do this before filling in the drill.

5 Rake the soil into the drill over the seed. Gently tamp down the soil along the row with the flat of the rake and then lightly rake over.

6 If the soil is heavy and is difficult to break into a fine tilth, draw out the drill and then line it with potting compost (soil mix).

depth of the drill depends on the size of the seeds, but most finer seeds should be sown at a depth of 1cm/½in. The seed packet usually gives the depth required.

Station sowing

With plants that grow quite large and therefore need to be spaced out in the row, it is wasteful to sow a continuous line of seeds. Station sowing involves sowing three seeds at distances that will be the eventual gap between plants – parsnip seeds, therefore, are sown at 20cm/8in intervals.

Wide rows

Some seeds, mainly peas and beans, are sown in wide rows – in effect, two rows are sown at once. A wide drill, 15cm/6in across, is made with the flat of the hoe. Two rows of peas or beans are sown, one down each side of the drill, and the soil is carefully raked back over the seeds so that they are not disturbed.

Broadcasting

This is the best method for sowing seeds in blocks. Rake the area to a fine tilth and scatter the seeds thinly but evenly over the surface. If the soil is dry, gently rake the seeds in and water with a fine-rose watering can.

Protecting

Fine earth is attractive to both birds and animals as a dust bath as well as a litter tray, and when it is used the seeds will be scattered far and wide. In addition, some birds find emerging seedlings an irresistible source of food. Protect the seeds by placing wire-netting guards along the rows. Alternatively, a few pea-sticks can be laid across the surface of the soil. Another possibility is to place short sticks in the ground and to twine cotton between them. This last method is the least convenient because the protection cannot be quickly removed and replaced to permit for hoeing and weeding.

Labelling

Before covering the seed with soil, mark the end of the rows with pegs and a label. Once the drill is filled in, it is difficult to see where it is. It may be some time before the seedlings emerge and the row can be easily disturbed by, for example, accidentally hoeing through it. Similarly, it is important to know what is sown where, so a label bearing the name and variety of the vegetable is important. Traditionally, many gardeners spike the seed packet on a peg but these quickly deteriorate and often blow away.

Sowing under Glass

Germinating seeds under glass is more tedious and time-consuming than sowing direct into the ground, but raising plants in this way has its advantages. It allows the gardener to grow reasonably sized plants that are ready to set out as soon as the weather allows, stealing a march on those sown in the soil by about two weeks. If there are pest problems, such as slugs or birds, the plants are better able to resist them if they are well grown when they are planted out than if they have to fight for their life as soon as they emerge through the soil.

ABOVE **There is a range of pots and trays now available that are suitable for sowing vegetable and herb seed. *Clockwise from top left*: individual cells or modules, a half tray, plastic pots, a fibrous pot and fibrous modules.**

Containers

Seeds can be sown in a variety of containers. Traditionally they were sown in wooden trays or flats. Some gardeners prefer to make their own, claiming that they are warmer and that they can be made deeper than the purchased equivalents. Plastic trays have, however, generally replaced the wooden varieties. They can be made of rigid plastic for multiple use or thin, flimsy plastic, and these are used only once before being thrown away.

Often, only a few plants may be required, and it is rather wasteful to sow a whole or half tray. A 9cm/3½in pot is usually sufficient.

More and more gardeners are using modular or cellular trays, in which one or two seeds are sown in a small cell. If both germinate, one is removed and the remaining seedling is allowed to develop without having to be pricked out. This method avoids a lot of root disturbance.

Even less root disturbance occurs if the seeds are sown in biodegradable fibrous modules. As soon as the seedling is big enough to be planted out, both pot and plant are inserted into the ground, and the pot allows the roots to grow through its sides into the surrounding earth.

Propagators

Propagators are glass or plastic boxes that help to keep the seed tray moist and in a warm atmosphere. The more expensive models have heating cables in them so that the temperature can be controlled. Although they are desirable, they are by no means absolutely necessary. Cheap alternatives can also be made simply by slipping the tray into a polythene (plastic) bag and removing it as soon as the seeds have germinated. Plastic jars can also be cut down to fit over trays or pots.

SOWING IN BLOCKS

Fill the cellular block with compost (soil mix) and tap it on the table to firm it down. Sow one or two seeds in each cell. Cover with a light dusting of compost. Remove the weaker of the two seedlings after germination.

SOWING IN POTS

Fill the pot with a good seed compost (soil mix), tap it on the bench and sow one to three seeds in each pot. Once germinated, the weaker seedlings will be removed, leaving one to grow on.

SOWING IN TRAYS

1 Fill the seed tray with seed compost (soil mix) and tamp down the compost lightly to produce a level surface. Sow the seed thinly across the compost.

2 Cover with a thin layer of compost (soil mix), lightly firm down and label. Labelling is very important because the seedlings of many vegetables look the same.

WATERING IN

Water the trays or pots by standing them in a shallow tray or bowl of water so that the water comes halfway up the container. Remove the tray or pot as soon as the surface of the compost (soil mix) begins to moisten.

USING A PROPAGATOR

1 Place the seeds in a propagator. You can adjust the temperature of heated propagators like this. Seed packets should indicate the best temperature, but you may need to compromise if different seeds need different temperatures.

2 This propagator is unheated and should be kept in a warm position in a greenhouse or within the house. Start opening the vents once the seeds have germinated to begin the hardening-off process.

Heat

A source of heat is useful for the rapid germination of seeds. It can be provided in the form of a heated propagator, but most seeds will germinate in the ambient temperature of a warm greenhouse or conservatory, or even within the house.

Sowing seed

Fill the seed tray with a good quality seed or potting compost (soil mix). Gently firm down and sow the seeds thinly on the surface. Spread a thin layer of potting compost over the seeds so that they are just covered. Again, firm down lightly. Water by placing the seed tray in a shallow bowl of water, so that the level of the water comes halfway up the sides of the seed tray. Once the surface of the compost shows signs of dampness, remove the tray and place it in a propagator or in a polythene (plastic) bag. A traditional alternative – and one that still works well – is to place a sheet of glass over the tray.

Subsequent treatment

As soon as the seeds begin to germinate, remove the lid from the propagator – or open the bag, depending on the method you are using – to let in air and after a couple of days remove the tray altogether. If you are using a propagator, turn off the heat and open the vents over a few days and then remove the tray.

Once the seedlings are large enough to handle, prick them out into trays, individual pots or modules. Hold the seedlings by the seed-leaves and not by the stem or roots. Make sure they are well spaced in the trays – at least 5cm/2in apart – and keep them warm and watered.

As the time approaches to plant them out, gradually harden them off by exposing them to outdoor conditions for a little longer each day until they can be safely left out overnight. They are then ready to plant out.

USING A COLD FRAME

1 Once the trays of seedlings or pricked-out seedlings are ready to plant out, harden them off by placing in a cold frame which is opened a little wider each day to let in more air.

2 Finally leave the lights of the cold frame off altogether so that the plants become accustomed to outside light.

Thinning and Transplanting

Outdoor-sown seedlings inevitably grow too thickly, no matter how thinly you try to sow them. In order to grow properly, they will need thinning. Seeds are often sown in a row that will not be their ultimate cropping position. Leeks, for example, are grown in a seed row and later transplanted to their final positions.

Why thin?

It is important that vegetables have enough space in which to develop. Plants that are too close together become drawn as they try to move to the light. In addition to not having room to develop, they become undernourished as they compete with their neighbours for moisture, nutrients and light.

Crops that are too tightly planted are more susceptible to disease because air cannot circulate freely around them, allowing fungal diseases, such as mildew, to get a hold. Half-starved plants are also more prone to disease than fully nourished ones. A little attention at this stage will pay dividends in producing healthy plants.

THINNING AND TRANSPLANTING SEEDLINGS

1 Water the row of seedlings, the night before if possible, but at least a few hours before transplanting.

2 Using a hand fork, dig up, rather than pull out, the excess plants. Only dig up the plants as you need them; do not dig them up all at once and leave them lying around.

3 Using a garden line to keep the row straight, and a measuring stick to get the distances equal, replant the seedlings using a trowel.

4 Gently firm in each plant and water around them. Rake the soil around the plants in order to tidy it up and to remove footprints and uneven soil.

Thinning distances

Beetroot (beets) 7.5–10cm/3–4in
Broad (fava) beans 23cm/9in
Carrots 7.5cm/3in
Dwarf French (bush green) beans 20cm/8in
Florence fennel 25cm/10in
Kohl rabi 20cm/8in
Lettuce 23cm/9in
Parsley 15cm/6in
Peas 5cm/2in
Parsnips 15–20cm/6–8in
Radishes 2.5–5cm/1–2in
Runner beans 25–30cm/10–12in
Salsify 15cm/6in
Scorzonera 15cm/6in
Spinach 15cm/6in
Spring onions (scallions) 5cm/2in
Swedes (rutabagas or yellow turnips) 30cm/12in
Swiss chard 30cm/12in
Turnips 15cm/6in

Thinning

The idea behind thinning is to remove all unwanted plants, leaving the best at regular intervals. Before you begin to thin, water the row to soften the earth and to make sure that the remaining plants have taken up enough water in case their roots are accidentally disturbed. Allow the water to soak in and the plants to take it up. If possible, water the evening before you plan to thin.

Go along the row, with a measuring stick if you are uncertain about the distances between the plants, removing the weaker seedlings and leaving one strong one at the correct planting distance for that variety – 15–20cm/6–8in for parsnips, for example. When you pull out the unwanted seedlings, gently press the ground around the one that is left so that the pulling motion does not disturb that one as well.

When the row is complete, gently water along its length so that soil is washed back around the roots of the remaining plants that may have been disturbed. Dispose of the unwanted seedlings on the compost heap.

Avoid thinning during hot or windy conditions because the remaining plants may become desiccated before their roots can become re-established if they have been disturbed. A slightly damp, overcast day is ideal.

In hot dry weather, you can snip the unwanted seedlings off with a pair of scissors so you do not disturb their neighbours' roots.

RIGHT **Thinning vegetables to the correct distances ensures healthy, full-sized plants: shown are rows of onions, beetroot (beets), potatoes, carrots, spinach.**

Transplanting

Plants for transplanting can either be grown from seed sown in pots or trays, or from seed sown directly in the open ground. Seedlings that have been grown in containers should be pricked out first into individual pots, or widely spaced trays, so that each plant has room to develop. Harden them off if they have been grown under glass before transplanting them into the open ground.

Damp, overcast weather conditions are ideal for transplanting seedlings because the plants will not dry out quickly in a muggy atmosphere. Again, as with thinning, it is essential to water the plants first before transplanting them. This will give them sufficient moisture to keep them going until they have re-established their root systems.

Dig up just a few plants at a time – there is no point in leaving plants lying around on the ground where they can dry out. Discard any that are weak or undernourished, and never use any that are diseased. Using a line to make sure that the row is straight and a measuring stick in order to get the planting distances correct, plant at the same depth as in the seed bed, except where stated under individual vegetables – leeks, for example, are planted deeper. Gently firm in around each plant and water in.

THINNING SEEDLINGS IN SITU

When thinning a row of seedlings that have been sown in situ, water the row the night before or at least a few hours before. Remove the unwanted plants, leaving the recommended gap between each retained plant. Try not to disturb the plants that are left. Water the seedlings after thinning and remove all the discarded seedlings to the compost heap.

USING A DIBBER

Cabbages (shown here), onions and leeks are planted out using a dibber. This makes a hole in the ground into which the plant is slipped before the earth is firmed in around it.

Planting distances

Asparagus 30–38cm/12–15in
Aubergines (eggplants) 60cm/24in
Broccoli 60cm/24in
Brussels sprouts 50–75cm/20–30in
Cabbages 30–50cm/12–20in
Calabrese (Italian sprouting broccoli) 15–23cm/6–9in
Cauliflowers 50–75cm/20–30in
Celeriac (celery root) 30–38cm/12–15in
Celery 23–30cm/9–12in
Courgettes (zucchini) 60cm/24in
Cucumbers 60cm/24in
Garlic 15cm/6in
Globe artichokes 75cm/30in
Jerusalem artichokes 30cm/12in
Kale 60cm/24in
Leeks 15cm/6in
Marrows (zucchini) 60cm/24in
Onion sets 10cm/4in
Peppers 45–60cm/18–24in
Potatoes 30–38cm/12–15in
Pumpkins 90–180cm/36–72in
Rhubarb 75–90cm/30–36in
Runner beans 25–30cm/10–12in
Seakale 30cm/12in
Shallots 15–18cm/6–7in
Sweet corn (corn) 30cm/12in
Tomatoes 60cm/24in

Harvesting and Storing

The great moment comes when the vegetables are ready to harvest; nothing tastes quite like fresh vegetables that you have grown for yourself. However, not all the produce can be eaten at once and it is prudent to store some, especially for the winter months when fresh vegetables are at a premium.

ABOVE **Harvest root crops by levering up the root with a fork and pulling on the stems or leaves.**

Harvesting

Try to resist the temptation to harvest vegetables too soon. Until they have developed fully, their taste might not be matured and some might even be bitter. Traditionally, parsnips, celery and Brussels sprouts should not be harvested until they have experienced at least one frost, which makes them taste sweeter. There are some plants that can be harvested prematurely, however, in particular leafy crops. For example, young turnip tops are worth eating, while the tips of broad (fava) bean shoots can be tasty, long before the beans themselves have matured.

When you are harvesting do not simply pick the best vegetables. If you also come across any that are diseased or rotting, harvest these as well and compost them. Do not leave rotting vegetables on the plant or in the ground because they will spread their problems to healthy fruit or the spores may remain in the ground until the following year.

ABOVE **Some vegetables are harvested by cutting through the stems as and when they are required. Swiss chard, shown here, is a good example of this method of harvesting. The stem is cut close to the base. Some gardeners prefer to twist or snap the stems off at the base rather than cutting them.**

RIGHT **Quite a number of vegetables are picked. This usually entails snapping or cutting the stem just above the vegetable so that either part of the stalk remains or there is a complete break at the junction between vegetable and stalk. Here, runner beans are being harvested.**

There is no hard and fast rule about when or at what time of day to harvest, although taking the vegetable straight from the garden to the pot does, of course, give the freshest tasting dish. If possible, try to harvest when you want a vegetable, rather than leaving it lying around for a few days before using.

Storing

There are several ways of storing vegetables for later use. If you pick or dig up a vegetable and are unable to use it right away, it can usually be kept a few days before use. The best way of keeping these is to store them in a cool, dark place, preferably a cellar or cold shed. However, this is not always possible and a refrigerator is the next best thing.

The traditional way of storing root crops throughout winter is to dig them up, clean off any dirt and remove the leaves. Then they can be placed in trays of just-moist peat (peat moss or peat substitute) or sand. The vegetables are covered with more peat and, if the tray is deep enough, another layer of root crops is placed on top and again covered in peat. Carrots, beetroot (beets), celeriac (celery root), turnips, swedes (rutabagas or yellow turnips) and parsnips can all be stored in this way.

STORING ROOT CROPS

1 Most root crops can be stored in trays of just-moist sand or peat (peat moss or peat substitute). Place a layer of peat in the bottom of the tray and then lay a row of carrots on top. Cover these with more peat.

2 Place another layer of carrots on top and cover these with more peat. Repeat with more layers until the tray is full, topping off with a layer of peat.

Unless the weather is extremely cold, parsnips, celeriac (celery root), swedes (rutabagas or yellow turnips), carrots and beetroot (beets) can simply be left in the ground until they are required. However, if a deep frost is likely to occur, it is best to lift at least a few and store them inside because it is difficult to get them out of the ground once it has frozen. Although not strictly a root crop, leeks can also be left in the ground until they are needed.

Trays of root crops should be stored in a cool, but frost-free, shed or cellar. This is also one of the best places to store many other vegetables. Squashes, pumpkins and marrows (zucchini) can be stored on shelves or wire racks. Bulbous onions, shallots and garlic can be kept in trays or in net sacks. The important thing about storing all these vegetables is that they should not touch one another and that air should be able to circulate freely around them.

Brassicas are not so easy to store, but some of the solid cabbages can be harvested and hung in nets or placed on shelves in the same cool, frost-free shed until they are required. Stored in this way, they will stay sound for several months. Some brassicas are winter hardy and can be left where they are until required. Brussels sprouts are a good example of this.

Many vegetables will freeze reasonably well. To maintain good flavour they should first be blanched (placed in boiling water) for a few minutes, the length of time depending on the type of vegetable. Details can be found in good cookery books.

Although some vegetables do not freeze well this way, many can still be frozen, simply by cooking them first – Florence fennel, for example, can be cooked and puréed before freezing.

Another, more traditional way to store vegetables and fruit is to turn them into chutneys, pickles or some other sort of preserve. Fruit is delicious when bottled.

LEFT **Many vegetables, such as these marrows (zucchini), can be stored in trays. It is best if they are not touching one another.**

Planting Herbs

There is no basic difference between planting herbs and planting vegetables. However, since herbs are often grown in their own beds it is worth considering them separately. Even if you do not have the space to grow vegetables, it is usually possible to find at least a little room for a few herbs.

ABOVE **Plants such as mint that spread rapidly underground should be planted in a large bucket or flowerpot, about 30cm/12in across or more, which is then sunk into the ground. The rim of the pot should be level with the surface of the soil.**

Siting herbs

There are many reasons for growing herbs. They can be purely decorative or they can be medicinal, but within the context of this book they are culinary. Herbs for the kitchen are usually required instantly, with the cook dashing out in the middle of cooking to grab a handful, and so the most convenient site for this type of herb is as close to the kitchen door as possible. From a horticultural point of view, most herbs like to be in an open, sunny position.

Soil preparation

Herbs will grow in the same soil you have in your vegetable garden, and, like vegetables, they prefer a rich, moisture-retentive soil. Dig and prepare the ground thoroughly, adding plenty of well-rotted organic material. At the same time, remove any perennial weeds. This is particularly important around permanently planted herbs, such as chives, mint and sage, because there will not be an easy opportunity for removing the weeds if they reappear.

Sowing

Some herbs, such as parsley, can be sown directly into the ground. This makes a great deal of sense if you want to have a whole row or block of them. However, make sure that the soil is warm enough before you plant. In cold springs, wait until the soil warms up first, even if it means missing the theoretical first sowing date. For example, parsley will not germinate if the soil is too cold, and you will have to re-sow because the first sowing of seeds will invariably rot. Thin the resulting seedlings to the appropriate distances.

For small quantities of herbs or in cold springs, it is a good idea to sow the herbs under glass and plant them out once they are big enough. They can be sown in modules to reduce the amount of root disturbance. Thoroughly harden off before planting out.

Planting

When you are planting out, remember that herbs need space to grow and you should allow for their increase in size. This is particularly important with shrubby plants such as sage and rosemary, which can grow from small cuttings when first planted out to up to 1.2m/4ft or more across. In addition, when you are deciding what to plant where, put the taller ones to the north so that they do not overshadow the smaller ones.

Plant the herbs at the same depth in the soil that they were in their pots. Gently firm them in, water and tidy up the soil to remove footprints. Loosen the soil if it is compacted.

Wayward herbs

Some herbs, mint in particular, are rampant. If they are planted in a bed they will rapidly spread and soon invade other, nearby

LEFT **Some time before planting, give the plant a thorough soaking.**

PLANTING OUT

1 Using a trowel, dig a hole in the prepared ground that is slightly larger than the rootball of the plant.

2 Insert the plant so that the top of the rootball is level with the surface of the soil. Fill in the hole around the plant and firm down.

3 Water the plant and the soil immediately surrounding the rootball.

ABOVE **Planting herbs next to a path means that the delightful scent of fresh herbs is released when someone brushes past them.**

plants. One way to cope with this is to plant the mint in a bottomless bucket or large plastic flowerpot. Dig a large hole and then place the bucket or flowerpot into it so that the rim is level with the surface of the soil. Fill the bucket or flowerpot with the excavated soil and fill in the remaining hole around the edge of the pot with the rest of the soil. Plant the mint in the centre of the container and water. The questing roots will now be prevented from moving far because of the walls of the pot. Since the roots do not grow far down, they will not be able to exit through the bottom of the bucket or the holes in the pot, which will permit free drainage so that the container does not become waterlogged. Containers used in this way will become congested, and a piece of the mint should be replanted with fresh soil every year. Planting mint in a corner that is confined by paths is another way of keeping it in check.

Growing Herbs in Containers

Containers are the perfect way to ensure that herbs are in just the right amount of light or shade. The mature herbs can later be transferred to the garden, or kept conveniently close to hand in their pots on a patio or kitchen window sill. Planting in pots also gives scope for adding height and depth to a border, and a group of pots can form an attractive garden feature or balcony arrangement.

ABOVE **Herbs can be planted in a variety of containers. This wooden box has useful handles for moving the herbs to different locations.**

Choosing pots

Herbs can be grown in any form of container – even old coleslaw cartons, ice-cream cartons or plastic picnic boxes – but they will always look better and more at home if you choose an attractive container that has been properly designed for growing plants.

There are plenty to choose from – nurseries and garden centres stock them by the hundred – and they are no longer as expensive as they once were. Always try to choose one that is big enough for your needs. Remember that plants need room to spread out their roots if they are to grow well and remain healthy, and if you are intending to grow several different types of herb you will need a large pot or several of them.

The shape does not matter too much as long as you do not choose an Ali Baba type pot, with a bulbous belly and a narrow neck, because the opening will not be large enough to get many herbs in (although such a pot could look beautiful with a single sage). Pot-bellied shapes work well if they are designed like strawberry pots with openings in the side to take individual herbs. Window-boxes also make good herb containers. They can be used on the ground or mounted outside the kitchen window or simply on a nearby wall.

Whatever type of container you choose, make certain that it has drainage holes in the bottom so that excess water can drain away.

Planting the herbs

If the container is large, it is likely to be heavy once it is full of damp compost (soil mix), so, if possible, position it before you fill it. Cover the bottom of the container with irregularly shaped stones to help any excess water find its way to the drainage holes. Fill the pot with a good quality compost and firm this down lightly. Then plant the herbs, making sure that they are the same depth as they were in their original pots. Smooth over the top of the compost and

LEFT **Mints are very rampant, so it is a good idea to grow them in pots. Here, a selection of mints is growing in terracotta pots.**

adjust the level of the surface, removing or adding some to bring it just below the rim of the container. Water herbs thoroughly.

Maintenance

The biggest task is to keep the herbs well-watered. During the summer months, when it is hot and dry, the container is likely to need watering at least once a day and even twice a day in some circumstances. All this watering means that nutrients quickly leach from the soil, so it will be necessary to add a liquid feed to the watering at least once a week. As an alternative, a slow-release fertilizer can be added to the potting compost (soil mix) before the container is filled.

Re-potting

Herbs will not last forever in a container, and if you are to be sure of a continuous supply it will be necessary to re-pot at least once a year. Many herbs are best thrown away and new ones planted in any case, and this applies even to perennials. Sage and rosemary will eventually get large, and it is better to replace these with new plants every year or every second year at the most, unless you have a container large enough to keep them for longer.

Always wash out a container thoroughly and refill it with new compost (soil mix), adding the old soil to the vegetable garden.

ABOVE **Even if you only have a small garden, you can still make room for a large container planted with culinary herbs.**

PLANTING HERBS IN A CONTAINER

1 To ensure that no stagnant water lies in the bottom of the container, place a layer of irregularly shaped stones in the bottom. This will ensure good drainage.

2 Fill the container with a good potting compost (soil mix). Firm it down gently.

3 Plant the herbs by digging holes in the compost (soil mix) and then firming them in. Top up or reduce the amount of compost so that it is just below the rim of the container.

4 To ensure that the plants are kept fed, insert one or more fertilizer sticks into the compost, following the manufacturer's instructions on the packet.

5 Water the container thoroughly and place in the shade for a few days until the herbs have recovered and become established.

Harvesting and Storing Herbs

Many herbs are seasonal and are not available for cutting all year round. One way of overcoming this problem is to grow some indoors, where they will survive the winter, but this is not always convenient and a better solution is to dry and store as many different types of your herbs as you can.

ABOVE **Harvest herbs when they are at their peak, usually before they flower. Cut them on a dry day, avoiding times when they are wilting in the heat.**

Harvesting herbs

Many herbs, such as parsley, rosemary and sage, are harvested on a cut-and-come-again principle: you take just as much as you want, when you want. With care, you can have parsley all year round. Sage and rosemary, being evergreen shrubs, should present no problems. Most other herbs, however, die back in winter and are not available unless you harvest and store them.

The time to pick herbs for storing is when they are fresh and at their peak, and with most herbs this is before they come into flower. (This, of course, applies to leaf herbs; if you want the seeds, obviously you must let the plants flower.) If you wait until after flowering, the leaves on most herbs will be tired, and will have lost their freshness and lack the sweetness of younger plants. On some plants the lower leaves are best avoided, because these are old and past their best. Avoid gathering herbs in the heat of the day, when the leaves may be limp. If you can, work early in the morning, as soon as any dew has disappeared. Do not harvest on wet days. It is easier to dry herbs if the whole stem is collected, so cut neatly with a pair of secateurs (pruners). Pick flowers on warm, dry days when they have just fully opened.

Seeds should also be collected on dry days and should be fully ripe before they are harvested. Tip the seeds into a paper bag or place the whole seedhead in the bag.

Root herbs, such as horseradish, should be harvested in autumn, once the above-ground parts begin to wither.

Drying herbs and flowers

The simplest way to dry any type of herb is to tie the stalks in small bunches and hang them in a warm, dark place where plenty of air can circulate. Although they can be hung in a light place, including indoors, do not place them in direct sunlight. An airing cupboard or a warm room is best, but kitchens and bathrooms, where there is a lot of steam, are not suitable. Do not put herbs into an oven, because they will dry too quickly. Individual leaves can be dried by placing them on mesh trays or sheets of muslin or on ordinary trays. Those with a mesh are preferable because air will circulate more freely around the leaves.

Do not dry different herbs in close proximity or you may find that they taint each other.

DRYING AND FREEZING HERBS

1 Pick seed just as it is ripening. At this stage it should readily come away from its stalks. Place it on a tray or muslin bag and leave the seed for a few days in a warm, dry place until it has completely dried.

2 Once herbs have been thoroughly dried, tip them into a glass jar with an airtight lid. Store in a cool, dry, dark place.

3 An alternative to drying is to freeze herbs. They can simply be packed into bags and frozen, or finely chopped and placed in ice-cube trays. Add water to the trays and freeze to produce ready-to-use cubes.

ABOVE **Oregano, which can be dried or frozen, is a useful herb for the kitchen.**

Drying roots

Roots should be cleaned and cut into small pieces and dried on a tray in the oven.

Storing

Do not attempt to store any herbs until they are completely dry. When they are dry, place them in airtight glass jars. Clear jars can be used if the herbs are to be kept in a cupboard, but dark glass is preferable for those to be left on open shelves. Keep the leaves whole if possible and crush them only just before use.

Freezing

A modern alternative to drying herbs is to freeze them. This has the advantage of keeping the plant's colour as well as being much quicker and easier to do. The cleaned herbs can be put into labelled polythene (plastic) bags and put directly into the freezer. Alternatively, the herbs can be finely chopped and placed in ice-cube trays. Add a little water to each and freeze. Individual frozen cubes can be added to dishes as required.

Infusions

Another possibility is to make flavoured oils and vinegars for using in cooking. A few sprigs of the herb are infused in a bottle of good-quality wine vinegar or in an olive or vegetable oil.

RIGHT **Herbs can be dried by tying them into bunches and hanging them in a warm, dry place such as near a stove or boiler. However, take care to avoid steamy places and direct sunlight.**

Growing Fruit Trees and Bushes

Fruit tends to be the poor relation in the garden, possibly because it can take up large amounts of space. However, fresh fruit is even more delightful than fresh vegetables and it need not take up as much space as you might think.

ABOVE **Strawberries can be grown in containers. If these are kept under glass, as here, then an early crop can be obtained.**

Where to grow your fruit

The traditional place to grow fruit is in a fruit garden, a separate area of the garden that is devoted to fruit. This has one especial advantage in that it can be completely protected in a fruit cage. Scattering the fruit over the whole garden means that individual plants have to be protected, which can be rather tedious.

Apart from the protection they require, however, there is no reason for keeping the fruit together. In a decorative kitchen garden, fruit can be mixed in with the vegetables, trees and standard bushes providing visual height in individual beds. Many fruit trees can also be grown along walls or fences, and they can be used as dividers or screens between various parts of the garden. If you have a small garden and want a shady tree to sit under, why not plant an apple tree rather than a species that is solely ornamental?

Choosing fruit

As long as it will grow in your garden, there is nothing to prevent you choosing whatever fruit you want. There is a slight complication in that some tree fruits need pollinators to make sure that the fruit is set, and this means that if you want a particular apple you may have to have another apple to act as a pollinator. This may not be necessary if your neighbour has a compatible tree.

Ground preparation

Most fruit trees and bushes are likely to remain in the ground for a long time and so it is important that the soil is thoroughly prepared. It is particularly important that all perennial weeds are removed. If any small piece is left in the ground it is bound to regrow and is likely to be difficult to extract from around the roots of the tree or bush without digging them up.

Another reason for preparing the ground thoroughly is to make sure that there is plenty of organic material tucked right down among the roots of the plants. This will help keep the soil moist as well as giving a continuous supply of nutrients until the plants are established. Once the tree and shrubs are planted, any organic material will have to be applied to the soil's surface and taken down by the worms. Double dig the soil if possible, incorporating as much well-rotted organic material as you can spare. Take this opportunity to make sure that all perennial weeds are removed. If the ground is heavy and it is

PLANTING A FRUIT TREE OR BUSH

When planting a fruit tree or bush, always ensure that it is planted at the same depth as it was in its container or in its nursery bed.

TYING IN A NEWLY PLANTED TREE

Using tree ties, ensure that a newly planted tree is firmly anchored to a stake. Attach the tie approximately 30cm/12in above the ground.

ABOVE **Even apple trees can be grown in containers. However, it is essential to water them every day, and at least twice on hot dry days.**

likely to be difficult to remove the weeds, spraying some time before digging may be the only answer to cleaning the soil.

Planting

As long as the weather is neither too wet nor too cold the best time to plant fruit trees and bushes is between late autumn and mid-spring. If bare-rooted plants are delivered when it is impossible to plant, heel them into a spare piece of the vegetable garden until they can be planted in their permanent position. Container-grown plants can be planted at other times of the year, but they need more attention to make sure that they survive.

Fruit trees and bushes should be planted to the same depth as they were in their pots or nursery bed when you purchased them. If a tree needs staking, place the stake in the ground before planting. Water the plants in thoroughly and keep them watered in dry weather until they are firmly established. Apply a mulch around the base of the plant in order to help preserve moisture as well as to keep the weeds down. Remove any weeds that do appear.

Try to keep a record of what you have planted. Fruit trees and bushes often outlive any label that comes with them, and it is often annoying when asked for the variety of an apple or raspberry, for example, when you cannot remember. A notebook with details of the variety, where you purchased the plant as well as the date on which you planted it, will be of future interest.

TOP-DRESSING FRUIT BUSHES

In the autumn, and again in the spring, top-dress fruit bushes with a layer of well-rotted organic material such as farmyard manure.

MULCHING STRAWBERRIES

Strawberries can be grown through a black polythene (plastic) mulch. This not only protects the fruit from mud-splashes, but also reduces the need for weeding and watering.

Supporting Fruit Trees and Shrubs

Once they are established, some fruit shrubs and most trees are free-standing, but most benefit from, and some require, permanent support. If this is provided adequately and properly from the start, these supports should last many years.

ABOVE **This apple tree is being supported by wires in a very decorative manner.**

Wall and fence fruit

Several types of trees and shrubs can be trained flat against walls or fences. The effects created can be decorative. These plants will need some means of holding them against the wall, and this usually takes the form of wires. To make sure that the framework lasts as long as possible use a galvanized wire, which will not corrode. The wire is held in place by vine eyes, of which there are several types available. Some are flat, metal spikes, which are hammered into the brickwork, while others are screw eyes, which are screwed into wall plugs that have been inserted into holes in the brick or stonework of the wall. They can be screwed directly into wooden fences. The eyes are placed 60–90cm/ 2–3ft apart and a wire led through the hole in each one. The wire is secured at the end eyes by pulling it back and twisting it around itself or by using a tensioning screw that can be tightened to tension the wire. The wires should be parallel to each other and 30–45cm/12–18in apart.

Free-standing wirework

Berried fruit – like raspberries, blackberries and the various hybrid berries – and grapes need a permanent framework. They are grown in the open, and it is necessary to build a structure that will carry the supporting wires. The end posts are the most important part of the structure because they take a strain in one direction only, and if they are not secured properly they can be pulled from the ground. Each post should be treated with a preservative to prolong its life. The end posts should be sunk into the ground by at least 60cm/ 24in and braced with another post set at an angle. Intermediate posts, every 2m/6ft or so, are set to a similar depth but do not need bracing. Galvanized wire is stretched along the length of the row, at 30cm/12in intervals, the first wire being 60cm/24in from the ground. These wires should be as taut as possible. They can be fixed with staples, or holes can be drilled in the posts and eye-bolts inserted, which can be used to tension the wire by tightening the nut on the outside of the end posts.

Individual support

Trees need individual support when they are first planted. In exposed positions some shrub fruit, especially standards, will also benefit from being supported.

SUPPORTING A TREE AGAINST A WALL

1 To support trees against walls, use wires held by vine eyes. Depending on the type of vine eye, either knock them into the wall or drill and plug before screwing them in.

2 Pass galvanized wire through the holes in the eyes and fasten to the end ones, keeping the wire as tight as possible.

The stake should be inserted before the tree is planted so that there is no chance of damaging the roots. Although the stake should be knocked well into the ground, there need only be about 45cm/18in above ground. Current practice is to support trees low down, at about 30cm/12in above the ground, so that the lower part of the tree and, more importantly, the rootball, are held in place, while the top is allowed to move freely, gaining strength as it does so.

Tie the tree to the stake, using a proper tree tie that will provide good support, but at the same time not cut into or chafe the trunk of the tree. It is important that you check at least twice a year that the tie is not too tight and cutting into the growing trunk. Adjust the tie if necessary.

If the tree is already in position, place the stake at an angle to the trunk so that it enters the ground some way from its base in order to avoid damaging the tree's roots. Alternatively, insert two posts, each some distance from, and on either side of, the trunk. Fix a crossbar between these two posts, and then tie the tree to this.

BELOW **The branches of small apple trees can be trained to spread by tying them down with string tied to the trunk.**

STAKING FRUIT

1 Knock a stout post well into the ground at the end of the row. An alternative is to dig a hole and insert the post before refilling and ramming down the earth.

2 Knock another post at a 45° angle to the vertical to act as a support to the upright post. Nail it firmly so that the upright post is rigid and will not be pulled by tight wires.

3 Fasten the wires around one end post and pull tight along the row stapling it to each post. Keep the wire as taut as possible. If necessary, use eye-bolts on the end posts to tension the wire.

4 Fasten the canes – in this case raspberry canes – to the wire with string or plant ties. Space the canes out evenly along the wire so that the maximum amount of light reaches the leaves.

Pruning Fruit Trees and Bushes

Pruning is a subject that terrifies many gardeners. Indeed, many gardeners fail to prune at all, to the detriment of the tree or the bush and to their subsequent crops. Like so many other things connected with gardening it is largely a question of experience. Once you have practised it a couple of times, you will be able to do it without any trouble at all.

Basic pruning cuts

Although trees and shrubs need different methods of pruning and training, the pruning cuts are the same in all instances. Always cut a stem just above a bud and make sure that the cut is angled away from the bud.

Branches that are large enough to be cut with a saw are usually cut across the branch at right angles. If the branch is thick and heavy and likely to break, thereby splitting the wood before the cut is complete, the sawing is done in three separate stages. The first cut is made on the underside of the branch, 5cm/2in from the final cutting position. The second cut is made slightly further out along the branch, this time from above, by sawing down until the branch splits along to the first cut and is then severed. The final cut can be made straight through from the top because there is now no weight to cause splitting.

Shapes

There are so many different ways of pruning and training fruit trees and bushes that it is impossible to explain every case here. Detailed pruning advice is given for individual fruits in the Fruit section

Rootstocks

The rootstock on which a fruit tree grows affects the size and rate of growth of the tree. It is important that you get the right stock for the type of tree you want to grow. Always check with the supplier that the tree or bush is suitable for your needs.

ABOVE **A standard apple tree is a particularly good shape for a traditional garden. It also provides shade in the summer.**

Fruit Tree and Bush Shapes

Standard trees are full-sized trees with a natural shape. These need space as they can grow large, but they create good shade for sitting under.

Half-standard trees are similar to standard trees, but, as the name implies, they are smaller.

Bush trees are much smaller than standards but are still quite large for a small garden. The trees are quite short but bushy with an open centre.

Spindle-bush trees are short – to 2.1m/7ft high – and cone shaped, with a central leader and side branches that are tied down to make them spread.

Dwarf pyramid trees are short growing and pruned into a pyramid shape. In general, more branches are retained than in the similarly shaped spindle-bush trees.

Fan trees or bushes are trained so that the branches are in a two-dimensional fan, radiating from the top of a short trunk. They are grown against a wall, a fence or post-and-wire supports.

Espalier trees or bushes are trained flat against a wall, a fence or post-and-wire supports. They have a main trunk and parallel branches coming from it at right angles.

Cordon trees or bushes consist of a single main stem. They are usually trained at 45° to the ground, but they can be also be vertical.

Double cordon trees or bushes are similar to ordinary cordons, except two shoots are trained vertically, forming a U-shape.

Triple cordons are similar to ordinary cordons, except three stems are trained vertically.

Standard bushes are grafted onto a single tall stem to give it a "lollipop" appearance.

ABOVE **Pears are the perfect fruit to grow in all manner of decorative shapes. Here, the pear is being trained into a crown shape.**

TOP LEFT **An espaliered pear tree on wire supports. Many other fruit trees can be trained in the same decorative way.**

OPPOSITE PAGE, TOP **This pear tree has been beautifully trained into a fan. The fan is supported on wires, but it could also be grown against a wall.**

Good and Bad Pruning Cuts

1 A good pruning cut is made just above a strong bud, about 3mm/⅛in above the bud. It should be a slanting cut, with the higher end above the bud. The bud should generally be outward bound from the plant rather than inward; the latter will throw its shoot into the plant, crossing and rubbing against others, which should be avoided. This is an easy technique and you can practise it on any stem.

2 If the stem has buds or leaves opposite each other, make the cut horizontal, about 3mm/⅛in above the buds.

3 Always use a sharp pair of secateurs (pruners). Blunt ones will produce a ragged or bruised cut, which is likely to introduce disease into the plant.

4 Do not cut too far above a bud. The piece of stem above the bud is likely to die back and the stem may well die back even further, causing the loss of the whole stem.

5 Do not cut too close to the bud otherwise the bud might be damaged by the secateurs (pruners) or disease might enter. Too close a cut is likely to cause the stem to die back to the next bud.

6 It is bad practice to slope the cut towards the bud as this makes the stem above the bud too long, which is likely to cause dieback. It also sheds rain on to the bud, which may cause problems.

Protecting Fruit

Gardeners are not the only animals to like fruit. Many others, birds in particular, do so as well, and the only way to make sure that there is enough left for the gardener to enjoy is to protect the fruit bushes and trees in some way. The only practical way to do this is to put some form of physical barrier between the predators and the fruit.

ABOVE **A tunnel of wire netting can be used to protect low-growing strawberries. The netting can be in short sections for easy removal and storage.**

Fruit cages

There is no doubt that the easiest way to protect fruit is with a complete cage. The advantage of this is that it covers the area completely and that the gardener can walk around within it, maintaining the bushes or harvesting the fruit. When individual protection is provided, each cover has to be removed in turn, which can be tiresome, especially if netting snags on branches.

The only problem with caging on a large scale is that it can be expensive. If you have every intention of leaving the fruit cage where it is, it might be more economical in the long term to build a cage with long-lasting materials. Use thick posts and make the covering from galvanized wire netting, which, although more expensive than plastic, will outlive many replacements of its plastic equivalent.

Ready-made fruit cages are expensive but they still probably work out cheaper than making one of your own, unless, of course, you have access to free materials, such as posts. Fruit cages are supplied in kit form and are easy to erect; they can usually be ordered to whatever size you require. Make sure that there are no gaps in the netting and that it is well pegged down or buried at the base because birds have a knack of finding the smallest hole to squeeze through.

A homemade fruit cage is time-consuming to construct, but you can make it fit any shape and cover any area you want. Metal posts, such as scaffolding poles, will last for ever but most gardeners find that wooden poles are more practical. They should be sturdy and treated at their base with preservative. Each should be let into the ground by about 60cm/24in for security, because the netting will act as a sail, putting great pressure on the posts in strong winds.

The covering can be plastic netting, but galvanized wire netting will last longer and be less likely to tear accidentally. Some gardeners like to remove the top covering to allow birds in to eat pests when the fruit is not actually ripening, and if you want to do this, use wire sides and a plastic netting for the top. Another reason for being able to remove the top covering in winter, especially if it is plastic, is that a heavy fall of snow can

LEFT **A fruit cage is expensive but it is the only really effective way of protecting fruit from birds.**

ABOVE **Strawberries can be protected against frost with cloches.**

LEFT **Fruit trees and bushes trained against a wall or fence can be protected with a home-made frame, as seen here. A similar frame can be covered with polythene (plastic) to protect the blossom from frosts.**

stretch and break it. The tops of the poles are best covered with a smooth rounded object – the bottom of a plastic drinks bottle is ideal – and although it may look ugly, it will prevent the plastic netting from being chaffed and worn as the wind moves it against the posts.

Make a door wide enough to get a wheelbarrow through and make certain that it fits well, or birds will get in.

Low-level protection

It is easier to provide protection for individual crops when low-level protection is required because less material is needed. The simplest method is to bend some wire-netting into an inverted U-shape and peg it to the ground with wires. This works well for strawberries. Alternatively, put short stakes in the ground at intervals all round and in the middle of the crop and drape plastic netting over this.

Draped netting

There is no satisfactory way of protecting taller, free-growing subjects, such as fruit bushes or trees. Draping them with netting is the only possible method, but gaps are usually left and the netting snags on twigs and shoots

If a fruit is growing against a wall or fence, then the netting can be held away from the plant by building a simple frame, and this can also be covered with polythene (plastic) in the spring in order to protect the blossom against frost.

Non-netting protection

Netting is the only satisfactory way to protect fruit crops in the garden. Commercial methods, such as bangers, are impracticable in a domestic garden. Humming wires have a limited success but do not really work. Covering the bushes with threads may keep the birds off but they make harvesting awkward and they are difficult to remove for pruning.

The traditional scarecrow makes a good feature in the garden, but it has no success in deterring birds and animals. Plastic birds of prey or owls at strategic points often work well for a while, but birds soon get used to them.

Harvesting and Storing Fruit

The best fruit is always the crop you pick and pop straight into your mouth. Given kind weather and a certain amount of skill on the gardener's part, however, there should be sufficient fruit not only to supply the kitchen but also to store for later use.

Harvesting

Fruit should be properly ripe before it is harvested for immediate use. There is little point in picking it early and leaving it to ripen – it will always ripen better on the stem. Fruit for storing should be mature and ripe – but do not pick at the very peak of ripeness, aim for just a little before. This is a matter of judgement and will come with experience. The time to pick is when the fruit comes away easily in the hand. Apples, for example, will come free with a little twist of the wrist, while raspberries will come away when twisted with the fingers.

With the exception of cane fruit, such as raspberries and blackberries, most fruit is picked with the stalks left on. Normally fruit is picked individually, but the various types of currant and grapes are usually picked in bunches. Pick fruit during dry weather and be careful not to bruise or otherwise damage it.

Storing

On the whole, the only types of fruit that can be satisfactorily stored without some method of preservation are apples, pears and quinces, and it is worth remembering that some varieties of fruit store better than others. 'Cox's Orange Pippin' apples, for example, can be kept until spring, but 'Beauty of Bath' apples have to be eaten right away, because they last not much longer than a week. As a general rule, early maturing apples do not store, but later ones do.

ABOVE **Apples are removed with a twist of the wrist. All fruits, other than cane fruit such as raspberries and blackberries, are picked with the stalks left on.**

Keep only fruit that is in perfect condition and throw out any that are marked or beginning to rot. Place the apples or pears in trays separated with paper so that they do not touch each other. Place the trays in a cool, dark place. Check periodically and throw out any fruit that is beginning to rot. Some apples will shrivel in storage and it is better to wrap these individually in greaseproof paper or to place several in a polythene (plastic) bag that has a few small holes in it.

ABOVE AND LEFT **Soft fruit, such as strawberries, raspberries and gooseberries should be carefully picked between thumb and finger. The fruit may then be placed in small individual containers so that they are not squashed or bruised.**

Storing Fruit

Apples, pears and quinces
Store in a cool place for up to 12 months, depending on the variety.

All other fruit
Eat immediately or freeze. Alternatively, preserve fruit by bottling or making into jam. Fruit can be kept for up to 12 months, depending on the method of preservation that has been used.

RIGHT **A filbert tree (*Corylus maxima*) is a rare but welcome sight in the garden. The variety shown here is 'Purpurea'.**

Do not place quinces close to apples and pears because the strong aroma will taint the other fruit. Store quinces in open trays.

Freezing

It is possible to freeze most fruit. However, although the taste will remain, many will lose their "solid" appearance when thawed and are, therefore, better used for cooking than for eating raw. Soft fruits are the easiest to freeze, but it is also possible to freeze apples, although it is best to cut them up or even cook and purée them before freezing.

Again, only choose sound fruit. Place the fruit on trays so that they are not touching each other and then put them in the freezer. Once frozen, they can be put into a bag. The fruit can be put straight into a bag before freezing, but they are likely to stick together and so the whole batch will have to be used at once. If you have no room for trays, split the fruit up into small usable quantities and place each batch of fruit in an individual bag.

Preserving

Freezing is a modern method of preserving fruit, but there are also a number of traditional ways. Some fruits, such as apples and pears, can be dried while others, such as plums and gooseberries, can be bottled. Another way is to turn the fruit into chutneys or jams. All these methods are dealt with in good cookery books.

ABOVE **Apples, pears and quinces can be stored in trays in a cool place. It is best if they are laid on paper so that the individual fruits do not touch. The length of storage time depends on the variety.**

ABOVE **With the exception of apples, pears and quinces, most fruit cannot be kept for any length of time without some form of preserving. The simplest method of preserving fruit is to freeze it.**

Propagation

While most gardeners do not have much space to increase their stock, and many do not need to replace their tree fruit, they need to know how to propagate soft fruits, so that they can be replaced from time to time. The techniques involved are all fairly simple to master.

ABOVE **This strawberry plant is producing plenty of runners, which root to produce a number of different plants.**

Hardwood cuttings

Currants, gooseberries, blueberries and grape vines are usually increased by taking hardwood cuttings. This process does not need any propagators or other equipment other than a pair of secateurs (pruners) or a sharp knife.

The best time for taking hardwood cuttings is autumn, preferably early autumn. Select a few shoots that have grown during the previous year and are now firm and well-ripened. They should be straight and about 30cm/12in long.

Choose a sheltered site, away from drying winds and hot sun. Make a narrow trench by inserting a spade into the soil and pushing it to one side to open up a narrow V-shaped slit. If the soil is heavy, trickle some clean sharp sand into the bottom of the slit and insert the cuttings. Place them about 15cm/6in apart, planting them so that about half of the cutting is below ground. Place the spade into the ground about 10cm/4in away from the initial slit and lever it so that the slit closes up, firmly holding the cuttings. Firm down the soil gently with your feet.

By the next autumn the cuttings should have rooted. They can be dug up and transplanted to their final positions or moved to a nursery bed for another year.

Layering

Blackberries and hybrid berries are best increased by the simple process of layering, as are strawberries, although the latter are usually obliging enough to do it themselves, leaving the gardener to transplant the new plants.

At some time during the growing season choose a healthy blackberry cane that is long enough to touch the ground. At the point where the tip makes contact with the soil, dig a hole about 10cm/4in deep. Place the tip in it and bury it by replacing the soil. If it is in an exposed position and it is possible that the cane will be blown or knocked out of the ground, you can secure it with a peg, although this is not normally necessary. By late autumn the tip will have rooted. Cut the new plant from its parent shoot, about 30cm/12in from the ground. Dig up the young plant and transplant it to its fruiting position.

If you want to grow a few new plants in pots, perhaps for selling, the young plant can be transplanted directly into a pot. However, it is possible to cut out this stage by burying the tip of the parent cane into a pot of potting compost (soil mix) instead of a hole in the ground; it will root just as easily. The pot can be let into the ground, which will prevent it from being knocked over and it will not dry out as quickly as it would if left standing on the ground.

Strawberries can be treated in a similar way. After fruiting they send out runners, which will drop roots at intervals along their length to produce new plants. To make sure that they root, you can peg them down or cover a short length of runner with soil, but

LAYERING

1 Blackberries, hybrid berries and strawberries can all be increased by layering. Choose a healthy shoot, dig a hole near the tip and then bury it.

2 After a short period the tip will have produced roots. It can then be cut from the parent plant and replanted where required.

3 If you would like to have potted specimens, then bury a flowerpot in the ground, fill it with compost (soil mix) and bury the tip in this.

this is usually unnecessary as the plant will root itself quite naturally. Again, the runners can be pegged into pots of compost (soil mix) if you want ready-potted plants.

Division

Raspberries are usually increased by division. It is a simple matter to lift some of the suckers that emerge a little way from the parent plant. In the autumn dig up a healthy, strong-growing sucker and cut through the root that is still attached to the main clump. Replant this in its fruiting position. It is advisable never to divide diseased plants for replanting. If you are in any doubt, it is always better to start from scratch, using certified disease-free stock that has been sold by a reputable nursery.

Methods of Propagation

Division Blackberries, hybrid berries, raspberries and strawberries

Layering Blackberries, hybrid berries and strawberries

Hardwood Cuttings Blackcurrants, gooseberries, grapes, red currants and white currants

Semi-ripe Cuttings Blueberries

Grafting Tree fruits

TAKING HARDWOOD CUTTINGS

1 Take the hardwood cuttings in the autumn, with each cutting measuring approximately 30cm/12in in length. Cut the cutting off just below a bud.

2 Dig a slit trench by pushing a spade into the ground and levering it backwards and forwards. If the ground is heavier, open the slit a bit more and part fill it with some clean sharp sand.

3 Place the cuttings vertically in the trench at about 15cm (6in) intervals.

4 Dig the spade in a short distance from the trench and lever it so that the slit closes up.

5 Firm down the soil around the cuttings with your foot and generally tidy up the surface of the soil with a rake.

common problems

Nothing is ever straightforward in the garden – perhaps if it were, many gardeners would give up through sheer boredom. Nature always throws in a few problems just to keep us on our toes. The weather is rarely consistent: it is either too wet or too dry, too hot or too cold. You turn your back for a few moments, and weeds seem to sprout up everywhere. Just when everything looks perfect, plagues of pests and diseases arrive. The gardener has a lot to contend with.

On the other hand, the situation is rarely as bad as many chemical companies would have you believe. Many of the problems are such that you can probably live with them, while others need only minor attention. Chemicals are only usually needed as a last resort.

RIGHT This informal vegetable garden, with its rows of onions, carrots, marrows (zucchini), spinach and beans, is a tribute to good garden hygiene.

Getting it in perspective

If the problems encountered by gardeners were insurmountable, no one would ever grow any vegetables at all. It cannot be denied that there are problems, but they often seem worse than they really are, particularly if you believe the literature issued by the chemical companies. Most of the problems that occur in the garden can be overcome by simple means that cost little in terms of either time or money. Many of the difficulties are insignificant and can, unless you are fastidious to the extreme, be ignored. A bit of rust on the leeks in a wet year doesn't look nice but it will not do a great deal of harm. A few minutes' contemplative hoeing will see off most of the weeds, and a sudden outbreak of caterpillars can soon be picked off by hand.

Do not let the thought of pests and diseases put you off in any way. An occurrence of either to the extent that serious action is needed is rare. Most gardeners find they survive season after season without any trouble. Anyway, if the worst comes to the worst, you can always give up and start afresh next year.

ABOVE Mulching with a layer of grass cuttings helps to preserve the moisture in the soil. You will need to water the ground before applying the mulch.

Be prepared

If you exercise a little forethought and adopt a good routine, you will be able to pre-empt many of the problems that might occur. Always practise good hygiene. Never leave rotten vegetables on the plants or in the ground. Remove them to the compost heap. Don't leave piles of weeds lying about, but put them on the compost heap or, if they are pernicious, burn them. Keep a close eye on your crops and take action as soon as possible if you see problems beginning to appear. Take out the tips of broad (fava) beans, for example, before they can be infested with blackfly. Cover your brassicas with fleece to keep off butterflies, and hence the caterpillars. If you notice one or two greenfly, crush them with your fingers before they can start breeding. Don't wait until they have multiplied and you have to resort to chemicals to control them.

Hoe as part of a regular routine. If you allow weeds to get too large, they will take longer to remove. Make your compost in such as way that it gets hot enough to destroy all weed seeds and fungal spores.

Stake peas and beans early, rather than leaving them until they are a tangled mass. Put up windbreaks in exposed areas, instead of waiting for things to blow over. Mulch to preserve moisture so that the soil does not dry out and you have to water. Foresight saves a lot of time and frustration.

ABOVE **Weeds use up a great deal of moisture and nutrients, and crowd out young plants, making them drawn and sickly. Weeds can also harbour disease.**

Chemical control

An increasing number of gardeners are becoming aware of the benefits of organic gardening and are avoiding the use of chemicals. There are times when chemicals can be useful, but these are less frequent than the large companies that manufacture them would have us believe. A weed-infested garden can probably only be cleared with chemicals, but if this is carried out properly, it should need to be done only once, and all subsequent control can be done by hand. Using chemicals on just one occasion will probably do no permanent harm to the soil, but do not become dependent on herbicides and reach for the spray every time you see a weed – that is not what gardening is about. You will end up creating a desert and a polluted one at that.

If you do use chemicals make sure that you follow the manufacturer's instructions. Take the necessary safety precautions and thoroughly wash all equipment. Never leave chemicals or associated equipment where children can get at them.

BELOW **A good mixed garden, with plenty of varieties of flowers and vegetables, is less likely to have problems than one restricted to a monoculture.**

Weather Problems

We cannot control the weather; we simply have to take what nature throws at us. Nevertheless, there are some ways in which we can limit the worst of its effects.

ABOVE **A maximum/minimum thermometer is ideal for keeping track of the temperature both in the open garden and inside a greenhouse.**

Wind

Winds can be destructive. Not only can they knock over and break plants, but also wind-rock can cause a plant to move about so that it becomes loose in the soil or it can create a hole around the point at which the plant enters the soil. This fills with stagnant water, and the plant can rot. A dry or hot wind can remove moisture from leaves, making them wilt. Cold winds can create wind-burn, which shrivels leaves. Winds can also make it unpleasant to work in the garden, frequently making the gardener not only uncomfortable but also irritable – not the best of moods to produce a good vegetable garden.

A long catalogue of woes, but the wind can be tamed to a large degree by creating windbreaks of some sort. By far the best defence is a hedge, which filters the wind, cutting down its speed considerably but at the same time not creating turbulence. A wall, on the other hand, stops the wind dead, but it escapes over the top and creates turbulence on the far side, and this can be more destructive than the wind itself. An alternative to a hedge is a form of plastic netting that is designed especially to be used as a windbreak. This is not the most beautiful of materials, but it is extremely functional.

BELOW **A hedge provides excellent protection from the wind. It allows some air to filter through, thus reducing the turbulence that occurs with solid features such as walls.**

TOP **Newspaper makes an excellent temporary insulation against sudden frosts in spring. Drop several layers, one on top of the other, to create air pockets. Do not leave on during the day.**

ABOVE **Fleece has a similar function to newspaper. It is very light and will not harm the plants. Unlike newspaper, it can be left on during the day as light penetrates though it.**

RIGHT **If a frost pocket is caused by a thick hedge, stopping cold air rolling down a hill, cut a hole in the base so that the air can pass through and continue down the hill away from the garden.**

Make sure that the poles supporting it are anchored securely because the netting will act as a sail and exert enormous pressure on its supports.

As a rule, a hedge or windbreak netting will create a "wind shadow" of about ten times the height of the barrier. In other words, a hedge 2m/6ft high will create a relatively wind-free area of about 20m/60ft from its base. The degree of protection decreases the further you get from the hedge, and at 20m/60ft from the hedge the decrease in wind speed is minimal.

Turbulence is reduced considerably by the use of double hedges or two rows of windbreak. Set a few yards apart, these give far greater protection than a single barrier.

Frost

There are two aspects to frost. The first is general winter cold; the second is those sudden unseasonable frosts that can wreak havoc among tender, newly put-out plants.

Winter cold is not generally too much of a problem in the vegetable garden because most of the things left in the garden are hardy. In particularly cold areas or in very cold spells, it is a good idea to give protection to some of the permanent crops, such as globe artichokes, by covering them with straw.

There is more of a problem if the garden is a cold one and the soil does not warm up until late in the spring. If your garden is like this, you will find it impossible to start gardening until then, and this makes early crops difficult to grow. There are several things you can do to help, however. If your vegetable garden is in a frost hollow – caused by cold air being trapped within it – it may be possible to "drain" it. Make a hole in the hedge or fence at the lowest point of the garden so that the air can flow through and continue down the slope. Alternatively, hedges may be placed higher up the slope to deflect the cold air as it moves downhill. Covering the soil with black polythene (plastic) or cloches will help warm up and dry out the soil so that you can start work on it earlier.

Sudden frosts can be a nightmare, especially if they are preceded by a warm spell that brings plants into early growth. Keep an ear or eye on the weather forecasts and cover tender plants if frost threatens. Use cloches, fleece or even newspaper.

ABOVE **Some plants, such as globe artichokes, are hardy but can be damaged by severe weather. They can be covered with straw to give them extra protection.**

ABOVE **Filling a box with straw makes a good form of insulation that can be removed and replaced. It also prevents the straw being blown about.**

ABOVE **Cloches produce longer-term protection than straw. They can be used to protect crops through the winter or as temporary cover in spring whenever frosts threaten.**

Drought

Few vegetables and fruit will grow without adequate moisture. Many plants will grow in dry conditions, but they quickly bolt (run to seed) and tend to be tough and often taste bitter. A constant supply of water is necessary so that growth is steady and uninterrupted. Irregular supplies of water will lead to irregular growth and many vegetables and fruit, in particular, will split.

Maintaining reserves

Throughout this book there is an emphasis on adding as much organic material as possible to the soil. Once again, this advice has to be repeated. Any free moisture in ordinary soil is likely to drain away or evaporate from the surface. However, fibrous material around the plant's roots will hold moisture in the same way as a cloth or a sponge. If there is excess moisture it will drain away, so that the plant is not standing in stagnant water, but enough will be retained to supply the plant's roots over a considerable time. Even if the water supply depends on irregular rain showers, the slow release will help to mitigate the dry periods.

Working as much organic material as possible into the soil is one way of pre-empting a dry summer. Add it to the soil when it is dug or, if you are using a non-digging, deep-bed system, add it as a top-dressing. Do this every year so that the water-retaining quality of the soil improves.

ABOVE **The best way to water a vegetable garden is with a watering can. Water can then be applied to exactly the right spot and in the right quantity with little water being wasted. However, watering by hand is both time-consuming and heavy work.**

Keeping water in

One way that moisture is lost from the soil is through evaporation from the surface. Hot sun and drying winds quickly take their toll on the soil and can dry it to a surprising depth, simply because more is drawn upwards to replace what has been lost nearer the surface. Covering the soil with a mulch helps to preserve this moisture.

ABOVE **A dribble hose is a good watering method because the hose is laid along the row of plants and it only waters the immediate area. The water slowly seeps out of the pipe, which means that it does not flood the area, but sinks well into the soil.**

LEFT **Place water butts beneath as many rooves as possible to catch the water as it runs off. It is the purest form of water to use and, being at ambient temperature, it does not chill the plants. It will also save water and, in most gardens, the money spent on water bills.**

RIGHT **Mulching with a layer of grass cuttings helps to preserve the moisture in the soil. Water before mulching and do not use too thick a layer as this may heat up and burn the plant – 7.5cm/3in is sufficient.**

Organic mulches are the best ones to use because they not only act as a barrier, but also eventually break down and are taken into the soil, much to its benefit. A mulch acts as a barrier partly because moisture does not evaporate from it quite as quickly as it does from ordinary soil, and partly because it acts as a thermal barrier, preventing the soil from getting too warm and thus speeding up the drying process.

Non-organic mulches – polythene (plastic), for example – prevent even greater loss as little moisture finds its way through, but, of course, it is not as easy for water to penetrate in the first place. Those to whom the aesthetic qualities of the kitchen garden are important may find that polythene looks ugly and will prefer to use an organic mulch.

It is important that the ground is thoroughly watered before any mulch is applied. If the ground is left dry the mulch will prevent it from getting wet unless a very large quantity of water is supplied.

Watering

Water is an expensive commodity – and becoming increasingly expensive in some areas – so you should use it only where and when it is really needed. Avoid, if possible, using sprinklers that waste large quantities of water on paths and other non-productive ground. If you have the time and strength use a watering can, supplying water to the base of individual plants. If you do this, you can be sure that the water goes where it is most needed. Sprinklers are especially useful when there is a large area of produce to cover or if watering by hand is difficult for physical reasons.

One efficient way of supplying water is to use a drip hose. This is a hosepipe (garden hose) with holes in it. It is laid along the line of plants and water constantly dribbles out. There is not enough water to flood the soil, but there is sufficient to provide a constant supply to the plants. If the ground is mulched, lay the pipe under the mulch. These hoses are best left on for several hours until the soil has taken up sufficient moisture, and then turned off, but there are gardens where they can be left on permanently. The system works best with permanent plantings, such as fruit bushes.

Whatever method you use, make certain that the ground is thoroughly soaked. A sprinkling of water on the surface will do little other than lay the dust. To be effective, a watering should supply at least the equivalent of 2.5cm/1in of rain.

LEFT **Black polythene (plastic) mulch is not attractive, but it is effective in reducing the water lost through evaporation. Special horticultural mulch can also be bought which allows water to pass through into the ground but prevents it escaping again.**

Weed Control

Many people are put off gardening simply because they do not like the idea of weeding. However, there are two points that they probably never consider. The first is that in a well-maintained garden there is far less weeding to do than they might think, and, second, weeding can be a rather relaxing, even therapeutic, task.

Keep it clean

Weeds in the right place can be a good thing, but the right place is not the vegetable garden. Weeds take nutrients and moisture from the soil, depriving the vegetables of their share. They can grow tall, smothering or drawing up the vegetables so that they do not grow properly. Many weeds harbour diseases, particularly rusts, and pass these on to your crops. So keep your kitchen garden clear of weeds if you want to produce the best crops.

Good preparation

One way to reduce the amount of weeding is to prepare the ground thoroughly in the first place. If all perennial weeds are removed, either by hand or with weedkillers, the only problem to cope with are new perennial and annual weeds that germinate from seeds. These are not much of a problem as long as they are hoed off soon after they have appeared. If you remove them before they can run to seed, gradually the number of seeds left in the soil – and hence the number of germinating weeds – will be reduced.

Keeping on top

As long as you keep on top of weeds they are not a problem. It is when you let things slip that it all becomes a chore. Hoe off weed seedlings as they appear and it will only take a few minutes of your time. Allow them to become fully grown and it will take hours to sort things out.

Hoeing

The method of hoeing is often a matter of personal preference. If you have a draw or swan-neck hoe, you scrape the weeds off by drawing the hoe towards you. If you have a plate or Dutch hoe, you push it forwards, slicing off the weeds. If you have a three-pronged cultivator, you pull it through the top layer of soil, disturbing the roots of the weeds. In dry weather a hoe of either kind is best because you do not want to open the soil too much or water will evaporate. In wetter weather, however, the cultivator can be extremely useful because it opens the soil and allows the water to drain through.

ABOVE **Avoid using chemical weedkillers in the vegetable garden. If necessary, use them to kill persistent weeds when initially preparing the plot. Always follow the instructions on the packet.**

Close work

Weeds do not always conveniently grow between the rows; they also grow in them where it is not as easy to hoe. With well-spaced

ABOVE **It is not always possible to hoe without damaging the vegetables, or because the weeds are too well advanced. Weeding with a hand fork is then the best alternative.**

BELOW **For delicate hoeing around plants that may be easily damaged, a small one-handed hoe, known as an onion hoe, can be used. It is a form of draw hoe.**

TOP **A push, plate or Dutch hoe is pushed forward, slicing either on or just below the surface, cutting off the weeds.**

ABOVE **A cultivator is a form of three-pronged hoe that is drawn between the rows of vegetables. This loosens the earth and with it any seedlings that have just germinated. As their roots are loose in the soil they cannot pick up moisture, and so die. This method is not as good in wet weather because the rain replants the weeds.**

LEFT **Hoeing is the traditional way of keeping a vegetable garden free of weeds. A draw hoe or swan-neck hoe is pulled towards the gardener in a series of chopping movements.**

crops, such as cabbages, it is possible to hoe around them, but this is impossible with vegetables such as carrots, and here you will have to weed by hand. Sometimes there is space to use an onion hoe, a small hoe with a short handle, which is held in one hand.

When you are working close to vegetables be careful not to disturb them. If a vegetable is disturbed when weeding nearby, firm down the soil and water in afterwards.

Non-digging methods

Gardening lore says that one year's weed seed means seven years' hard work, spent removing the resulting seedlings. What actually happens is that the seeds get mixed with the soil and germinate only when they come to the surface – one year's worth of weed seeds, therefore, will continue to be a nuisance until they have all been used up. However, if you do not bring the seeds to the surface in the first place they cannot germinate, and in non-digging methods only the surface layer is disturbed and the store of weed seeds is quickly used up. In consequence, if you regularly scrape off any weeds that appear, then the amount of work will soon be reduced because the only new weeds will be those blown in on the wind – the rest will be left underground, out of harm's way.

Pests and Diseases

Some gardeners get terribly worried about pests and diseases, but in reality they are rarely a real problem. Common sense and good management mean that you should be able to go for years without feeling the need to reach for the spray gun.

Gardening books always include long lists of pests and diseases and make it look as if these problems are lurking around every corner, just waiting to burst in on your garden and ruin your crops. In fact, it is unlikely that most gardeners will ever see a fraction of these during his or her lifetime, and, if they do, they are probably not really worth worrying about.

A mixed garden

One of the best ways of keeping the garden pest free is to grow a wide range of crops. If you only grow carrots and carrot root fly turns up and devastates your crop, you have nothing left. However, if you grow 20 different types of vegetables, you are only going to lose a twentieth of your total crop, which is relatively insignificant.

A mixed garden, which contains plenty of flowers – particularly the old-fashioned varieties – will attract a host of wildlife such as ladybirds, hoverflies and plenty of other predators, which will attack any pests that arrive in the garden. I have a large cottage garden with several large flower gardens within it and I am rarely troubled by even such common pests as aphids. Indeed, I cannot actually remember the last time any chemicals were used on my garden, not because I am against using chemical treatments, but because it has just not been necessary to do so.

ABOVE **Rabbits can devastate a garden overnight, leaving nothing but chewed off stumps as a result of their visit.**

ABOVE **Birds are one of the worst pests in the garden. Here large bites have been taken out of a brassica.**

LEFT **Nets can be used to guard your crops against rabbits and rodents.**

Animals

There is one type of pest that is very difficult to control – mammals. They can rarely be killed and are difficult to deter. The only real action that you can take is preventative, and this means building a barricade around your garden. Wire netting, which will keep out most animals, should be partially buried in the ground to prevent burrowing species, such as rabbits, getting underneath. For the more athletic species, such as deer, the barrier will need to be at least 2.4m/8ft high if you are to prevent them from jumping over it. Fortunately, there is no need to take action unless you live in an area where these pests are a problem. You will rarely be troubled, for example, if you garden in a town.

Birds

While only relatively few gardeners have deer to contend with, birds are everywhere, and even if things are quiet one day, a large flock of pigeons can appear the next, even in a town. The only real recourse against pigeons is to net everything. A fruit cage that is tall enough to allow the gardener in is the best,

ABOVE **Damage to trees can be prevented by using wire guards.**

RIGHT **Birds and butterflies can be kept at bay with fine-meshed nets.**

ABOVE **Insect damage can cause a wide range of problems. Aphids, like these, not only distort and kill plants by sucking the sap from leaves and stems, but can also introduce diseases.**

ABOVE **The caterpillar stage in the development of butterflies and moths causes a great deal of damage to leaves, especially to members of the cabbage family.**

ABOVE **Mechanical methods are often easier and cause less harm than using chemicals. Here, fleece is used to cover brassicas to prevent butterflies from laying eggs.**

but this is expensive. Low level netting can be used as temporary protection when crops are at their most vulnerable.

Bird scarers are also a possibility, but they are not especially effective. Humming tapes are probably the most effective solution, but they do not always work.

In addition to eating fruit, buds and leaf vegetables, birds can also cause damage to crops by dust-bathing in the seedbeds of the garden. These can be covered with netting as a deterrent. The birds are usually also deterred if several pea-sticks are laid temporarily on the bed.

LEFT **Biological controls are an increasingly successful way to fight pests. They are mainly used in greenhouses, but others are now becoming available for the open garden. The control insects are released, here from a sachet, in order to attack the pests.**

LEFT **Sticky traps are another form of non-spray control that is becoming popular for a wide range of pests. Here, pheromones attract insect pests to the trap, where they get stuck. Other sticky traps consist of sheets of yellow plastic covered with a non-drying glue. These are mainly used in greenhouses.**

Insects

A wide range of insect pests can attack vegetables. Some of these, such as aphids, attack virtually anything; others, such as carrot fly, restrict themselves to one type of crop. Many pests can be deterred by taking simple precautions. Cabbage root fly, for example, can be deterred by placing a piece of roofing felt or plastic on the ground around the plant to prevent the adults from laying their eggs next to the stem. Black fly can be a pest of broad (fava) beans, but if you remove their favourite part of the plant, the succulent tips, before they appear, the blackfly usually do not stop. Small outbreaks of insects can usually be removed by hand before they get out of control.

If the worst comes to the worst, you can use a chemical control. There are types that are safe to use with vegetables, but it is essential to read the instructions on the packaging, especially any advice about safety. Use chemicals only when and where they are needed; do not automatically drench everything. Make sure that spray or powder does not drift onto other plants, especially those that may be ready to be harvested.

Caterpillars

There are three ways of dealing with caterpillars. The first is preventative. Cover the plants with fleece or small-mesh netting so that butterflies and moths cannot lay their

LEFT **Slugs and snails have few friends among gardeners. They make holes in just about any part of a plant, often leaving it useless or even dead.**

eggs. The second is to check susceptible plants regularly and remove any eggs or caterpillars by hand. You may miss a few, but this usually keeps the problem within reasonable bounds. The third is to use chemicals. Again, be certain that they are suitable for vegetables and follow the instructions scrupulously.

Slugs and snails

Mollusc are probably the gardener's worst enemy. There are many traditional ways of ridding the garden of them, including using containers of beer sunk into the beds, but one of the most effective ways is to go out after dark with a torch (flashlight) and round up as many as you can see – and you will be surprised how many you will find. Kill them by putting them in a container of water with added washing-up liquid, or capture and release them on waste ground away from your garden. Doing this for a few nights should help to keep the problem under control.

If you must, you can use slug bait. There are organic baits available if you prefer, but they do not seem to be as effective as the non-organic type. Always follow the manufacturer's instructions to the letter and do not leave either bait or dead slugs around because they may be eaten by wildlife. Biological control is available, but it is expensive, the supply is erratic, and it does not always work; but things should improve on this front.

Diseases

Good housekeeping can prevent many diseases. Remove diseased or rotting material as soon as you see it. Deter aphids, which are often the carriers of disease, and, as a matter of practice, do not use the same ground two years running for the same crop. Wet, ill-drained soil may be the cause of some diseases, so improving the condition of the soil can be an important factor in keeping disease at bay. Healthy, well-fed and watered plants are less likely to fall prey to disease. Never buy, or accept as gifts, diseased plants.

Many modern hybrids are less susceptible to certain diseases than some of the older ones, so choose your varieties with care, if you are worried about possible diseases.

Some diseases can be treated with chemicals, but if there is any doubt, dig up the affected plants and burn them as soon as possible. If you do use chemicals, be careful and follow all instructions, especially the safety ones. Store chemicals well out of the reach of young children.

Burning is the only solution for plants suffering from viral diseases, such as mosaic virus on marrows (zucchini) and cucumbers or on spinach, because there is no known cure. Burning vegetables may seem a waste, but it is far better to safeguard the unaffected plants as well as to prevent spores from getting into the soil. If this does happen, next year's plants might be affected as well. To avoid this, use a rotational system of growing crops.

Remember not to put diseased plants on the compost heap. In theory, the compost should get hot enough to kill off any spores, but you can never be quite certain that all parts of the heap are sufficiently hot, and you might end up spreading the disease over the whole garden.

BELOW **Many of the diseases that affect vegetables are fungal ones, such as this rust on leeks.**

vegetables

Vegetables are the mainstay of any kitchen garden. The quantities and varieties as well as the way in which the crops are laid out will be determined by the preferences of the gardener. However, there are a few principles that apply to the growing of each type of vegetable, and these are described in this section of the book.

The gardener is spoilt for choice when it comes to the range of varieties available. At first it will be a question of experimenting to find the varieties whose taste you prefer as well as those that are best suited to the soil and climate in your garden. Once they have identified these varieties, many gardeners tend to stick with them. There is no harm in this, although it pays to be adventurous and to try not only a few new varieties, but also some types of vegetable that you have not grown before.

As well as buying seed, many gardeners collect their own. In this way they are certain to continue using the varieties that do well in their garden, especially if they collect seed from the best plants each time. F1 hybrids will not come true and it is not worth collecting seed from them, but it is worth experimenting with ordinary open-pollinated seed. Some plant seeds, like beans and peas, are easy to collect, but other plants, such as carrots, are biennial and do not set seed until the second year. Leaving plants in the ground for two years takes up valuable space and so it may not be worth it for these. Experiment, it will add to the fun of gardening, especially if you end up with your own strain of vegetables.

Shallots

Allium cepa Aggregatum Group

Shallots have been grown for almost as long as onions. They were originally named scallions after Asculon (Ashqelon) in Israel, the place from where the Greeks thought the vegetable originated, but shallots probably originally came from Central Asia.

Shallots are widely used in cooking, especially in France, where small onions are preferred. Although they lack the strong smell of onions and do not make your eyes water, the taste is often more intense yet sweeter than that of onions, and they are used where delicate flavours are needed. The leaves are sometimes used as a substitute for chives, and in country areas shallots are often used as a substitute for pickling onions.

Shallots are a small form of onion, but instead of growing as single bulbs they tend to grow in bunches or clusters. The shapes and colours of shallots vary considerably, and France in particular has a great number of cultivars. Some are torpedo-shaped, others are rounded. The colour varies from yellows through browns to reds, and flavours range from delicate to strong.

Cultivation

An open, sunny position is required for growing shallots, and a light soil, which has been dug and manured during the previous autumn, is preferable. In the northern hemisphere the traditional day for planting shallots in many regions is

PLANTING

Plant the shallot bulbs in rows at 15–18cm/6–7in intervals with 30cm/12in between each row. Using a dibber or trowel, bury the bulbs so that only the tips are showing.

Boxing Day, but this is too early for most areas, and late winter or early spring is a better time. Set them out in rows, planting the individual bulbs at 15–18cm/6–7in intervals. Use a dibber or trowel, and bury the bulbs so that only the tips are showing. The rows should be 30cm/12in apart.

Keep weeded. Water in early summer if necessary.

Harvesting

When the foliage shrivels in midsummer, ease the shallots from the soil with a fork. Place them on staging in a greenhouse or on racks of wire netting to dry. Once the leaves have completely dried, remove any

LEFT **Rows of shallots with garlic growing in the background.**

BELOW **Shallots drying on netting in the sunshine before being stored.**

dirt and dead foliage and break them up into individual bulbs before leaving to dry further.

Storage

Place shallots on wire racks or trays or in netting bags. Store them in a dark, cool but frost-free place, such as a cellar or garage. They should keep through the winter. Check on them regularly and throw out any that show signs of rotting.

Pests and diseases

On the whole, shallots are relatively trouble free, but they may succumb to the same problems in terms of pests and diseases as onions. The main pest is likely to be onion eelworm, which produces distorted leaves. Onion fly may also be a problem. They lay their eggs in the bulbs, and the maggots then go on to eat the shallots, turning the leaves yellow and eventually killing them. Companion planting with parsley is a traditional deterrent. In both cases you will have to burn or destroy any infected bulbs.

Various fungal diseases, such as neck rot and white rot, can affect shallots. Burn or destroy all infected bulbs.

ABOVE **A vigorous crop of young shallots with the individual bulbs just beginning to form.**

Cultivation

Planting time late winter to early spring
Planting distance 15–18cm/6–7in
Planting depth just below the surface
Distance between rows 30cm/12in
Harvesting midsummer

Varieties

'Atlantic' yellow skinned
'Delicato' red skinned
'Dutch Red' red skinned
'Dutch Yellow' yellow skinned
'Giant Red' red skinned
'Giant Yellow' yellow skinned
'Golden Gourmet' yellow skinned
'Hâtive de Niort' brown skinned
'Pikant' yellow skinned
'Sante' yellow skinned
'Success' red-brown skinned
'Topper' yellow skinned

shallots

Garlic

Allium sativum

Garlic is a very individual form of onion, characterized by its distinctive smell and flavour. It is widely used throughout the world for cooking and medicinal purposes and has been so for thousands of years. It is thought to have originated in Central Asia, but it can no longer be found in the wild. Even in cultivation it has ceased to set seed, and existing cultivars are thought to be very old indeed.

Garlic forms a bulb made up of numerous individual cloves. There are several different cultivars available worldwide, but they are very similar, the main differences being taste and pungency. The skins are usually white but can be tinged to a lesser or greater extent with purple. The only other differences are the size and number of cloves, hardiness and storage qualities. Garden-grown garlic is often bigger and more pungent than purchased bulbs.

Most seed merchants sell one or two varieties, sometimes just listed as "garlic bulbs". It is possible to plant bulbs purchased through a greengrocer or supermarket, but sometimes these have been "treated" and fail to sprout or, if they do sprout, produce distorted leaves. It is, however, worth trying if you find a variety you particularly like.

BELOW **This is a healthy crop of garlic plants. Unlike onions, the garlic bulbs form out of sight below the ground.**

ABOVE **Young garlic in spring before the bulbs begin to form.**

PLANTING

1 Use a dibber to make holes in the ground for each clove, at 10–15cm/ 4–6in intervals. A line of string will help you to keep the row straight.

2 Plant the cloves just below the surface, firming them in so that they are covered to their own height with soil.

RIGHT **Garlic can be started off by planting the cloves in individual pots.**

Cultivation

A sunny open position is required and, as with other members of the onion family, a light soil is preferred. Use soil that has been manured for a previous crop or, if you are planting in spring, dig in the manure in the preceding autumn.

If possible plant in mid- to late autumn. In colder districts, however, and in heavy cold soils it is better to wait until spring. Remove the outer skin and break the bulbs into individual cloves. Use a dibber to plant the cloves at 10–15cm/4–6in intervals, burying them so that they are covered to about their own height with soil. Alternatively, draw out a drill about 5cm/2in deep and plant the cloves in this at 10–15cm/4–6in intervals. Allow 30cm/12in between each row.

Keep well weeded, but avoid damaging the bulbs with the hoe.

Harvesting

Lift the bulbs when the leaves have turned yellow. Spread them out in a sunny place, preferably under cover – on greenhouse staging is ideal. When they have dried out thoroughly, remove any dirt and any long roots. If you are plaiting them or tying them in bunches, the leaves will need to be left on. If you are keeping them in net bags or trays, remove the dead foliage, leaving about 2.5cm/1in of stem.

Storage

Tie the stems together so that the garlic can be hung in bunches. A more sophisticated method is to plait the leaves together so that a chain of garlic is formed. Although these ropes of garlic are decorative, resist the temptation to hang them in the kitchen because the warmth and moist air will soon bring them into growth. Hang them in a cool, but frost-free, shed or cellar. Alternatively, place the garlic in trays and keep them in a similar position.

Pests and diseases

Garlic is relatively pest free. It can, however, suffer from various fungal or viral diseases. If the problem is a minor attack of rust, it can be ignored. If it is anything else, you will have to remove the bulbs, and burn or destroy them.

LEFT **A simple way of "stringing" garlic is to thread a stiff wire through the dry necks of the bulbs. The bulbs can also be tied on string.**

Varieties

Frequently just listed as garlic.
'Long Keeper'
'Long Keeper Improved'
'Marshall's Mediterranean'

Cultivation

Planting time mid-autumn (milder areas); early spring (cold areas)
Planting distance 10–15cm/4–6in
Planting depth twice height of the clove
Distance between rows 30cm/12in
Harvesting mid- to late summer

garlic

Spring Onions (Scallions)

Allium cepa

Spring onions (scallions) are small onions that are eaten fresh; they are not dried. They produce small bulbs that are little more than a slight swelling at the base of the stem. The bulb and the base of the stem is white; the cylindrical leaves are green. A young form of large, bulbous onions, they originate from the same part of the world, Central Asia. They are called spring onions (scallions) because they are ready to eat in spring, unlike other onions, which do not mature until later in the year.

ABOVE **Spring onions (scallions) can be pencil-slim or have a slight swelling at the base, forming a small bulb.**

The Welsh onion is similar to spring onions (scallions) but derives from a different species, *Allium fistulosum*. It has little to do with Wales, since it has been introduced to the West only relatively recently, although it has been in cultivation in China since prehistoric times. It found its way westwards through Russia in the early 17th century, possibly picking up its name from the German *welsche* (foreign) on the way. Welsh onions are somewhat coarser in appearance than spring onions. They are perennials, rather like coarse chives, and the foliage can be used in the same way as that of chives.

Bunching onions are similar again and have been derived from Welsh onions. These can be used as annuals, like spring onions (scallions), or as perennials, like Welsh onions.

Spring onions (scallions) can be used in cooking but they are more frequently eaten raw, especially in salads. The leaves can be used as a substitute for chives, and the onions themselves are often used as a garnish. Welsh and bunching onions are used in much the same ways.

Many gardeners use shallots for pickling. However, there is also a special type of pickling onion (also called a cocktail onion) that can be grown. These are similar to spring onions (scallions) except that the bulb develops more fully. They are small, white-skinned onions. Like spring onions, they are grown from seed sown in the spring and are usually ready for harvesting after two months. They are treated in the same manner as spring onions and can be left unthinned for smaller bulbs or thinned for larger ones. The smaller ones can be used as a substitute for bulbous spring onions. Although usually pickled they can be stored like other bulbous onions.

Cultivation

Like the rest of the family, spring onions (scallions) need an open, sunny site. The soil should preferably be light, but they will grow in most soils as long as they are manured. Dig in manure in autumn for spring sowing. Sow the seed in spring and then at three-week intervals for a succession. Late summer sowings can be overwintered under cloches for an early spring crop.

Sow thinly in drills 1cm/½in deep and 15–20cm/6–8in apart. If sown thinly enough, there should be no need to thin. This is important because the smell of bruised plants that is caused by thinning attracts onion fly.

Spring onions (scallions) should be grown quickly or they become tough, so they will need watering in dry weather. Welsh onions are grown in the same way but should be left in situ – only the leaves are cropped. Lift and divide every few years when the clumps get congested.

Harvesting

Spring onions (scallions) are ready for use at about eight weeks from sowing. Simply pull them from the ground. If the soil is compacted, they can be eased out with a hand fork.

Storage

Spring onions (scallions) cannot be stored for more than a few days. Keep in a cool place or in a refrigerator. The leaves can be chopped

THINNING

Although it is advisable to avoid thinning spring onions (scallions) where possible, it is often necessary to thin out congested rows.

HARVESTING

Spring onions (scallions) can be harvested either by pulling them from the ground by hand or, as is shown here, by gently forking them out.

ABOVE **Spring onions (scallions) that have been newly harvested.**

and frozen, either in bags or in ice cubes, for use in winter in the same way as chives.

Pests and diseases

The main pest is onion fly, whose maggots eat the onions, turning the leaves yellow and eventually killing them. The dangerous period is when the onions are damaged by thinning or weeding because the flies smell the odour that is given off. Burn or destroy any affected onions. Onion eelworm produces distorted leaves. Again, burn or destroy affected plants.

Various fungal diseases can affect spring onions (scallions) but because their life is so short any diseased plants should be destroyed and a fresh start made in a new position in the garden.

Cultivation

Sowing time early spring
Sowing distance sow thinly
Sowing depth 1cm/½in
Distance between rows 15–20cm/6–8in
Thinning distance avoid thinning if possible
Successional sowing three-week intervals
Harvesting eight weeks after sowing

spring onions (scallions)

Varieties

'Guardsman' for summer use
'Hikari Bunching' for summer use
'Ishikura' for summer use
'North Holland Blood Red' red skinned, for summer use
'Santa Claus' red skinned, for summer use
'Savel' for summer use
'White Knight' for overwintering
'White Lisbon' for summer use and overwintering
'Winter White Bunching' for overwintering

Leeks

Allium porrum

Like most forms of onion, leeks have been grown since ancient times. They were probably derived from Allium ampeloprasum, *which grows in the Near East and in countries of the Mediterranean littoral. Its traditional connection with Wales arose because Welshmen were said to have worn leeks in their hats in a battle against the Saxons in AD640 to distinguish them from their enemies.*

Although leeks belong to the onion family, they do not have such a pronounced basal swelling nor the pungent flavour and smell of the other culinary members of the genus. They consist of cylinders of tightly wrapped leaves, white where they have been blanched and green above soil level. It is the white section that is mainly used. Unlike the other culinary onions, which are mainly used as flavourings, leeks are used as a vegetable in their own right in a wide range of dishes and soups. They can also be used, of course, as a simple vegetable accompaniment.

A wide range of varieties is available, some are hardier than others (those with bluer leaves tend to be hardier), and some are ready earlier, while others stand better until spring. Some varieties have been bred specifically for their appearance on the show bench.

BELOW **A good block of leeks, with their rich green leaves, looks decorative in its own right.**

PLANTING

1 Make a hole with a dibber and drop the plant in. Do not fill in the hole.

2 Fill each hole along the row with water.

Cultivation

Leeks like an open, sunny position and a rich, fertile soil that is reasonably free draining. Dig well-rotted organic compost into the soil in autumn for planting in spring. Leeks like a long growing season, so start them off by sowing in nursery-bed rows in early to mid-spring. Sow thinly in drills 1cm/½in deep and 15cm/6in apart if you need more than one row. Transplant

Cultivation

Sowing time early to mid-spring
Sowing distance sow thinly
Sowing depth 1cm/½in
Distance between sown rows 15cm/6in
Planting distance 15cm/6in
Distance between planted rows 30cm/12in
Harvesting early autumn to late spring

when the seedlings are 15–20cm/6–8in high, which will be two or three months after sowing. Water the row the day before lifting and then dig out in batches with a hand fork. Plant into their permanent rows using a dibber. The plants should be 15cm/6in apart and the rows should be 30cm/12in apart. Make a hole about 15cm/6in deep and drop the leek in so that about 5cm/2in of the leaves show above the soil. Do not fill in the hole with soil, but fill it with water. This will wash sufficient soil around the roots.

As the leeks grow, earth (hill) them up by pulling soil up around the stems to blanch them. Alternatively, plant the leeks in the bottom of a trench and gradually fill the trench as the leeks grow. Keep weeded and watered in the early stages of growth.

Harvesting

Leeks can be lifted for use at any time between early autumn and late spring. Dig them out with a fork. Autumn varieties are not as hardy and should be harvested before midwinter.

Storage

Leeks are generally hardy and can be left in the ground until they are required. In cold areas they can be covered over with a cloche. They are best used fresh from the ground, but they can be dug several days before use and kept in a cool place. There is no method of storing leeks out of the ground. If the piece of ground they occupy is needed for some other purpose in the spring, then they can be lifted and heeled in elsewhere until they are needed. Simply dig a trench and insert the leeks to the same depth as they were in their original planting position. Dig them up as and when they are required.

EARTHING (HILLING) UP

Earth up the plants as they grow in order to blanch the stems. Alternatively, plant the leeks in a trench and fill it in as the plants grow.

HARVESTING

Harvest the leeks by digging under them with a fork. As you do this, pull them from the ground with the other hand.

Pests and diseases

Leeks are not usually troubled by pests and diseases. Rust is the most likely problem. Infected plants can be burned or destroyed; if the rust is not too severe it can be ignored, although it is best to plant leeks elsewhere for the next year. Other onion pests and diseases may occasionally be a problem; destroy any affected plants.

Varieties

Autumn
'Albinstar'
'Autumn Giant Startrack'
'Autumn Mammoth-Argenta'
'Elephant'
'Pancho'
Mid-season
'Carentan'
'Cortina'
'Grenvilliers-Splendid'
'King Richard'
Winter
'Alaska'
'Giant Winter-Cantalina'
'Giant Winter-Royal Favourite'
'Giant Winter-3'
'Kajak'
'Musselburgh'
'Wila'
'Yates Empire'

leeks

LEAF VEGETABLES

ABOVE **This is a very well-grown specimen that would do as well on the show bench as it will on the kitchen table.**

Cabbages

Brassica oleracea Capitata Group

Cabbage has been in cultivation for 3,000 years or so, but the cabbage as we know it today is a comparatively recent development, probably dating from the Middle Ages. Cabbage can be found growing in the wild throughout Europe, from Britain to Spain, but the wild form is more akin to broccoli than the hearted varieties with which we are now familiar.

Cabbages come in various forms, mainly depending on the time of year they are harvested – spring, summer, autumn and winter varieties are self-evidently named. These are all hearting cabbages, although spring cabbage is also available as "greens", which are loose heads of green leaves, unlike the typical tight heads of blanched leaves. There are also a few other winter varieties, which are sometimes considered separately, such as the savoys (with their distinctive, crinkly leaves), hybrids between the savoys and winter cabbages and 'January King'. The most distinctive of this group of cabbages is the red cabbage.

Some people have been put off cabbage by having to eat overcooked leaves, but it has always remained a staple winter vegetable for gardeners, especially in country areas, and nowadays it is enjoying a revival in popularity as people increasingly appreciate its culinary potential.

PROTECTING YOUNG CABBAGES

Young cabbages need protecting from birds. Wire guards are light and easy to erect. They are also easy to store if they are made in short sections.

Cultivation

Cabbages do best in an open, sunny site in a soil that is fertile but reasonably free draining. They do not like a soil that is too acid, and acid soil may need liming to bring it to pH6.5–7. This should be done immediately after digging and before planting. Most gardeners sow cabbages in nursery beds and transplant them; others prefer to sow them in trays under glass; still others buy them as young plants from nurseries and garden centres. The methods are basically the same for all types; it is just the timing that varies.

Thinly sow seed in shallow drills about 1cm/½in deep. Thin seedlings if necessary to prevent them from becoming drawn. After about five weeks, when they have four or five leaves, transplant them to their final position. Final spacing depends on the type and size (see Cultivation). Plant using a dibber or trowel and firm the soil in well around the roots. Water well and keep watered until they have become established.

Spring cabbages can be sown in situ and initially thinned to 10cm/4in. In spring thin again to 30–38cm/12–15in.

Hoe regularly and keep free of weeds. Draw up some soil around the stems of overwintering varieties. Remove any dead leaves.

Harvesting

Cut the hearting cabbages when they have become firm. Use a knife to cut through the stem, just below the firm head but inside any loose leaves. Savoy cabbages taste better if they are harvested after they have experienced at least one frost. The leaves of spring cabbages are cut as required, a few being left to heart up if required.

Storage

Most cabbages are winter hardy and can be left where they are until required. Those with solid heads can be cut and stored in a cool place, where they will keep for a couple of months. Some varieties of red cabbages may not be as hardy and can be harvested in early winter and stored.

PREVENTING CABBAGE ROOT FLY

Cabbage root fly can be kept at bay by placing a felt or plastic collar around the base of the cabbage in order to stop the fly laying its eggs.

Cultivation

Spring cabbage
Sowing time late summer
Sowing distance sow thinly
Sowing depth 1cm/½in
Distance between sown rows 15cm/6in
Planting distance 30–38cm/12–15in
Distance between planted rows 50–60cm/20–24in
Harvesting spring

Summer cabbage
Sowing time early to mid-spring
Sowing distance sow thinly
Sowing depth 1cm/½in
Distance between sown rows 15cm/6in
Planting distance 35cm/14in
Distance between planted rows 60cm/24in
Harvesting midsummer onwards

Autumn cabbage
Sowing time late spring
Sowing distance sow thinly
Sowing depth 1cm/½in
Distance between sown rows 15cm/6in
Planting distance 50cm/20in
Distance between planted rows 60–75cm/24–30in
Harvesting autumn

Winter cabbage
Sowing time late spring
Sowing distance sow thinly
Sowing depth 1cm/½in
Distance between sown rows 15cm/6in
Planting distance 50cm/20in
Distance between planted rows 60–75cm/24–30in
Harvesting winter

Varieties

Spring cabbage
'April'
'Durham Early'
'Greensleeves'
'January King'
'Offenham 1-Myatt's'
'Offenham Compacta'
'Pixie'
'Spring Hero'

Summer cabbage
'Castello'
'Derby Day'
'Hispi'
'Minicole'
'Primo'
'Quickstep'

Autumn cabbage
'Autoro'
'Bingo'
'Castello'
'Minnicole'
'Rapier'
'Winnigstadt'

Winter cabbage and savoys
'Best of All'
'Capriccio'
'Celtic'
'Christmas Drumhead'
'Duncan'
'Hidena'
'Ice Queen'
'January King'
'Novusa'
'Ormskirk 1-Ormskirk Late'
'Tundra'
'Wivoy'

Red cabbage
'Kissendrup'
'Metro'
'Red Drumhead'
'Red Dutch'
'Ruby Ball'
'Vesta'

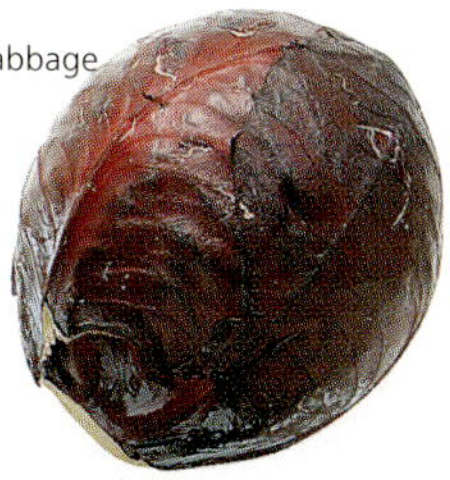
red cabbage

loose-leaf cabbage

Pests and diseases

Cabbage root fly are a nuisance, but they can be deterred by placing a collar of roofing felt or a similar material around the plant's stem. This prevents the adults from laying their eggs near the plant. Caterpillars are another problem. Cover the plants with netting or fleece to stop butterflies laying their eggs. Caterpillars can be removed by hand, but if you decide to spray, follow the manufacturer's instructions. Flea beetles make small holes in young leaves and should be prevented by dusting with the appropriate chemical. Slugs and snails should be controlled. The most serious disease is club root, which causes the roots to swell up. Any affected plants should be burned or destroyed. Liming helps to deter club root, as does growing cabbages in a different bed each year.

RIGHT **A block of cabbages in very good condition.**

Brussels Sprouts

Brassica oleracea Gemmifera Group

Brussels sprouts are so called because they are thought to have originated in Belgium, where they are recorded as growing in the mid-18th century. By the beginning of the 19th century they had spread to France and Britain. Even after 200 years of cultivation, Brussels sprouts still seem to be an acquired taste. Not everybody likes them, and children in particular seem to find that they have too strong a taste. When cooked properly, however, they are a very tasty and valuable part of winter meals, and few would consider their Christmas dinner complete without a bowl of them.

Cultivation

Sowing time early to mid-spring
Sowing distance sow thinly
Sowing depth 1cm/½in
Distance between sown rows 15cm/6in
Planting-out time when 13cm/5in high
Planting distance 50-75cm/20-30in
Distance between planted rows 75cm/30in
Harvesting mid-autumn to spring

Brussels sprouts are usually categorized according to season: early, mid and late. If plants are grown from each group, there can be a continuous crop from autumn right through to spring.

The sprouts themselves are the tight buds that form where the leaves join the main stem. As well as the sprouts, the succulent tops of the plants can be harvested once the sprouts are finished. The size of the plant varies according to cultivar, and some that have been bred as dwarf or compact plants are best suited to smaller gardens where space is at a premium. Another intriguing type is the red-leaved variety, 'Rubine', which is ideal for decorative kitchen gardens.

ABOVE **These Brussels sprouts are just beginning to develop. Soon the lower leaves will be removed, exposing the sprouts.**

Cultivation

An open position is required, but it should be protected from strong winds. The ground should be manured in autumn and limed if necessary to bring the acidity to within pH6.5–7. The seed can be sown in the open ground or started in trays under cover. For a late-summer picking, the seed should be sown in late winter or early spring – soil and weather conditions would generally mean that these seeds should be sown inside. For the more usual autumn-onwards harvest, sow in the open in early to mid-spring. Sow the earliest varieties first and the latest a few weeks later to make sure that they crop successionally. Sow thinly in shallow drills (see Cultivation). Plant out in the final position about five weeks after sowing, when the plants are about 13cm/5in tall. Plant the taller varieties at 75cm/30in intervals and the dwarfer forms at 50cm/20in intervals, with 75cm/30in between rows. Use a dibber or a trowel and firm the soil lightly around the plant. Water well.

Keep the plants well watered until they are established. Because there is such a large amount of space between plants they can be intercropped with a fast-growing crop such as radishes or lettuces. Keep the weeds down. If the site is exposed, stake the plants against the wind, and drawing soil up around the stems also helps. Remove the bottom leaves as they turn yellow.

Harvesting

Harvest when the Brussels sprouts are large enough to pick but while they are still tight. Start at the bottom of the plant, picking a few off each plant and snapping off each one with a downward twist. Move up the stems as the sprouts fill out. When all the sprouts are removed, pick the loose heads or tops and cook them as greens. Most gardeners prefer not to start harvesting until after the first frosts because this improves the flavour. As you harvest, remove any sprouts that have "blown" – that is, those that have not formed tight sprouts but are just a loose collection of leaves – and put them on the compost heap.

BELOW **Here, purple-leaved Brussels sprouts make an impromptu, but striking, combination with *Dahlia* 'Bishop of Llandaff' on the other side of the fence.**

Storage

Brussels sprouts are hardy and can be left on the stems until they are required. They cannot be stored after picking for any length of time unless they are frozen. Freeze early maturing varieties before the weather damages the outer leaves. Choose only good quality, uniform sprouts for freezing.

Pests and diseases

Brussels sprouts are prone to the same problems as cabbages. The worst problem is clubroot. Aphids will also take shelter in the tightly packed sprouts.

ABOVE **This healthy block of Brussels sprouts has been planted with red cabbages to create a highly decorative effect.**

Brussels sprouts

Varieties

Early	'Mallard'
'Lancelot'	'Roger'
'Oliver'	**Late**
'Peer Gynt'	'Fortress'
Mid-season	'Icarus'
'Bedford Fillbasket'	'Sheriff'
'Citadel'	'Trafalgar'
'Evesham Special'	'Widgeon'

Broccoli

Brassica oleracea Cymosa Group

Broccoli was developed from the wild cabbage in the 17th century in Italy, from where it spread through the rest of Europe. It is also known as sprouting broccoli or purple sprouting broccoli. Calabrese (Italian sprouting broccoli) and romanesco (Roman broccoli) are very closely related, but in the garden and kitchen they are considered separately because they grow at a different time of year and are cultivated in a slightly different way. In the past, gardeners also referred to winter cauliflowers as broccoli, and in some areas they may still do so.

Cultivation

Sowing time mid-spring
Sowing distance sow thinly
Sowing depth 1cm/½in
Distance between sown rows 15cm/6in
Planting-out time when 13cm/5in high
Planting distance 60cm/24in
Distance between planted rows 60–75cm/24–30in
Harvesting late winter to mid-spring

It is the flower shoots of broccoli that are gathered and eaten, just as the buds are forming and before the yellow of the opening flowers is seen. The flower-heads appear both at the top of the plant and as side shoots. In most varieties the flower-buds are purple – hence one of the alternative names, purple sprouting – but there are also creamy-white varieties, on which the flower-buds appear like miniature cauliflowers. The purple varieties are generally considered to be hardier than the white forms. There is one variety – 'Nine Star Perennial' – which, as its name suggests, is perennial in habit. If all the heads are picked each year it should last up to about five years, producing white heads each year.

In addition to the flower-heads, the stalk just below the buds and their associated leaves can also be eaten. Even more stalk may be eaten if the tougher outside is first removed.

The harvesting period for broccoli varies slightly, but it fills the "hungry" gap between late winter – 'Rudolph' is one of the earliest varieties – and mid-spring, when fresh vegetables are at a premium. The problem is that they are large plants and occupy the land for the best part of the year. Use the space between plants when they are first planted out for cultivating catch crops such as radishes. Each plant usually produces plenty of shoots and if space is very limited, it is worth growing just a couple of plants.

Cultivation

An open position is required, preferably one not buffeted by strong winds. The ground should be reasonably rich as well as manured in autumn and limed if necessary to bring the acidity to pH6.5–7. The seed can be sown in spring in the open ground or started in modules or trays under cover. Sow thinly in shallow drills 1cm/½in deep. If necessary, thin to 5cm/2in apart. Transplant the young broccoli when they are about 13cm/5in high. Water the row of plants the day before transplanting. Plant out the young broccoli at 60cm/24in intervals with the same distance between rows, using a dibber or trowel. Firm them in well with your heel and water.

Keep watered until they are established. Remove any weeds as soon as you notice them. In windy areas it may be necessary to stake the plants to prevent wind-rock. Earthing (hilling) up the stems will also help.

LEFT **This purple-sprouting broccoli is now ready for cutting.**

Harvesting

Depending on variety, harvesting starts in late winter to mid-spring. Snap or cut off the shoots as they begin to bud up but before they come into flower. Shoots should be about 15cm/6in long. Pick the shoots from all parts of the plant. Do not allow any to come into flower, or they will quickly run to seed and exhaust the plant.

Storage

Broccoli is perfectly hardy and should be left on the plant until required. It will not keep for more than a few days after picking, although it can be stood in a jug of water to keep it fresh or placed in a cool place such as a refrigerator. It can be stored for longer periods by freezing, a good way of coping with excess heads, which should always be picked and not left on the plant to flower.

Pests and diseases

Broccoli is susceptible to the same problems as cabbages.

Varieties

'Claret' late season
'Early Purple Sprouting' early to late season
'Nine Star Perennial' mid-season
'Purple Sprouting' mid- to late season
'Rudolph' early season
'White Sprouting' mid- to late season

broccoli

Calabrese (Italian Sprouting Broccoli)

Brassica oleracea Italica Group

Although calabrese (Italian sprouting broccoli) is in many ways very similar to broccoli, it is usually considered as a separate vegetable. Its origins are the same: it originated in the countries of the eastern Mediterranean littoral and in Italy, before moving to the rest of Europe. It is sometimes known as Italian broccoli or American broccoli. A similar vegetable, which is usually bracketed with calabrese, is Romanesco (Roman broccoli).

Unlike broccoli, calabrese (Italian sprouting broccoli) is quick growing but not very hardy, and it is grown so that the edible heads, which are much larger than those of broccoli, are produced in late summer and autumn. Calabrese forms a large central head, rather like a loose cauliflower, and when this is picked, side shoots develop, each carrying a slightly smaller head. Not all varieties seem capable of producing side shoots, however, and these varieties are finished once the main head is picked. The colour is different from broccoli in that it has a blue-green tinge. Another major difference to broccoli is that it is important that growth should not be checked so it is sown where it is to grow and not transplanted.

Romanesco (Roman broccoli), which is sometimes known as green cauliflower, is similar to calabrese (Italian sprouting broccoli) and is, in fact, often listed as a variety of calabrese. The main difference is that it is hardier and can be grown to produce heads from late autumn into early winter, covering at least part of the gap between calabrese and broccoli. Unlike calabrese and broccoli, romancesco only produces a single head and is then finished. The shape of the head is also different. It is distinctly conical-shaped, with little eruptions over the surface, creating further small whorls or pinnacles. It is an attractive plant, with yellowish, lime-green buds.

STATION SOWING

Calabrese (Italian sprouting broccoli) needs to be sown where it is to grow. Station sow the seed at intervals of 30cm/12in.

Cultivation

Sow in an open site in a fertile soil that has either been manured for a previous crop or manured during autumn digging. It is important to sow calabrese (Italian sprouting broccoli) and romanesco (Roman broccoli) where they are to mature, because they do not transplant well. Station sow in shallow drills about 1cm/½in deep at 30cm/12in intervals. Sow three seeds at each station. Rows should be 30cm/12in apart. Seeds can be sown closer together but this results in smaller heads. After germination, remove surplus seedlings so that only one, the strongest, remains at each station.

Keep well watered, especially in dry spells, so that the plants' growth is not checked. Keep them free of weeds.

Harvesting

Depending on variety, calabrese (Italian sprouting broccoli) is ready for harvesting from summer until well into autumn, usually 10–12 weeks after sowing. Romanesco (Roman broccoli) is ready from late autumn to the turn of the year or even later if protected with cloches.

Calabrese (Italian sprouting broccoli) first produces a single head, which should be cut while it is still tightly closed. Some varieties will subsequently produce side shoots with smaller heads. Romanesco (Roman broccoli) produces only one head, and when this is harvested the plant can be disposed of.

Cultivation

Calabrese (Italian sprouting broccoli)
Sowing time successional sowings from mid- to early summer
Sowing distance station sow at 30cm/12in
Sowing depth 1cm/½in
Distance between sown rows 30cm/12in
Harvesting late summer to autumn

Romanesco (Roman broccoli)
Sowing time early summer
Sowing distance station sow at 30cm/12in
Sowing depth 1cm/½in
Distance between sown rows 30cm/12in
Harvesting late autumn early winter (later if protected)

Storage

Neither calabrese (Italian sprouting broccoli) nor romanesco (Roman broccoli) keeps for more than a few days in a cool place and both are best eaten straight from the plant. They can be preserved for longer by freezing.

Pests and diseases

Both vegetables are susceptible to the same problems as cabbages.

Varieties

Calabrese (Italian sprouting broccoli)
'Caravel'
'Corvet'
'Green Comet'
'Mercedes'
'Ramosa'
'Trixie'

Romanesco (Roman broccoli)
'Romanesco'
'Temple'

calabrese (Italian sprouting broccoli)

Kale

Brassica oleracea Acephala Group

Because kale is a leafy, rather than a headed, brassica, it is much closer than many of the others to the original wild cabbage, and it is, therefore, probably one of the oldest forms. There are several different types, because the name is used to refer to any leafy brassica, including a whole group of coloured varieties that are used purely as ornamental plants. The main edible group is the curly kales, which are also known as borecoles. Another group, particularly popular in the southern United States, is the plain-leaved collards.

Although kale is one of the least favourite of brassicas as far as culinary uses are concerned, it does fill the period in midwinter when there are very few fresh vegetables around. Kales are very hardy and withstand winter weather well, and they will also tolerate wet and even poor soil conditions.

The edible varieties are decorative and are often grown for that attribute rather than for their flavour. The leaves of the traditional curly kale are so curled that they look like froth. In recent times the dark, narrow-leaved 'Nero di Toscana' (palm-tree cabbage) has become very popular for its visual qualities, and it is frequently seen in decorative potagers. In addition, there are some non-edible forms that are used purely as decoration both in the kitchen garden and in flower borders. Ornamental kales come in a wonderful range of purple, pinks, reds and creamy-whites. They are at their best in the winter when there is very little else of interest in the garden.

The leaves of kale are eaten, especially the young leaves from the centre of the plant. Some of the resistance to eating kale arises from the fact that some kales are used as cattle and sheep fodder in winter. Some people dislike its strong flavour, which can be rather bitter if the leaves are not cooked properly. Cooked well, however, kale makes a very good winter dish and is well worth growing.

BELOW **This informal vegetable garden includes a block of young curly kale plants.**

WATERING

It is important that kale plants are kept growing, so make sure that you do not let the soil dry out. Water well, as and when required.

Cultivation

Kale needs an open situation in which to grow. Although it prefers a fertile soil, it will grow in poorer soils than most other cabbages. If possible, however, incorporate manure when digging in autumn. Thinly sow the seed in late spring in the open ground in drills that are about 1cm/½in deep and 20cm/8in apart. Thin if necessary so that the young plants are about 5cm/2in apart. Transplant to their final positions when they are about 13cm/5in high. The final planting distances vary depending on the variety – for smaller varieties 45cm/18in will do, but the largest may need to be 60cm/24in apart. Allow 60cm/24in between the rows.

Kale needs to be kept steadily growing because it is slow to recover from any checks. It is, therefore, necessary to water during dry spells, especially when the plants are young. Weed regularly and remove any yellowing leaves.

Harvesting

With early varieties, harvesting can begin in autumn and continue through winter and into spring. Pick the young leaves but do not strip plants, which will take time to recover. It is better to remove just a few leaves from each plant. In spring pick the emerging shoots before they come into flower. Leaves and shoots are picked simply by snapping them off.

Storage

Kale is extremely hardy, and the leaves can be left on the plants until required. It cannot be stored for any length of time, although it can be frozen for use between spring and the first of the summer vegetables.

Pests and diseases

Kale is generally the most pest free of all the brassicas, but it is still prone to the same problems as cabbages. Caterpillars can be a particular problem with autumn-picked varieties, especially because they hide within the curly leaves. Treatment with a spray or powder may help if it gets into the creases. Soaking the leaves in salted water before you cook them is a good way to remove caterpillars.

Cultivation

Sowing time late spring
Sowing distance sow thinly
Sowing depth 1cm/½in
Distance between sown rows 20cm/8in
Planting-out time when 13cm/5in high
Planting distance 45–60cm/18–24in
Distance between planted rows 60cm/24in
Harvesting autumn to mid-spring

curly kale

HARVESTING

Narrow-leaved black kale is being harvested here by removing the younger, more succulent leaves.

Varieties

'Cottagers'
'Dwarf Blue Curled Scotch'
'Dwarf Green Curled'
'Fribor'
'Frosty'
'Hungry Gap'
'Nero di Toscana'
'Pentland Brig'
'Tall Green Curled'
'Thousandhead'

Cauliflowers

Brassica oleracea Botrytis Group

Cauliflowers are not the easiest of crops to grow, but they are one of the most rewarding, both in a sense of achievement and in the eating. Like so many of our vegetables, their origins are rather obscure. The Romans are thought to have cultivated a type of cauliflower, but the vegetable as we know it today originated in the countries at the eastern end of the Mediterranean at a much later date. It was introduced into Italy in the late 15th century and finally reached Britain about a hundred years later. However it was another two hundred years before it came to be widely grown.

Cauliflowers are characterized by their large, dome-shaped heads of creamy-white flowers (which are generally known as "curds"). When well-grown, these should be tight, evenly shaped and unblemished. The typical cauliflower has creamy-white curds, but there are also other colours for those who want something a bit different. Purple is the most common alternative colour, but there are also various shades of green and orange, although most of these are not true cauliflowers but hybrids, often produced using broccoli. The heads are usually 15–20cm/6–8in across, but there are now modern hybrids, often known as mini-cauliflowers, which develop very quickly and have heads to only 10cm/4in or less across.

LEFT **Harvest the cauliflower by cutting the stem with a sharp knife just below the first ring of leaves.**

PLANTING

Cauliflowers must be firmed in well when they are planted. Plants in loose soil run to seed quickly.

For those with the space to grow them there are cauliflowers for almost every season of the year. The only gap comes in winter, because most of the so-called winter cauliflower are not, in fact, ready until spring.

Cauliflowers can be awkward to grow, but, with care and attention, all gardeners should be able to produce good-quality crops. The main factor is to make sure that the plants' growth is not checked, because this causes irregular and undersized curds. An irregular water supply can be one cause. Late transplanting may be another. The one aspect that is difficult for the gardener to control is high summer temperatures, which are not conducive to growing good cauliflowers, since they prefer cool conditions. In hot areas you may have to abandon the idea of summer cauliflowers and concentrate on winter varieties.

Cultivation

Cauliflowers should be planted in an open, sunny position. To grow cauliflowers well it is essential that you have a fertile soil, preferably manured during digging in autumn. The manure is important, because the soil should be moisture-retentive so that the plants are not checked during dry periods. The soil must not be too acid; if possible adjust the pH level to 6.5–7 by liming in autumn.

Cauliflowers can be sown in the open ground or in modules or trays. They should be sown thinly in shallow drills about 1cm/½in deep and 20cm/8in apart. For the timing for the various seasons, check the Cultivation box. If necessary, thin the seedlings to about 5cm/2in apart. Transplant them when they have five leaves, which should be about six weeks after sowing. Water the rows of seedlings on the day and then transplant them using a dibber or trowel. Firm the soil around the plant down well with your heel. The planting distances vary from 50–75cm/20–30in, depending on the variety: compare Varieties with Cultivation box.

Keep cauliflowers well watered, especially in warm, dry spells. Once the curds begin to form, snap the larger outside leaves down over them to protect them. This will prevent discoloration.

Harvesting

The curds are ready when they form an even dome shape. Summer and autumn varieties mature in about 16 weeks from sowing and winter ones in about 40 weeks. Mini varieties are ready in about 15 weeks. When they are ready, cut through the stem with a sharp knife just below the head, leaving one or two leaves around the curd to protect it on its way to the kitchen. If you are storing them for a while, cut them so that they have a short length of stem from which you can hang them. If the leaves are occasionally sprayed with water, they will keep for several weeks in cool conditions.

PREVENTING SUN SCORCH

Protect the curds from discoloration by the sun by covering them with the inner leaves.

Storage

In general, it is best to leave the cauliflowers on the plants until they are required, but they can be cut and placed in a cool place for up to three weeks. They store best if they are hung upside down, otherwise cauliflowers will freeze well.

Pests and diseases

Cauliflowers are susceptible to the same problems as cabbages.

cauliflower

Cultivation

Early summer
Sowing time midwinter
Sowing position under glass
Planting-out time spring, when 13cm/5in high
Planting distance 50cm/20in
Distance between planted rows 60cm/24in
Harvesting early to midsummer

Summer
Sowing time mid-spring
Sowing distance sow thinly
Sowing depth 1cm/½in
Distance between sown rows 20cm/8in
Planting-out time early summer, when 13cm/5in high
Planting distance 60cm/24in
Distance between planted rows 60–75cm/24–30in
Harvesting late summer

Autumn
Sowing time late spring
Sowing distance sow thinly
Sowing depth 1cm/½in
Distance between sown rows 20cm/8in
Planting-out time early summer, when 13cm/5in high
Planting distance 60cm/24in
Distance between planted rows 60–75cm/24–30in
Harvesting autumn

Winter
Sowing time late spring
Sowing distance sow thinly
Sowing depth 1cm/½in
Distance between sown rows 20cm/8in
Planting-out time summer, when 13cm/5in high
Planting distance 70–75cm/28–30in
Distance between planted rows 60–75cm/24–30in
Harvesting late winter to early spring

Mini-cauliflowers
Sowing time spring
Sowing distance station sow 15cm/6in
Sowing depth 1cm/½in
Distance between sown rows 45cm/18in
Harvesting late summer to autumn

Varieties

Early summer and summer
'All Year Round'
'Alpha'
'Mayflower'
'Montana'
'Snow Crown'
'Snowball A'
'White Summer'

Late summer and autumn
'All Year Round'
'Autumn Glory'
'Castlegrant'
'Dok Elgon'
'Plana'
'Violet Queen'
'Wallaby'

Winter
'Arcade'
'Cappacio'
'Early Feltham'
'Jerome'
'Purple Cape'

Mini-cauliflowers
'Candid Charm'
'Mini-Cauliflower King'

Spinach

Spinacia oleracea

Spinach is the bane of most children and many adults, and yet when it is cooked properly it is a magnificent vegetable and a key ingredient in many classic and modern dishes. Spinach is related to the beetroots (beets) and chards and not to the cabbages or lettuces, to which it bears a superficial resemblance. It was first cultivated in Asia by the Persians, and it spread along the trade routes to China and eventually to Spain by the 11th century. It was five centuries later that it arrived in Britain.

Spinach is really a plant for a cool climate. It dislikes hot, dry summers, when it will very quickly go to seed, often before it is fully developed and ready to harvest. However, if you make sure that your plants are properly watered and that you select cultivars that suit your area, you can produce a crop that should last for two or three weeks and, with successional cropping, this can be extended considerably.

The plants look rather like a loose lettuce, with stalked leaves rising from a central stem. When the plant bolts, this stem quickly elongates. Supplying the plant with plenty of moisture and nourishment can postpone the tendency to bolt.

Alternatives to spinach

Spinach has a relatively short life, especially in hot, dry summers, when it is likely to bolt, and so many gardeners (erroneously one can't help feeling) think it is not worth growing. There are other vegetables that are cooked in the same way as spinach and have the advantage of having a longer season. These are generally known as "perpetual spinach", and the chief of them is Swiss chard. Another good alternative is New Zealand spinach (*Tetragonia tetragonioides*), which is not related botanically to spinach but makes a good substitute, both in the garden and kitchen. It is grown as an annual, but unlike true spinach it can be picked throughout the summer months and also way into autumn. Sow in trays or modules under glass and plant out after the danger of frosts has passed. Alternatively, station sow at 45cm/18in intervals in shallow drills, 1cm/½in deep, where they are to grow, again after the last frosts. It is more tolerant of drought than spinach but it does best if watered during dry periods. Pinch

Cultivation

Summer
Sowing time successional sowings from early to late spring
Sowing distance thinly
Sowing depth 1cm/½in
Thinning distance 15cm/6in
Distance between sown rows 30cm/12in
Harvesting early to late summer

Winter
Sowing time late summer to early autumn
Sowing distance thinly
Sowing depth 1cm/½in
Thinning distance 15cm/6in
Distance between sown rows 30cm/12in
Harvesting winter and spring

HARVESTING

Spinach is a very easy crop to harvest. When you require some, simply cut away the young leaves with a pair of sharp scissors.

LEFT **This beautifully maintained walled potager includes a healthy crop of spinach.**

RIGHT **This row of healthy looking spinach is now ready for harvesting.**

out the tip to make it bush out and harvest the leaves when they are big enough. Carry on doing this for as long as the plants last. Do not allow them to set seed or they may self-sow and possibly keep coming up for several years.

The young leaves of red orache or red mountain spinach (*Atriplex hortensis*) can also be used in the same way. In spring, sow seed where they are to grow either in shallow drills or by broadcasting. Thin to 30cm/12in apart. It is worth growing in a potager for its decorative qualities alone.

Cultivation

Grow spinach in an open, sunny position but preferably one that does not get too hot. The soil should be fertile and contain as much organic material as possible so that it is moisture retentive. Permanently wet soils should be avoided, however. Dig in manure or compost in autumn.

Thinly sow the seed in early spring, with successional sowings at two-week intervals through to late spring. It is better to sow several short or part-rows at intervals than one long one if there is the possibility that most of the plants will run to seed before they are harvested. Sow in shallow drills, about 1cm/½in deep and 30cm/12in apart. As soon as the seedlings are big enough to handle, thin them out to 15cm/6in apart. Keep well watered and keep weeds under control.

A crop for overwintering can be sown in late summer or early autumn. This will benefit from being covered with cloches from autumn onwards. The cloches will not only protect the plants, but will keep the leaves tender.

Harvesting

Start harvesting as soon as the leaves are big enough, which is usually 8–12 weeks after sowing. Don't strip the plant, but just take a few leaves to start with and until the plants are mature. Break or cut the stems, but avoid pulling because this may loosen the plant and precipitate bolting. Continue harvesting until the plants start to run to seed – when the central stem starts to elongate. When harvesting winter spinach, do not overpick.

Storage

Spinach should be picked and used as fresh as possible because it does not store. The leaves can, however, be frozen.

Pests and diseases

Spinach should be grown so fast that there can be few problems (apart from bolting) and, in any case, there is little time for the gardener to satisfactorily correct any problems that do occur. The best solution in this case is to scrap the affected plants and start again.

To avoid slug damage, clear the ground of slugs before sowing and at regular intervals thereafter.

The most likely diseases to affect spinach are downy mildew (choose resistant varieties) and spinach blight. Destroy the affected plants.

Varieties

Summer	Winter
'Bloomsdale'	'Broad-leafed Prickly'
'King of Denmark'	'Norvak'
'Long Standing'	'Sigmaleaf'
'Medana'	'Symphony'
'Monopa'	
'Melody'	
'Triathlon'	

spinach

Swiss Chard

Beta vulgaris Cicla Group

Swiss chard has a number of alternative names, including chard and seakale beet. The red-stemmed forms are additionally known as rhubarb chard, red chard or ruby chard. Spinach beet or perpetual spinach is essentially the same but has thinner stems. Although it is called Swiss chard, the plant originates from around the Mediterranean and dates back long before the modern state of Switzerland was thought of. Both the Greeks and Romans grew chard including red-stemmed forms. Although not grown much in England until recently, it has been around since at least the 16th century.

ABOVE **The vibrant colour of the stems of Swiss chard can be relied upon to make a strong decorative statement in the kitchen garden.**

Swiss chard has large, glossy, dark green leaves on wide creamy-white stalks. Both parts can be eaten, although they are often cooked separately, because the stems take much longer than the leaves. Ruby chard is similar, but the stems are a brilliant red and the leaves are a deep purple-green in some varieties and green in others. A third variant are those with striped stems, which can be in a range of colours, including red, yellow and orange. All three versions are very decorative and can be used in any ornamental scheme. Unlike some other brightly coloured vegetables – ornamental kale, for example – these chards are eminently edible as well as being decorative.

Perpetual spinach is relatively dull in comparison. It has smaller, less shiny leaves and stems that have no ornamental value at all. However, it makes a very good alternative to spinach. Both are easy to grow and maintain and produce an abundance of leaves for harvesting over a long period. Both can be used as a straightforward vegetable dish or combined with ingredients to make something a bit more special.

Cultivation

Swiss chard and perpetual spinach need an open site and a fertile soil. Manure the soil while digging it in the autumn. Station sow the chard in spring in shallow drills 1cm/½in deep and 38cm/15in apart. The stations should be 45cm/18in apart for larger plants, although for smaller plants they can be closer together. For perpetual spinach the intervals should be 30cm/12in. Germination is rapid, within a few days. Thin out unwanted seedlings at each station. A sowing can be made in late summer to provide a crop that goes on until the following summer, thus together with the spring sowing, providing leaves all year round.

Water and keep weed free. Both can be sown in trays or modules and planted out when they have reached an adequate size, at the same intervals as above. In very cold areas it may be necessary to give the plants protection of cloches or fleece, but they are generally hardy enough to need no protection.

Harvesting

Both forms, the Swiss chard and perpetual spinach, are perpetual in that once they have matured (usually 8–12 weeks after sowing) leaves can be cut from them as you wish, right through from summer until the following spring when they are likely to start running to seed (Swiss chard in seed is a very decorative vegetable indeed, so do not be in too much of a hurry to get rid of it unless you desperately need the space). Snap or cut off the leaves at the

WINTER PROTECTION

In cold areas Swiss chard needs some form of winter protection. Any form of cloche or portable cold frame can be used.

HARVESTING

Swiss chard is harvested by cutting the stalks at the base with a sharp knife. Like perpetual spinach, it can be harvested from summer until the following spring.

Cultivation

Swiss chard
Sowing time late spring
Sowing distance station sow at 45cm/18in
Sowing depth 1cm/½in
Distance between sown rows 38cm/15in
Harvesting late summer to spring

Perpetual spinach
Sowing time mid spring
Sowing distance station sow at 30cm/12in
Sowing depth 1cm (½in)
Distance between sown rows 38cm/15in
Harvesting late summer to spring

base of the plant. Take the leaves as soon as they are big enough and continue to harvest them so that the outer leaves do not get too large and coarse.

ABOVE **This row of mixed colour Swiss chard is ready for harvesting.**

Storage

Neither Swiss chard nor perpetual spinach stores well and should be cooked straight from the plant. Both can be frozen if necessary.

Pests and diseases

On the whole, both Swiss chard and perpetual spinach are pest and disease free. However, it is difficult to grow perfect Swiss chard (the leaves always seem to have holes in them), but while this may be a problem on the show bench, once cut up in the kitchen, no one will notice, so it isn't something to worry too much about. Slugs, earwigs, caterpillars, flea beetles and birds may all be to blame, but apart from getting rid of the slugs there is little need for action. If planted too close together they may suffer from downy mildew, especially in a damp season.

ABOVE **A perfect specimen of Swiss chard, clearly showing the white ribs that can be cooked separately from the leaves.**

Varieties

Swiss chard
'Argentata' deep green leaves, silvery white stems
'Bright Lights' dark green leaves, red, pink, orange, creamy silver and yellow stems
'Charlotte' purple-red leaves, bright red stems
'Feurio' red leaves, red stems
'Fordhook Giant' deep green leaves, white stems
'Lucullus' pale green, ruffled leaves, white stems
'Rainbow Chard' red, pink, orange, creamy silver or yellow stems.
Sometimes listed simply as "Swiss Chard" (with white stems) or "Rhubarb Chard" (with red stems) with no varietal name given.

Perpetual spinach
No varieties normally simply listed as "Perpetual Spinach" or "Leaf Beet".

red-leaved Swiss chard

Swiss chard

Chinese Cabbage

Brassica rapa var. *pekinensis*

Chinese cabbage is rather like a cos (romaine) lettuce, with crisp, crunchy leaves that can be eaten either raw or cooked. It is also a convenient name under which to group several other oriental greens, such as pak choi (bok choy) and mizuna, in which gardeners are becoming increasingly interested.

ABOVE **Young pak choi (bok choy) planted in a block, ready for harvesting. They can be cut on a cut-and-come-again basis.**

Chinese cabbage has been developed over centuries, particulary in China, since it was first recorded in the 5th century. It had reached America by the end of the 19th century but had to wait until the last decades of the 20th century before it arrived in Europe.

The original Chinese cabbages were loose headed, but the varieties we grow today are mainly hard headed and mostly derive from cultivars raised in Japan. They are tightly packed with dense leaves, which are a very pale creamy-yellow, blanched through lack of light, and sweet tasting. They last well if kept cool after harvesting, and one head seems to last several days of liberal helpings as a salad leaf. It can also be cooked, but its delicate flavour can be lost or overpowered by stronger flavours if the cook is not careful. Not many new vegetables have been introduced into gardens in the last couple of hundred years, but this one is most welcome.

Other new introductions have also appeared from the Far East, although they are perhaps not as popular as Chinese cabbage. Pak choi (bok choy; *Brassica rapa* var. *chinensis*) is one such. The common varieties are looser headed than the more commonly grown forms of Chinese cabbage and look more like a small Swiss chard, with dark green leaves and wide white stems. There is more flavour in pak choi (bok choy) than in Chinese leaves. They can be used raw or cooked.

Another plant that is creating increasing interest is mizuna (*Brassica rapa* var. *nipposinica*), which originated in Japan. This is unlike other greens in that the leaves are feathery, which makes them useful for the decorative kitchen garden as well as the purely productive one. They, too, can be cooked or used in salads.

LEFT **Like the original Chinese cabbages, this specimen is loose-headed.**

Cultivation

As with most vegetables, Chinese cabbage and other oriental greens like an open position and a fertile soil that is moisture retentive. Dig in plenty of well-rotted organic material during autumn digging. They do not do well on poor soils. Sowing in the open is best because they resent disturbance, which may cause bolting. They will also bolt if sown too early. Sow in early to midsummer in shallow drills 1cm/½in deep and 25cm/10in apart. Station sow the seed at 30cm/12in intervals, or sow thinly and thin to that distance. Take care not to disturb the roots too much when transplanting, and to avoid this, seed can be sown in modules. Keep weeded and well watered at all times.

Cultivation

Chinese cabbage
Sowing time early summer
Sowing distance station sow at 30cm/12in
Sowing depth 1cm/½in
Distance between sown rows 25cm/10in
Harvesting late summer to late autumn

Pak choi (bok choy)
Sowing time late spring
Sowing distance thinly
Sowing depth 1cm/½in
Distance between sown rows 15cm/8in–45cm/18in
Harvesting summer to late autumn

Mizuna
Sowing time spring
Sowing distance thinly
Sowing depth 1cm/½in
Distance between sown rows 38cm/15in
Thinning distance 15–45cm/6–18in
Harvesting summer to winter

RIGHT **The hard-headed Chinese cabbage is derived mainly from cultivars raised in Japan.**

Similar sowing conditions prevail for pak choi (bok choy), which can be sown a bit earlier as it is slightly less prone to bolt. Sowing distances vary from about 15cm/6in for smaller varieties to 45cm/18in for the larger. Mizuna, which does not bolt, can be sown at any time during the season, and it can be easily transplanted from seed trays if so desired. The spacing is the same as for pak choi. It can be harvested in winter from a late summer sowing, although it does best with some form of winter protection.

Harvesting

Chinese cabbage is ready to harvest after about seven weeks and can be cut as required through until late autumn. It can also be cut on a cut-and-come-again basis at a much earlier stage. However, it is more usual to remove the whole head by cutting just below the lowest leaves. If the stump is left in the ground, more leaves may develop, and these can be harvested as required.

Leaves of pak choi (bok choy) can be cut at any stage once they are big enough, usually after about three weeks. Whole heads can be removed when ready and the stumps left to reshoot. Flower-heads can also be eaten. Mizuna leaves can be cut at any stage from three weeks onwards, although the older leaves are not as succulent. The flower stalks can be eaten.

Storage

Chinese cabbage and other oriental greens should be used fresh from the garden.

Pests and diseases

The main pests are likely to be slugs, snails and caterpillars. Apart from these, there are usually not too many problems, although Chinese cabbage and the other oriental greens can be prone to any of the cabbage diseases.

Varieties

Chinese cabbage
'China Express'
'Eskimo'
'Harmony'
'Jade Pagoda'
'Kasumi'
'Mariko'
'Michihili'
'Tip Top'

Pak choi (bok choy)
Frequently listed simply as pak choi/bok choy.
'Joi Choi'
'Mei Quing'
'Shanghei'
'Tai-Sai'

Mizuna
Usually listed simply as mizuna greens.

Chinese cabbage

Lettuce

Latuca sativa

Lettuce is an odd vegetable, which is as often used for decorative purposes as for taste and nutrition. Shop-bought lettuces have much to answer for in this respect, as are the oft-repeated scare stories about their being full of chemicals. Home-grown lettuces not only have flavour, but you also know what they have been fed on. Another advantage of growing your own lettuces is that you can grow several different types and colours so that you can make a really attractive salad – and, of course, they are fresh. You can pick just as many leaves as you want right at the last minute.

ABOVE **A block of developing lettuces shows how decorative this varied crop can be.**

Lettuces have been popular for a long time and were even depicted in carvings and paintings in Ancient Egypt. They were popular among the Romans, who are reputed to have introduced them to Britain. The original lettuces were probably quite bitter and needed blanching to make them palatable, much like endives today.

Modern gardeners are fortunate in having so many different types as well as a wide range of varieties. The main type is the cabbage or headed lettuce. These are either loose balls of soft leaves – butterhead lettuces – or those with much firmer, crinkly-edged leaves – crispheads. Cos or romaine lettuces are more upright and have long, crisp leaves and a succulent heart. Then there are the loose-leaved or non-heading varieties, which do not produce a heart but just a mass of loose, individual leaves. These lettuces are very good when you want to be able to take leaves as and when you require them. There has recently been a great deal of interest in these cut-and-come-again lettuces, and many new varieties have appeared. This method of growing lettuces is far from new, however.

The mainstay of salads, lettuce is usually eaten raw, although an increasing number of recipes include cooked lettuce. Lettuce leaves are also widely used as a garnish, for which the coloured forms of the loose-leaved varieties are particularly useful. There is now quite a wide range of red- and bronze-leaved forms, as well as green forms with decorative leaves.

Lettuces are not difficult to grow and, in theory, can be harvested all year round, but some type of protection is required for winter varieties. They grow relatively quickly and will be ready from 5 to 12 weeks after sowing, depending on the variety. This means that they can be grown among slower growing crops or used to replace another crop that has already been harvested.

HARVESTING

Harvest lettuces when the "heart" feels firm.

Cultivation

Lettuces need an open, sunny position, although light, partial shade during the heat of the day can be an advantage in hot areas or during hot summers. The soil needs to be fertile and, preferably, moisture retentive, and this is best achieved by incorporating plenty of manure during the autumn dig. Lettuces can be sown straight in the ground or grown in trays and transplanted. It is a good idea to sow a short row of lettuces and then, instead of throwing away the thinnings, to transplant them to make up the rest of the row. The advantage of this is that the transplants will take a few days to settle down and will produce a slightly later crop than the sown plants. If the whole row is sown at once, the lettuces will mature at the same time, which will probably mean that many are wasted. Transplanting is difficult after midsummer, because lettuces often rapidly run to seed.

Start early sowings in trays or modules under glass in late winter or early spring. Plant these out under cloches or in cold frames to get an early crop. Seed can be sown directly in the soil from early spring onwards. Sow in shallow drills 1cm/½in deep, each row about 30cm/12in apart. Thin the lettuces to 15–30cm/6–12in apart, depending on the size of the variety. Transplanted lettuces should be planted at the same distances. Keep the soil moist and do not allow the plants' growth to be checked or they will rapidly run to seed. Sowings after midsummer will provide lettuces for autumn and early winter, but cover them with cloches when necessary from around mid-autumn. Special winter varieties can be overwintered under cloches or grown in greenhouses or in cold frames.

Harvesting

Lettuces can be harvested whole or leaves can be taken from the plants as required. The loose-leaved varieties are usually picked leaf by leaf, but cabbage-type varieties can be picked in the same way if you wish. Hearted varieties are usually ready for harvesting as soon as they feel plump and firm. Do not leave them too long in the

ground after maturing or they may bolt. Pull the whole lettuce from the ground or cut below the bottom leaves if you want the plant to resprout. Loose-leaved varieties mature earlier, and leaves can be picked as soon as they are large enough, which is usually from about seven weeks after sowing.

Storage

Whole lettuces can be kept in a refrigerator for a short time, but they are best used straight from the garden.

Pests and diseases

Slugs and greenfly (aphids) are two of the worst problems and should be dealt with by your preferred methods. Other pests can include root aphids and cutworms.

The main disease is downy mildew, and lettuces also tend to suffer from a few other fungal diseases. These occur mainly in wet seasons and are best avoided by making sure that individual lettuces are not planted too close together. This will ensure that there is plenty of air movement around the plants. If pests or diseases do get out of control, do not spend a lot of time and money on chemical control. Simply get rid of the plants and start again.

ABOVE **A block of decorative lettuces, showing the rich variety of colours available.**

Cultivation

Sowing time late winter (under glass) to early spring onwards
Sowing distance thinly
Sowing depth 1cm/½in
Distance between sown rows 30cm/12in
Thinning distance 15–30cm/6–12in
Harvesting early summer onwards

Varieties

Butterhead
'Avondefiance'
'Buttercrunch'
'Continuity'
'Dolly'
'Hilde II'
'Musette'
'Sabine'
'Tom Thumb'

Crisphead
'Avoncrisp'
'Beatrice'
'Iceberg'
'Lake Nayah'
'Malika'
'Minetto'
'Saladin'
'Warpath'
'Webb's Wonderful'

Cos
'Balloon'
'Bubbles'
'Corsair'
'Little Gem'
'Lobjoits Green Cos'
'Paris White'
'Wallop'

Loose-leaved
'Cerise'
'Cocarde'
'Frisby'
'Lollo Rosso'
'Red Fire'
'Red Sails'
'Redina'
'Salad Bowl'

Winter
'Arctic King'
'Kellys'
'Novita'
'Valdor'
'Winter Density'

Salad Leaves

Although lettuces, perhaps supplemented by leaves such as endives and chicory, provide the traditional greenery for most salads, there is an increasing number of small leaves that play their part. Some are available during the winter months, when lettuce from the garden may be scarce, and as well as adding bulk, each adds an individual flavour to pep up the overall interest of the salad. The two most important of these salad leaves are rocket (arugula; Eruca vesicaria*), which is also known as salad rocket, rucola and Italian cress, and lamb's lettuce (mâche;* Valerianella locusta*), which is also known as corn salad.*

Neither rocket (arugula) nor lamb's lettuce (mâche) is new – indeed, both have been eaten for centuries – but their popularity seems to be on the increase, particularly in the United States, where numerous varieties are available. The choice is also increasing in Europe, where it has always been particularly popular in France, from where many of the varieties come.

Young rocket (arugula) leaves have a sharp taste, and the older the leaves, the hotter and spicier the taste. They are usually eaten raw in salads, but older leaves are sometimes cooked, and the flowers can be eaten too. They make an excellent winter crop. Lamb's lettuce (mâche) is also used as a winter crop. The leaves are milder than those of rocket, and it is also much slower growing, taking up to 12 weeks before being ready to cut, compared with three weeks for rocket.

Several other leaves can be grown, each needing similar cultivation to rocket (arugula) and lamb's lettuce (mâche). The leaves of land cress (*Barbarea verna*) have a similar flavour to watercress. Mustard (*Brassica hirta*) and the similar tasting salad rape (*Brassica napus*) are also worth growing. Cress (*Lepidium sativum*), also known as garden or curly cress, can be grown to complement the other leaves, and winter purslane (*Claytonia perfoliata*) is another mild leaf for the salad bowl.

ABOVE **Chinese leaf mustard, in this case the variety 'Red Giant', will add a zing to any salad with its pungent flavour.**

Cultivation

All these salad leaves are plants for a cool climate and will rapidly run to seed in hotter areas. Because of this and because other salad materials are scarce at that time, they are mainly grown for autumn and winter use. In cooler areas they can be sown in spring for summer use. Although they are hardy, they need to be protected by cloches to be at their best.

Both rocket (arugula) and lamb's lettuce (mâche) are sown in late summer; rocket can also be sown in early autumn. Sow in drills 1cm/½in deep and 30cm/12in apart. Thin the resulting seedlings to 15cm/6in apart for rocket and 10cm/4in for lamb's lettuce. Keep lettuces watered if the weather is dry. Cover with cloches in late autumn or early winter.

LEFT **Land cress, often known as upland cress, is similar in taste to watercress and is often used as a land-grown substitute. This makes a welcome contribution to most salads.**

Cultivation

Rocket (arugula)
Sowing time late summer to early autumn
Sowing distance thinly
Sowing depth 1cm/½in
Distance between sown rows 30cm/12in
Thinning distance 15cm/6in
Harvesting late autumn onwards

Lamb's lettuce (mâche)
Sowing time late summer
Sowing distance thinly
Sowing depth 1cm/½in
Distance between sown rows 30cm/12in
Thinning distance 10cm/4in
Harvesting winter

Harvesting

Either pick individual leaves or cut off the lot as soon as they are large enough. They will sprout again.

Storage

Both plants should be picked as required because they will not store.

Pests and diseases

Both plants should be free of both pests and diseases, although rocket (arugula) may be attacked by flea beetle. If the tell-tale marks appear on the leaves, dust with derris.

ABOVE **Curled cress, or simply cress, is grown for its sprouts, but can also be used when fully grown, as is the case here.**

LEFT **Lamb's lettuce or mâche is a mild-flavoured leaf that is useful in autumn and winter salads.**

Varieties

Rocket (arugula)
Sold under one or other of its common names – rocket (arugula), rucola, salad rocket – rather than as varieties.
'Jade'
'Verte de Cambrai'
'Volhart'

Lamb's lettuce (mâche)
Frequently sold simply under its common name.
'Cavallo'
'Grote Noordhollandse'

Endives

Cichorium endivia

ABOVE **These curly-leaved endives, whose foliage creates a textured effect, have been grown in a block rather than in rows.**

Endives and chicory (Cichorium intybus) *are very closely related. So close, in fact that they can often be confused. The confusion is not helped by the fact that in France endive refers to what an English-speaking gardener would call chicory, while chicorée frisée is, in fact, the frilly-leaved form of endive. When it comes to growing them in the garden, however, there is rarely any confusion.*

There are two main types of endive. Curly endive is a flat-growing plant with frilly leaves; it is not very hardy and is mainly grown as a summer salad vegetable. Batavian endive or escarole is a more upright plant, with broad, wavy (rather than frilly) leaves. It is much hardier than curly endive and is, therefore, the type to choose for winter growing, although in milder areas both can be grown. Both types are annuals, unlike chicory which is a perennial.

Endives have been used as a salad vegetable for many centuries – in fact, civilizations as far back as the Ancient Egyptians are known to have enjoyed them. They are thought to have originated somewhere in the Near East but have long been grown in southern Europe, before eventually moving northwards. They are still not cultivated as widely as lettuces, probably because they have a rather bitter taste, which deters many people from growing them. The flavour can be dramatically improved, however, by blanching the leaves and the bitterness is more intense in hot conditions, so it is worth remembering that summer varieties are likely to have a sharper taste than the winter ones. This bitter taste contrasts well with other flavours in a mixed leaf salad.

One advantage that endives have over lettuce is that some varieties can be used in winter when lettuces are scarce. In summer, particularly in late summer, endives have the added advantage that they are less likely to bolt in dry weather, and they are also less prone to diseases, making them a reliable choice all the year round for the vegetable garden.

LEFT **Broad-leaved endives or escaroles are more cold-tolerant than the curly-leaved varieties.**

Cultivation

Endives generally prefer an open, sunny position, but in very hot areas they will benefit from a little light shade. The soil should be fertile and moisture retentive. Both curly-leaved and broad-leaved forms can be sown in open soil from spring onwards, and broad-leaved forms can also be sown in late summer for winter cropping. Sow in shallow drills 1cm/½in deep and 38cm/15in apart. When the seedlings appear, thin them to 25cm/10in apart for curly varieties and 38cm/15in for broad-leaved forms. Make sure that the soil does not dry out because it is very important not to check their growth.

Cultivation

Curly-leaved
Sowing time spring to summer
Sowing distance thinly
Sowing depth 1cm/½in
Distance between sown rows 38cm/15in
Thinning distance 25cm/10in
Harvesting summer

Broad-leaved
Sowing time spring to late summer
Sowing distance thinly
Sowing depth 1cm/½in
Distance between sown rows 38cm/15in
Thinning distance 38cm/15in
Harvesting summer, autumn and winter

Cover the winter varieties with cloches at the onset of winter. Alternatively, they can be grown in a greenhouse or covered cold frame.

Curly-leaved forms can be blanched by slipping a porous pot (terracotta is best) over the plant for about a week in summer or for up to three weeks in the colder weather of autumn and winter. Cover only a few plants at a time because they do not keep for long under these conditions. Place the cover over them when the leaves of the plant are dry. The taller broad-leaved varieties can also be covered, but it is often enough simply to tie the plant with raffia or soft string so that the outer leaves exclude the light from the inner ones.

Harvesting

Cut the blanched plants as required. Both can either be cut complete or just a few leaves can be used. The cut stalks will reshoot.

Storage

Neither form stores well and should be cut as required.

Pests and diseases

On the whole both forms of endive are trouble free. The most likely problem to occur will be attacks from slugs and snails, especially during the blanching process. Place a few slug pellets under the cover or lift it regularly and remove any slugs or snails that you find.

TOP **The leaves of endives can be used in salads or cooked. Unblanched leaves like these are more bitter than blanched ones.**

ABOVE **Blanching makes the leaves of endives taste sweeter. A plate laid over the centre of the plant is one way to achieve this.**

Varieties

Curly-leaved	Broad-leaved
'De Ruffec'	'Batavian Broad-leaved'
'Frisée de Namur'	'Batavian Green'
'Green Curled'	'Cornet de Bordeaux'
'Monaco'	'Full Heart Italian'
'Moss Curled'	'Golda'
'Riccia Pancalieri'	'Stratego'
'Wallone'	

curly-leaved endive

Chicory

Cichorium intybus

Although it is very closely related to the endive, chicory is quite distinct, both in the kitchen and the garden. Both vegetables are salad leaves, both can be bitter and both are useful as winter vegetables, but whereas endive is an annual, chicory is a perennial, even though it is often grown as an annual.

ABOVE **The Witloof or Belgian chicories are mainly grown for their chicons, but the leaves can also be eaten.**

Chicory dates from at least Roman times, when it was eaten as a salad leaf and a cooked vegetable. It has always been most widely used in Italy, which still grows more varieties than most countries. Left unharvested, chicory produces blue dandelion-like flowers, which set plenty of seed. The seeds spread easily, and chicory has become naturalized in many places, including North America, where it did not formerly grow.

As with endive and lettuce, the name chicory is, in fact, used to describe several distinct types. The best known is probably Witloof or Belgian chicory, which has green edible leaves but is grown mainly for the tight-leaved shoot or "chicon". This is produced in winter by blanching and can be used raw in salads or cooked.

Another type is the sugar loaf chicory, which has an upright head, looking rather like a cos (romaine) lettuce. Its large outer leaves envelop the inner ones, so that these are blanched naturally and thus lose some of their bitterness. Sugar loaf chicory is usually harvested from late summer onwards and can be used as a winter crop if given protection.

Radicchio or red-leaved chicory is another group. Unlike the sugar loaf type, this is a low-growing plant, but again, the outer leaves protect the tight, crisp heart, thus blanching it naturally and improving the taste. As well as flavour, radicchio adds colour to winter salads. It is harvested in the autumn and on through winter if given protection.

Traditionally, chicory has also been grown for its root, which has been used, roasted and ground, to bulk up coffee. Today few gardeners grow chicory for this purpose, although there is no reason why they should not.

Although it is not a chicory, dandelion (*Taraxacum officinale*) is often treated and eaten in exactly the same way, with the blanched leaves providing salad material. Sow in spring, removing any flower-heads that subsequently appear. Early in the following spring, cover and blanch the leaves. Keep the plants for another year or discard and start again.

Cultivation

Grow chicory in an open, sunny position. Although it will grow in any soil, it does best in fertile ground, into which manure has been incorporated during the previous autumn. Sow Witloof chicory in late spring or early summer in drills 1cm/½in deep and 30cm/12in apart. Thin the subsequent seedlings to about 15cm/6in. Remove any flowering stems.

To blanch chicory cut off all the leaves in late autumn and cover the remaining stumps with 15cm/6in of free-draining soil or compost (soil mix). The chicons are ready to pick as they appear. To blanch them indoors, lift a few roots from late autumn onwards. Cut off the leaves and trim back the base of the roots so that they fit into a 23cm/9in pot. Put three or four roots in the pot and fill with damp compost so that just the tops show. Cover with another pot or a bucket and place in a dark, preferably warm place. The chicons should be ready in about three weeks. Cut and cover again to get a second crop.

Sow sugar loaf from spring to late summer in 1cm/½in drills set 30cm/12in apart. Thin to 25cm/10in. Do not allow soil to dry out.

Radicchio can be sown in a similar way from early to midsummer. Thinning should be the same, although some of the larger

LEFT **Radicchio or red-leaved chicory produces a tight, self-blanching head that can be eaten like a lettuce.**

ABOVE **Radicchio chicories do not need the same care as Witloof or Belgian chicories.**

varieties may need more space. Protect with cloches once winter arrives.

Harvesting

Chicons should be cut complete when they are about 15cm/6in long. Harvest individual leaves of other forms as required or remove the complete head. The inner leaves are always the sweetest.

Storage

Chicory does not store well, so cut as needed. They can be kept for a few days in a refrigerator but wrap them so that no light reaches them or they will turn green and become bitter.

Pests and diseases

Slugs and snails are likely to be the only problem.

Cultivation

Witloof
Sowing time spring to early summer
Sowing distance thinly
Sowing depth 1cm/½in
Distance between sown rows 30cm/12in
Thinning distance 15cm/6in
Harvesting late autumn and winter

Sugar loaf
Sowing time spring to summer
Sowing distance thinly
Sowing depth 1cm/½in
Distance between sown rows 30cm/12in
Thinning distance 25cm/10in
Harvesting autumn

Radicchio
Sowing time early to midsummer
Sowing distance thinly
Sowing depth 1cm/½in
Distance between sown rows 38cm/15in
Thinning distance 25–30cm/10–12in
Harvesting late autumn to winter

Varieties

Witloof
'Normato'
'Witloof'
'Witloof Zoom'

Sugar loaf
'Bianca di Milano'
'Crystal Head'
'Poncho'
'Snowflake'
'Sugar Loaf'
'Winter Fare'

Radicchio
'Cesare'
'Medusa'
'Palla Rossa Zorzi Precoce'
'Rossa di Treviso'
'Rossa di Verona'

Witloof chicons

ROOT CROPS

Parsnips

Pastinaca sativa

Parsnips were developed in Europe from the widespread wild parsnip. It is possible that the Greeks and Romans cultivated them, but there is confusion over whether they were referring to parsnips or carrots in their writings. However, parsnips were certainly being eaten in Europe in the Middle Ages, although they subsequently went into something of a decline (except as cattle food), and it is principally in Britain where they remain popular. Parsnips have always been part of country fare, but they are now regaining a rightful place as vegetables for discerning palates.

ABOVE **Parsnips can be left in the ground until they are required.**

There is not much to see of the parsnip above ground, except for its inedible leaves. It is the large, swollen root that is the part that is eaten. Some varieties, especially when they are in light, fertile soil, can grow very big, to 45cm/18in or even longer. For most purposes, however, smaller roots are more than adequate.

There are more than 30 different varieties of parsnip. They differ little from each other, although some are more resistant to canker, while others have less hard cores. Certainly, none is more decorative than any other, either in the garden or on the plate. Ultimately, your choice of variety will be based on which grows best for you and which taste you prefer, although, in truth, there is not a great deal of difference.

Cultivation

An open, sunny position is required. Parsnips can be grown in heavy soils, but they prefer light ones, and although they do best in a fertile soil, do not sow them on freshly manured ground (the parsnips fork). Sow in soil that was manured the previous season or dug in the autumn. Always use fresh seed; last year's is unlikely to germinate. The seed should be station sown at 15–20cm/6–8in intervals in 1cm/½in drills. The rows should be 30cm/12in apart. Do not sow too early – the soil should be at least 7°C/45°F – but they do need a long growing season, so sow as soon as you can. Parsnips are slow to germinate so sow a few radishes between the stations of parsnips. These will appear quickly and mark the line of the rows, making it easier to hoe without accidentally disturbing the germinating parsnips.

In heavy or stony soils the parsnips may fork and produce stunted growth, rather than the desired conical shape. To avoid this, make holes with a crowbar at each sowing station, moving it in a circle to make an inverted conical hole in the ground. Fill this with potting compost (soil mix) or good loam and sow the seeds in this.

Thin the seeds to one to each station as soon as they are big enough to handle. Keep

PLANTING IN STONY GROUND

1 At the required sowing intervals, make an inverted conical hole with a crowbar.

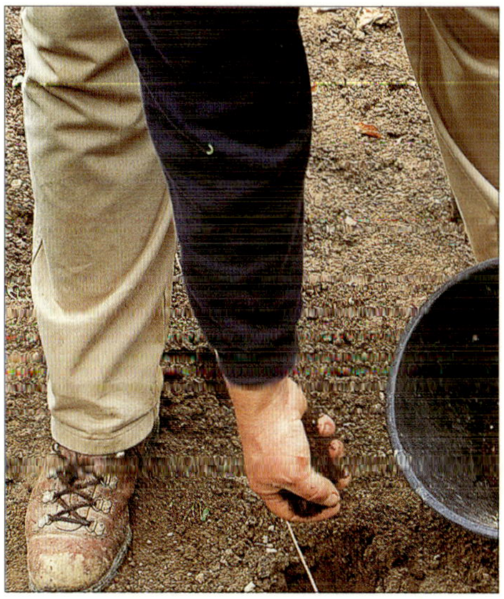

2 Fill the hole with potting compost (soil mix) and sow in the centre, covering the seed with more compost.

Cultivation

Sowing time early spring
Sowing distance station sow at 15–20cm/6–8in
Sowing depth 1cm/½in
Distance between sown rows 30cm/12in
Harvesting late autumn until spring

free from weeds. Water in dry spells because sudden rain after a prolonged dry spell may cause the roots to split. In very cold climates cover the rows of parsnips with straw during the winter.

Harvesting

Parsnips can be harvested from autumn onwards. Although they can be harvested before the leaves die back, most gardeners wait for this. Many gardeners also wait until after the first frosts, because these make parsnips taste sweeter. Dig the roots from the ground with a fork. In heavy soil or if the parsnips have deep roots, take care or the fork may slash through the flesh rather than lifting it out of the ground.

Storage

Parsnips are very hardy and should be left in the ground until they are required. If a frosty spell is forecast, however, it can be a good idea to lift a few while you can still get them out of the ground, and place them in trays of just-moist peat (peat moss) or sand until they are required. They are a late crop and may be harvested in spring well beyond the time that the ground may require preparing for the next crops. The parsnips can be dug up and temporarily heeled into another piece of ground or stored in sand or peat as described.

Varieties

'Avonresister' small, some canker resistance
'Bayonet' long-rooted, some canker resistance
'Cobham Improved Marrow' medium
'Gladiator' long-rooted, some canker resistance
'Hollow Crown Improved' long-rooted
'Intermediate' small
'Tender and True' long-rooted, some canker resistance
'White Gem' medium, long-rooted
'White Spear' long-rooted

ABOVE **Harvest parsnips by digging a fork well under the root and levering them out.**

Pests and diseases

Parsnips can be attacked by such pests as celery fly or carrot flies, but on the whole they are usually pest free.

Parsnips are also prone to canker, but you can help reduce the chances of this occurring by choosing one of the increasing number of varieties that have been grown with a resistance to this problem.

SOWING

Parsnips are best station sown in groups of three, eventually reducing the seedlings to one by thinning out the weakest.

parsnips

Carrots

Daucus carota

Many people may wonder if it is worth growing carrots when they are so cheap to buy. The answer must be an emphatic "yes". Fresh carrots, whether old or young, that are taken straight from the ground before being cooked taste infinitely better than shop-bought ones; there is no comparison. You may have to put up with them being covered in mud and perhaps with slug and carrot fly holes in them, but this is a minor consideration compared with the superior taste.

Wild carrots appear throughout Europe and well into Asia. The exact origin of domestic carrots is rather obscure, but they probably originated in the countries of the eastern Mediterranean, possibly even in Afghanistan. The original domesticated ones were various colours, including white, yellow, purple and red, and carrots of these colours are currently being re-bred and will soon be re-introduced by seed merchants. The orange ones, with which we are all familiar, were developed in Holland and France at a much later date.

The edible part of the carrot is below ground, while above are the attractive filigree leaves. Although mainly grown for the kitchen, they are well worth growing as purely decorative plants.

Although carrots bought in supermarkets are more or less identical, there is a lot of variety available to the gardener. Not only are there early carrots (often grown in frames) that are round, looking almost like radishes, there are some that are long and tapered. Others are just as long but are cylindrical, with parallel sides and a rounded end. Shorter varieties are best for immediate use, while the longer ones are better for storing over winter. Although the other colours are being bred, the majority of carrots are the familiar orange, but there are a few pale yellow and creamy-white forms available.

THINNING

Thin the carrots only if necessary. Do so on a still, muggy evening to prevent the smell of the carrots travelling and betraying their presence to carrot root flies. Water after thinning.

Cultivation

Choose an open, sunny position. Carrots will grow in heavier soils, but they do best in light ground – sandy soils are perfect. The soil should be free from stones and fresh manure because both will cause the carrots to fork. If the soil is stony, make individual holes with a crowbar, fill them with compost (soil mix) and sow into these. Avoid freshly manured soil by using a plot that was manured for a previous crop or by manuring in the autumn. Sow very thinly in drills 1cm/½in deep and set 15–20cm/6–8in apart. Sow under cloches in late winter or in the open from early spring, but not before the soil has warmed up to at least 7°C/45°F. Sow successionally, with the last sowing in early summer.

When the seedlings appear, thin the earliest to 8cm/3in and the maincrop to 5–8cm/2–3in apart, depending on the size of carrot required. It is best to thin on a muggy, windless evening in order to avoid attracting carrot fly. For the same reason, remove all thinnings and bury them in the compost heap. Weed regularly but avoid disturbing the young carrots – a mulch of grass cuttings will help keep weeds down. It will also help to keep the soil moist. Water in dry weather.

SOWING WITH SAND

Carrots must be sown thinly. To help with this mix the seed with a little silver sand and "sow" the mixture.

Harvesting

Harvesting can begin at a very early stage as the thinnings can be very delicious, although they are rather tedious to clean. Early carrots can be dug up from late spring onwards, approximately seven weeks after sowing. Maincrop carrots take a bit longer and are ready from ten weeks onwards. Shorter varieties can be pulled, but longer ones and those that have been grown in heavier soils will need digging out with a fork.

HARVESTING

Shorter varieties can be pulled out by hand, but longer ones and those grown on heavier soils will need digging out with a fork. Try to avoid piercing the roots with the tines of the fork.

Storage

Carrots are usually left in the ground until they are required. They may even be left in the ground over winter unless there are a lot of slugs or the winter is very harsh. Instead, they can be lifted, cleaned and placed in a tray of just-moist sand or peat (peat moss).

Pests and diseases

The worst pest is undoubtedly carrot fly, the maggots of which burrow into the carrots. There are an increasing number of varieties that are resistant to this pest and these may be worth trying. Be careful when thinning, because the flies are attracted by smell, and the bruising of any part of the carrot will release the tell-tale odour. Planting garlic nearby is a traditional way of disguising the smell. Another, cumbersome but successful, method is to erect a fine mesh barrier, up to 90cm/3ft high, around the carrots. This deflects the flies, which fly quite close to the ground.

The principal disease from which carrots are likely to suffer is violet root rot, in which, as its name suggests, the root rots, becoming a violet colour. Burn or destroy all affected plants and make sure that you do not use the same ground for carrots for at least a couple of years.

carrots

ABOVE **A flourishing row of carrots, coming to maturity. These will be ready for harvesting a few at a time, whenever required for the kitchen.**

Cultivation

Sowing time early spring and successionally to early summer
Sowing distance very thinly
Sowing depth 1cm/½in
Distance between sown rows 15–20cm/6–8in
Thinning distance 5–8cm/2–3in
Harvesting late spring onwards

Varieties

Early
'Amsterdam Forcing 3' cylindrical
'Amsterdam Sweetheart' cylindrical
'Early Nantes' stump-rooted
'Rondo' round

Maincrop
'Autumn King' cylindrical
'Chantenay Red Cored' tapered
'Favourite' stump-rooted
'Fly Away' cylindrical
'Ingot' cylindrical
'James Scarlet Intermediate' tapered
'Nantes' stump-rooted
'Nantes Express' stump-rooted
'St Valery' tapered

Beetroot (Beets)

Beta vulgaris

Beetroot (beets) originated around the shores of the Mediterranean and was spread northwards into the rest of Europe by the Romans. Once the Romans reached northern and eastern Europe, the vegetable seems to have been taken to heart, and many of the recipes in use today come from these areas.

Beetroot (beets) is related closely to Swiss chard and shares its distinctive bright red coloration. This is not only manifest in the leaves and stems of the plant but also in the roots themselves, and when they are cut or bruised they exude a wonderfully deep red juice. When it is cooked, the flesh is still a very deep colour, even though it loses a lot of colour in the water if it is boiled (baking preserves it). Not everyone likes this coloration, because it has a tendency to stain not only other food, but lips and clothes as well.

However, although you never see them in greengrocers, there are also white and golden varieties, which are equally delicious but do not cause the staining. There are also a few fancy ones in which the roots are made up of concentric rings of white and red flesh. The general shape is round or near round, but cylindrical or even tapered varieties are available.

The green or reddish-green leaves can also be eaten when they are young, either in salads or cooked.

Unlike parsnips and carrots, the bulk of the vegetable's swollen root sits on top of the ground so that you can watch its progress and easily determine when it is ready to harvest.

Many of the older varieties have a tendency to bolt, particularly if they are sown early, but there are now ample alternatives that have had this characteristic bred out of them. Another aspect of choosing varieties is related to germination. Most seed is, in fact, made up of a cluster of seeds, which means that when they germinate they produce several seedlings close together. However, if you find that thinning these is fiddly, look out for monogerm varieties, which usually have the word "mono" somewhere in their name.

BELOW **Beetroot growing in a block in a raised bed. This method enables you to control the growing medium and grow crops unsuited to your soil.**

Cultivation

Sowing time early spring and successionally to early summer
Sowing distance thinly or in stations at 8cm/3in intervals
Sowing depth 1cm/½in
Distance between sown rows 20cm/8in
Thinning distance 8cm/3in
Harvesting early summer onwards

Cultivation

Beetroot (beets) needs an open, sunny position. They will grow in heavy soils, but do best in light ones. The soil should be fertile but not freshly manured. Use a plot that was manured for the previous crop or one into which manure was dug during the

HARVESTING

Harvest beetroot by pulling it by hand from the ground. In heavier soils a fork may be needed to loosen the roots.

PREPARING FOR COOKING

Remove the leaves by twisting them off, 3–5cm/1–2in from the root. This prevents the beetroot (beets) losing their colour by "bleeding" when they are cooked.

previous autumn. Sow directly into the open soil into shallow drills 1cm/½in deep and set 20cm/8in apart. The seed should be station sown at 8cm/3in intervals or sown thinly and thinned to that distance when they have germinated. Beetroot (beet) seed is slow to germinate but it can be speeded up by soaking for an hour in warm water before sowing. Seed can be sown in early spring, once the soil has warmed up to 7°C/45°F, and successionally sown at two-week intervals until early summer. An earlier sowing can be made under cloches.

Keep beetroot (beet) weed free but avoid damaging them with a hoe. Keep them supplied with constant moisture. Avoid alternating dry and wet periods, or they may split.

ABOVE **Even a small garden such as this can accommodate a selection of crops, including onions and beetroot (beets).**

Harvesting

Pull the young beetroot (beets) from the ground while they are still quite small. This will be about seven weeks after sowing. Continue to pull as required. You may need to use a fork to help ease later crops or those in heavy soils from the ground. If possible, do not break the thin root attached to the bottom of the globe, because this will "bleed", causing the beetroot to lose a lot of its colour. For a similar reason do not cut off the leaves; instead, twist them off, leaving about 5cm/2in on the beet.

Storage

Beetroot (beets) can be left in the ground until they are required, except in cold districts, where they can be lifted, cleaned and placed in trays of just-moist sand or peat (peat moss). Store these trays in a cool, frost-free shed or garage.

Pests and diseases

On the whole, beetroot (beets) are reasonably trouble free in terms of possible pests and diseases. Birds may eat the young seedlings when they first appear, so keep these off with netting of some sort. If any diseases occur, burn or destroy the affected plants and re-sow them elsewhere.

Varieties

'Action' miniature
'Albina Vereduna' white flesh
'Boltardy' round
'Burpee's Golden' gold flesh
'Cheltenham Green Top' cylindrical
'Cheltenham Mono' monogerm
'Chioggia Pink' pink and white stripes
'Cylindra' cylindrical
'Detroit-Little Ball' miniature
'Dorée' golden
'Forono' cylindrical
'Moneta' monogerm
'Monodet' monogerm
'Monogram' monogerm
'Monopoly' monogerm
'Red Ace' cylindrical
'Tardel' miniature

Swedes (Rutabagas or Yellow Turnips)

Brassica napus

Swedes are one of those vegetables that never seem to get into ready-prepared, convenience dishes and yet are still popular with cooks who prepare their own food. They belong, perhaps, to what one might call the category of "wholesome food" (such as stews) rather than high cuisine, but they are increasingly used in a wide range of dishes, including delicate soups. Swedes are convenience food in their own right – it takes only a matter of seconds to pull one from the ground, peel, chop and put it to cook.

Swedes (rutabagas or yellow turnips) are not very old as vegetables go, although no one is certain about their origins. It seems likely that they appeared in Europe as a random cross between turnips and cabbages sometime in the Middle Ages. They did not find their way to Britain until the latter part of the 18th century, and it is thought that they were introduced from Sweden, hence the name. The American name "rutabaga" also has Swedish origins, being derived from *rotbagga*, which is Swedish for "ram's foot", an apt visual description of small or immature swedes.

LEFT **This is a typical swede, with lots of spreading leaves. This plant should stand in the ground throughout the winter.**

Cultivation

Sowing time late spring to early summer
Sowing distance thinly
Sowing depth 1cm/½in
Distance between sown rows 38cm/15in
Thinning distance 23cm/9in
Harvesting autumn onwards

Although they are usually considered a rootcrop, swedes (rutabagas or yellow turnips) actually belong to the cabbage family and, as such, suffer from similar pests and diseases. For this reason, they should be included with the cabbages when you are planning a rotational system. The swollen root of the swede is mainly above ground, with just a small amount being buried. In the better garden varieties, the top of the globe is usually purple, while the lower section, which is hidden from the light, is white. The flesh is a creamy-yellow, usually deepening during cooking. The appearance of the foliage clearly shows its close alliance to the cabbage.

Many gardeners used to sow a later crop of swedes (rutabagas or yellow turnips) around midsummer in order to provide "tops", or the leaves, which can be used as greens during spring. These can be grown closer together than suggested above for conventional use.

Cultivation

An open site is required. Like most root crops, swedes (rutabagas or yellow turnips) prefer a light soil, although they can be grown on heavier ground. As with most brassicas, the soil should not be too acid. Lime, if necessary, to bring it to about pH6.5. The ground should not be freshly manured, but it is important that it contains as much organic material as possible because the soil should be moisture retentive. Add manure during autumn digging. Sow thinly in late spring or early summer into drills that are 38cm/15in apart and 1cm/½in deep. Thin the swedes

ABOVE These healthy looking swedes have just been harvested. The spreading stems can be clearly seen. This variety is 'Acme'.

RIGHT Swedes are generally round, but can vary in shape depending on the growing conditions. This variety, 'Marian', has become elongated.

to 23cm/9in apart, preferably doing this in stages. Make sure that the soil is kept moist throughout summer, otherwise any check in the growth may result in woody or split globes. Keep the weeds down.

Harvesting

Swedes (rutabagas or yellow turnips) can be harvested from autumn onwards, throughout the winter, once they are large enough to use. Lift the globes as they are required. In most soils they can simply be pulled from the soil, but in heavier ones they may need loosening with a fork first.

Storage

Swedes (rutabagas or yellow turnips) are completely hardy and can be left in the soil as long as necessary. Some varieties become woody if they are left in the ground beyond the turn of the year, however, so these should be lifted and stored in trays of just-moist sand or peat (peat moss) and placed in a cool, frost-free shed or garage.

Pests and diseases

Being brassicas, swedes are prone to the same diseases as the rest of the cabbage family. Flea beetles are a particular scourge and the leaves should be dusted with derris as soon as they are spotted. Mildew can also be a problem, but there are now varictics that are resistant. Club root is another problem to look out for.

Varieties

'Best of All'	'Marian'
'Brora'	'Ruby'
'Devon Champion'	'Western Perfection'

purple-topped swedes (rutabagas or yellow turnips)

Turnips

Brassica napa Rapifera Group

Like swedes (rutabagas or yellow turnips), turnips are members of the cabbage family. The origins of the turnip go back so far that they are obscure, but the wild plant from which it is derived is still commonly found throughout Europe and Asia and is thought to have been cultivated as far back as prehistoric times. The long history has meant that many forms have appeared in cultivation, particularly in China and Japan. The popularity of the turnip has waned in the West, and with it a number of different forms, although there are still some 30 varieties from which to choose.

The Western form of the turnip is round, sometimes an almost perfect globe, sometimes slightly flattened. It has one thickish root or several roots emerging from the base. The skins are a creamy-white, and the top of the globe can be green, purple, white or creamy-yellow. The flesh is white or yellowish. The globe is partly sunk into the ground, but most of it is above ground. In Asia long-rooted varieties are also grown, and seed of this form is sometimes available in the West. It is also possible sometimes to find old European varieties with long roots.

The fleshy ball is cooked and eaten, but many gardeners also enjoy the young leaves, which are cooked as spring greens. Summer turnips are more succulent and lend themselves to a range of dishes. Those that are overwintered are generally not quite as tender, but they are useful in casseroles, stews and soups. In Japan they are often eaten raw.

BELOW **A well-shaped, purple-topped turnip. It is advisable to keep turnips moist so that they will grow quickly.**

Cultivation

Because turnips are a member of the brassica family, they should be included with cabbages in the rotational sequence. They need an open, sunny situation and, preferably, a light soil, although they can be grown in heavier ground. There must be plenty of organic material in the soil so that it does not dry out. The manure should either be left from a previous crop or be dug in during the previous autumn.

Cultivation

Summer
Sowing time late winter (under cloches) to early spring
Sowing distance thinly
Sowing depth 1cm/½in
Distance between sown rows 23cm/9in
Thinning distance 13cm/5in
Harvesting summer

Autumn and winter
Sowing time mid- to late summer
Sowing distance thinly
Sowing depth 1cm/½in
Distance between sown rows 30cm/12in
Thinning distance 20cm/8in
Harvesting autumn and winter

Greens
Sowing time late summer
Sowing distance thinly
Sowing depth 1cm/½in
Distance between sown rows 8–10cm/3–4in
Thinning distance none
Harvesting spring and early summer

Sow early varieties of turnip under cloches in late winter for early crops or in open ground from early spring onwards. Sow seed 1cm/½in deep in drills 23cm/9in apart. When the seedlings are big enough to handle, thin them to about 13cm/5in apart. Continue to sow at two- to three-week intervals for a continuous

HARVESTING

Turnips can be harvested by simply pulling them from the ground.

ABOVE **These turnips – a variety known as 'Tokyo Cross' – have just been harvested and will grace any dining table.**

ABOVE **The distance between the plants in this row of red-topped turnips is just right for growing them successfully.**

supply of small, tender turnips throughout the summer. For varieties to be harvested from the autumn and winter, sow in midsummer. They should be at the same depth, but rows should be about 30cm/12in apart. Thin the seedlings to 20cm/8in.

If you want to grow turnips just as "greens", sow thinly in late summer and there should be no need to thin. Rows can be as close as 8–10cm/3–4in.

The secret of growing good turnips is to keep them moist so that they can grow quickly. Keep them weeded.

Varieties

'Golden Ball'	'Milan White Forcing'
'Green Top Stone'	'Orange Perfection'
'Hakutaka'	'Presto'
'Imperial Green Globe'	'Purple Top Milan'
'Jersey Navet'	'Red Milan'
'Manchester Market'	'Snowball'
'Market Express'	'Stanis'
'Milan Early White Top'	'Stone'
'Milan Purple Top Forcing'	'Tokyo Cross'
	'Tyfon'
	'Veitch's Red Globe'

Harvesting

Harvest the early and summer varieties as soon as they are the size of golf balls. They can be eaten when they are slightly larger, but they are at their best at this size. Larger and older turnips become woody, so rather than sowing one long row, it is better to sow short rows at different times to provide a steady supply of young turnips. Varieties sown in midsummer can be harvested from autumn onwards as they are required. The "greens" can be harvested as young leaves from spring into summer.

Storage

Turnips can be left in the ground until they are required. In very cold areas or if they are likely to be frozen in the ground and impossible to extract, they can be lifted, the tops removed and the globes stored in trays of just-moist sand or peat (peat moss), and kept in a frost-free place.

Pests and diseases

Turnips suffer from the same problems as cabbages. Flea beetle, which is likely to be the worst pest, should be treated with derris dust.

Diseases can include violet root rot and club root. Destroy any affected plants.

green-topped turnips

Kohl Rabi

Brassica oleracea Gongylodes Group

Although it is not strictly a root vegetable, kohl rabi is placed in this group because of its similarity to the turnip. In reality, it is a short-stemmed cabbage, but the stem has swollen into a round ball. The fact that it is a stem can be seen from the cabbage-like leaves that sprout out from all around the swelling, unlike those of a turnip, which grow on top. The skin is either green or purple, depending on variety, and the flesh is white. Because it is a stem, kohl rabi sits on or just above the ground, with a taproot descending into the soil.

This curious vegetable is a relative newcomer to gardens, and it is thought to have originated in Europe as late as the 15th or 16th century, although it may have developed earlier – Pliny describes a similar type of vegetable being grown by the Romans in the 1st century AD. No matter when it originated, kohl rabi is not as popular today as it should be. Even after four centuries it is still considered something of a rarity in France and Britain, although it is more widely grown in Germany and Austria – as is testified by varieties such as 'Purple Vienna' and 'White Vienna' – as well as in Eastern Europe.

Kohl rabi has a fresh, mild taste, which is somewhat similar to that of turnips, and it is useful in a wide range of dishes, including soups, as well as being eaten as a vegetable in its own right. It can also be eaten raw – in salads, for example. From the gardener's point of view it has the advantage over the turnip in that it can be grown in drier conditions yet still retain its succulence. Most varieties should be harvested while they are still quite small – about the size of a tennis ball – but some varieties, such as 'Gigante', which comes from the Czech Republic, usually grow to 4.5kg/10lb or more but remain succulent. Unfortunately, 'Gigante' is not an easy variety to get hold of, but it is definitely worth growing if you come across any seed. Purple-skinned varieties of kohl rabi are slightly hardier than white-skinned forms.

ABOVE **The leaves of these healthy looking kohl rabi are in perfect condition. The kohl rabi have been planted in a block.**

Cultivation

Kohl rabi needs an open, sunny situation, preferably with light soil, but they will grow on heavier ground. The soil should be well manured, ideally from an earlier crop or during the previous autumn. The seed should be sown thinly in drills, about 1cm/½in deep and 30cm/12in apart. Sowing can start under cloches in late winter for an early crop or early spring in the open ground. Continue to sow at three-week intervals until late summer for a continuous crop of tender roots. Thin to about 15cm/6in for earlier crops and to 20cm/8in for later ones. Watering is not as crucial as for turnips, but they are less likely to split if the moisture supply to the roots is constant. Keep weeded, but avoid damaging the roots with the hoe.

Harvesting

The stems are best harvested when they are about the size of tennis balls. Most varieties get rather woody after that. Later crops can be left in the ground until early winter and

LEFT **This is a perfect specimen of kohl rabi, which is ready for harvesting. Use in soups, for example, or eat as a vegetable in its own right.**

Cultivation

Sowing time late winter (under cloches) and early spring to late summer
Sowing distance thinly
Sowing depth 1cm/½in
Distance between sown rows 30cm/12in
Thinning distance 15–20cm/6–8in
Harvesting summer onwards

possibly even later in milder areas. They are very easy to harvest as they can be simply pulled from the ground. When harvesting, shorten the root and cut back the leaves, leaving short stems before taking them into the kitchen for preparation.

Storage

There is no need to store kohl rabi because they should be pulled from the ground as required. In colder areas the last crop can be pulled, cleaned and stored in trays of just-damp sand or peat (peat moss), but they do not keep as well as other root crops as they tend to shrivel.

Pests and diseases

Kohl rabi suffers from the same kind of pests and diseases as cabbage. Flea beetles can be one of the worst pests, and leaves should be dusted with derris if an infestation occurs.

ABOVE **A purple-skinned kohl rabi, showing the soft bloom that appears on the skin.**

LEFT **Grow kohl rabi quickly, with plenty of moisture. This one was grown in conditions that were too dry.**

Varieties

'Adriana'	'Purple Vienna'
'Gigante'	'Quickstar'
'Green Early Ball'	'Rapidstar'
'Kolpak'	'Roblau'
'Kongo'	'Rowel'
'Lanro'	'Trero'
'Purple Danube'	'White Danube'
'Purple Early Ball'	'White Vienna'

white-skinned kohl rabi

Salsify and Scorzonera

Tragopogon porrifolius and Scorzonera hispanica

Although salsify and scorzonera are different plants, they are closely related, not only botanically but also in the manner in which they are grown and used. Neither is in the mainstream of vegetables, which is surprising because both are delicious. Salsify is, in fact, also known as vegetable oyster or oyster plant because of its taste. The roots are, however, not among the easiest to prepare – they are relatively narrow with plenty of smaller roots, which makes peeling difficult. In addition, they discolour very quickly once they have been peeled. In the kitchen, despite the fine taste, they are not very versatile since they are usually used as vegetables in their own right rather than as part of other dishes.

ABOVE **A basket of salsify just after the crop has been harvested, showing the small side roots that make the roots "hairy" and difficult to clean.**

Salsify originated from the countries around the Mediterranean, although garden escapees have naturalized over a large part of Europe and North America. Scorzonera is not quite as rampant and is still restricted to Europe, from the warm Mediterranean countries to the arctic wastes. As with most vegetables their history is rather uncertain, but salsify is thought to have been first cultivated in Italy in the 16th century, while scorzonera was grown in Spain and Italy even earlier.

Both vegetables have long, narrow tap-roots, which are covered in thinner side roots. Salsify has a yellowish skin, rather like that of a parsnip, and scorzonera has a dark brown or black skin. They are grown mainly for the roots, but the young shoots and flower-buds can also be eaten. Salsify is also grown as an ornamental plant for its attractive purple flowers, although the leaves can be rather untidy. The flowers produce copious amounts of seed, which soon drifts away and germinates. Scorzonera has inconspicuous yellow flowers.

These vegetables are usually sold by their name rather than under the name of a cultivar, since few of the latter have been bred. However, one variety of salsify is well known – 'Sandwich Island'.

Cultivation

Choose a site that is sunny and open. As with most root crops, both vegetables like a light soil, although they will grow in heavier conditions. The soil should be deeply dug and have humus added well in advance of sowing because they do not like freshly manured ground. To be sure of having a sufficiently large crop, both must be sown as early as possible to give a long growing season, although scorzonera should not be sown too early or it will run to seed. Seed should be sown by mid-spring, 1cm/½in deep in drills set 25cm/ 10in apart. Use fresh seed rather than any left from a previous season. Thin the seedlings to 15cm/6in apart. Although they can be grown closer together, they are more difficult to dig up individually.

Neither vegetable needs a great deal of attention, apart from being kept weeded. On the whole, they will not require watering, although if there is a prolonged drought, give them a good soaking once a week.

Harvesting

Like parsnips, salsify and scorzonera taste best after they have experienced a frost. This is not to say that you cannot harvest earlier, and they are usually ready from mid-autumn onwards. Dig the roots

LEFT **This block of salsify shows clearly how untidy and unattractive the foliage is. The resulting crop, however, is its own reward.**

Cultivation

Sowing time early to mid-spring
Sowing distance thinly
Sowing depth 1cm/½in
Distance between sown rows 25cm/10in
Thinning distance 15cm/6in
Harvesting autumn and winter

ABOVE **Scorzonera leaves are wider and more glossy than those of salsify, which are quite untidy in appearance.**

RIGHT **Salsify is worth growing for its flowers alone.**

up with a fork as required, taking care not to bruise or damage them. Salsify should be harvested and used during the first winter because it is a biennial. Scorzonera, however, is a perennial and can be left in the ground and harvested in the following autumn and winter, which gives the roots the chance to get larger.

Storage

Both plants are very hardy and can be left in the ground until needed, although it can be a good idea to lift a few and store them in trays of just moist sand if a hard frost is forecast, because it may then be difficult to get them out of the ground.

Pests and diseases

Neither salsify nor scorzonera tends to suffer from pests or diseases.

Varieties

Salsify
Most are listed simply as salsify or vegetable oyster.
'Mammoth'
'Sandwich Island'

Scorzonera
Most are listed simply as scorzonera.
'Duplex'
'Lange Jan'
'Maxima'
'Russian Giant'

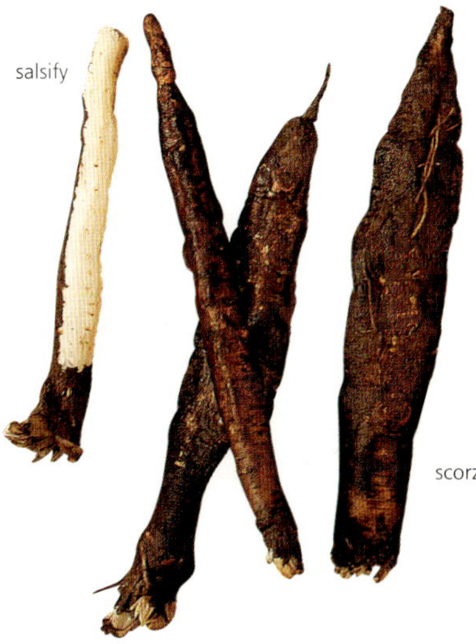

salsify

scorzonera

Potatoes

Solanum tuberosum

The potato is one of the most important food crops in the world. The family to which it belongs, Solanaceae, is found worldwide, although the potato itself originates from a fairly restricted area in the Andes, spreading up into Mexico. There are many species involved in the botanical development of the potato, which is very complicated, and the history of the potato in cultivation is almost as complicated as its botanical history.

ABOVE **Potatoes have attractive flowers. In early crops, the opening of the flowers is an indication that the tubers are ready.**

The potato has been grown as a vegetable in the Andes for thousands of years, and the Incas were discovered to be eating it by the conquering Spanish in the late 16th century. Taken to Italy, it eventually spread to the rest of Europe. The original cultivars were not particularly hardy, and it took a long time for the potato to catch on in northern Europe and two centuries before it was widespread in Britain.

The tubers – that is, the swellings on the roots – are eaten. All other parts, including the leaves and the fruit, are poisonous. If the potatoes themselves are exposed to light for any length of time, they turn green, and this, too, is poisonous unless cooked.

Potatoes are grown from "seed potatoes". These are not seeds in the conventional sense, but potato tubers that have been selected for growing. Once they have been planted, the seed potatoes start to sprout, producing roots and leaves. As the roots grow, new tubers are formed on them, and these are harvested when they are large enough.

Because potatoes are so widely distributed, there are hundreds of varieties from which to choose. Many are suited to particular climates, and different types will be found in different countries. The varieties differ in a number of respects. The first main difference is the timing of the crop, and there are two main groups, earlies and maincrop, which are further subdivided into first earlies and so on. The next main difference is use. Some are better for baking or roasting; others are better for boiling or frying; others are suitable for salads. Finally, and in some respects the most important criterion, is flavour. Most varieties taste quite different from each other, and many gardeners have their own favourites, although this does not stop them from experimenting with different ones.

Given these characteristics, it might be supposed that gardeners would grow several cultivars. However, potatoes can

LEFT **This row of potatoes shows the earth drawn up around the stems.**

BELOW **A crop of newly dug salad potatoes, "drying" in the sun.**

Cultivation

First earlies
Planting time early spring
Planting distance 30cm/12in
Planting depth 10–15cm/4–6in
Distance between rows 45cm/18in
Harvesting early summer

Second earlies
Planting time mid-spring
Planting distance 38cm/15in
Planting depth 10–15cm/4–6in
Distance between rows 60cm/24in
Harvesting summer onwards

Maincrop
Planting time mid- to late spring
Planting distance 38cm/15in
Planting depth 10–15cm/4–6in
Distance between rows 75cm/30in
Harvesting autumn

ABOVE **This large kitchen plot contains rows of neatly earthed- (hilled-) up potatoes. Frosts can be a problem for the emerging foliage.**

take up a lot of space in the garden and they are relatively inexpensive to buy. Many gardeners, therefore, prefer to restrict themselves to growing a few earlies, which have an incomparable flavour when taken straight from the ground to the kitchen, and to go to the greengrocer for the rest of the year. The ground on which the earlies were grown can be used for later crops, such as cabbages or leeks.

There are so many varieties that it could take more than one gardening lifetime to get through them all by sowing one or two varieties each year. One way of trying as wide a range as possible is to get together with two other gardeners and to buy bags of, say, three potatoes each and to divide them up between yourselves so that each of you can grow a small number of nine varieties rather than a large number of three varieties. Keep a note of those you like best and make them your maincrop for the following year.

It is possible to enjoy new potatoes at Christmas too by planting a few in large pots in early autumn and keeping these in the greenhouse.

LEFT **A recently harvested uprooting of red-skinned potatoes, all evenly shaped and with good-quality skin.**

Cultivation

Potatoes are best grown in an open, sunny position. As earlies are likely to emerge through the ground before the last of the frosts, try to choose a warm, protected spot away from frost pockets. They will grow on most soils, although they prefer slightly acid conditions. The soil should be fertile but avoid planting potatoes on newly manured grounds.

Earlies should be chitted. This involves standing the seed potatoes on a tray so that the eyes are facing upwards. Place the tray in a cool but frost-free place that is in the light although out of direct sunlight. Short shoots will appear, and this gets the crop off to a good start. Maincrop can be treated in the same way, although it is not essential.

First earlies are planted in early spring followed by second earlies two weeks later. Draw out a row with a hoe about 10cm/4in deep and place potatoes at 30cm/12in intervals. Rows should be 45cm/18in apart.

ABOVE **This harvesting of early potatoes is now ready for transferring to the kitchen. They will make delicious "new potatoes".**

Alternatively, the potatoes can be planted in holes dug with a trowel or with a special potato planter. Whichever method you use, cover the potatoes with soil and then draw up more soil to form a low ridge above them. When the shoots reach heights of 23–25cm/9–10in, draw earth up around them along the rows to make certain that all the tubers are well covered; otherwise they turn green. Continue to do this until the foliage touches across the rows.

Second earlies and maincrop are treated in the same way, except that they are planted in the second half of spring and the potatoes are set 38cm/15in apart and in rows 60cm/24in apart for second earlies and 75cm/30in apart for maincrop.

Keep an eye on weather reports, and if frost is forecast cover any shoots with newspaper or horticultural fleece. Keep all potatoes, especially earlies, watered if there is a prolonged dry spell forecast.

CHITTING POTATOES

Before planting, place the potatoes in a tray in a light place (but out of direct sunlight) in order to "chit". This means that the potatoes produce shoots.

PLANTING

Hoe out a trench 10cm/4in deep and lay the tubers about 30–40cm/12–15in apart, depending on the type. Cover with soil and earth (hill) up into a low ridge.

EARTHING UP

When the shoots reach 23–25cm/9–10in long, draw the soil around them along the rows.

An alternative method of growing potatoes is to plant them under a sheet of black polythene (plastic). Place the polythene along the row and anchor it by burying the edges in the soil. Cut slits at the relevant intervals and plant potatoes through them.

FROST PROTECTION

Once the potato shoots have emerged through the soil, it is important to take note of any frost forecasts. The shoots will need protecting from possible frost damage. Cover them over with horticultural fleece or even with newspaper.

HARVESTING

To harvest, dig a fork well under the potatoes and draw it up through the soil, bringing the tubers up with the earth.

Varieties

First earlies

'Arran Pilot' white skin, early
'Epicure' white skin, early
'Foremost' white skin, waxy yellow flesh
'Maris Bard' white skin, waxy texture, very early
'Pentland Javelin' white skin, waxy flesh last of the earlies to crop
'Ulster Chieftain' white skin, floury texture

Second earlies

'Estima' white skin, waxy yellow flesh, good boiler
'Kondor' red skin, yellow flesh, good boiler
'Marfona' white skin, heavy cropper, good for baking
'Maris Peer' white skin, waxy texture, good boiler
'Wilja' white skin, waxy yellow flesh, good salad potato

Maincrop

'Cara' pink skin, white floury flesh, late
'Desiree' pinkish red skin, waxy yellow flesh, good for baking and for fries
'King Edward' pink and white skin, creamy floury texture, good for baking and roasting
'Maris Piper' white skin, floury texture, heavy cropper, good for baking
'Pentland Dell' white skin, floury texture, heavy cropper, good for baking and roasting
'Pink Fir Apple' pink skin, yellow waxy flesh, wonderful salad potato
'Ratte' white skin, yellow waxy flesh, excellent salad potato
'Romano' red skin, firm white flesh, good boiler

Harvesting

Early potatoes are harvested in early summer, usually just as their flowers are opening, which should be about 12 weeks after planting. They are usually lifted as they are required. Maincrop are left in the soil until the autumn and are usually all lifted at once and stored. To harvest earlies, dig a fork in well below the potatoes and lever them out of the soil, at the same time pulling on the haulm (stems and leaves). For maincrop, remove the haulm about two weeks before harvesting so that the skins on the potatoes harden. Lift the maincrop on a dry, warm day and leave them lying in the sun for an hour or two to let them dry and to harden the skins.

Storing

Do not leave potatoes in the light for too long. Pack them into hessian (burlap) or paper sacks and store them in a dark, cool but frost-free place. Alternatively, they can be stored in trays as long as no light gets to the tubers. Regularly check all potatoes and remove any that have started to rot.

Pests and diseases

The worst problem that can occur is blight, which is particularly prevalent in wet years. The leaves go yellow and brown and start to curl. Eventually the haulm seems to fall to pieces. The potatoes develop black patches, which eventually turn into a slimy, evil-smelling rot. Do not plant potatoes on ground that was affected the year before (either from potato or tomato blight). Earth (hill) them up well to keep the spores from the tubers. If necessary, spray with the appropriate copper-based fungicide, preferably in wet years before blight appears. Look out for resistant varieties.

Another common disease is potato scab, which disfigures the surface of the tubers. To avoid it occurring, do not grow potatoes on ground that has been recently limed or manured. Other diseases include spraing, violet root rot and blackleg.

The main pests are slugs and wireworms, both of which eat holes in the tubers. Other pests can include cutworms and potato cyst eelworms.

Jerusalem Artichokes

Helianthus tuberosus

Surprisingly, these potato-like tubers are grown on plants that are sunflowers. Unlike the dinner-plate-sized flowers of its relative, however, the flowers of the Jerusalem artichoke are small, but borne on equally tall stems. The knobbly tubers are found below ground, and they can used as a vegetable in their own right and cooked in the same way as potatoes or parsnips – roasting is a particularly good way of cooking them. They have a lovely distinct flavour but also combine well in other dishes, especially soups, and can be eaten raw. The tubers should be about the size of a chicken's egg; larger ones can be cut into pieces.

ABOVE **Here, an uprooted Jerusalem artichoke plant clearly shows the tubers that are now ready for harvesting.**

Jerusalem artichokes have no connection with Jerusalem nor with globe artichokes. They originated in North America and were brought to Europe in the 16th century, eventually finding their way to Britain via Holland in the early 17th century. The name Jerusalem could be a corruption of the Italian word for sunflower, *girasole*, or it may be derived from the name of the town in Holland, Terneuzen, from where they were sent to Britain.

This is a very easy vegetable to grow. It is not particular about the soil and it is troubled by few pests and diseases. The only real problem is getting rid of it if you decide to stop growing it at any stage. A single piece of one of the many tubers left in the ground will resprout to produce a new plant, and it is, unfortunately, easy to miss one or more pieces. The regrowth normally appears in the row, however, and it will not spread throughout the garden unless you are careless enough to distribute the tubers about.

Although Jerusalem artichokes are grown primarily as a vegetable, they can also be grown to provide a temporary windbreak. They grow rapidly, sometimes to 3m/10ft, and make a dense hedge of wiry stems that needs no support except in exposed sites.

The mature plants make excellent windbreaks within the kitchen garden, as well as creating visual screens that can be used to divide up the garden.

LEFT **A basket of recently harvested Jerusalem artichokes. These are perfect easy-to-peel specimens that are not too knobbly.**

Cultivation

Unlike most vegetables, Jerusalem artichokes are tolerant of light shade. They are also tolerant of a range of soils, even growing in poor ones, although best results will be obtained from ground that has been manured during the previous autumn. Do not overfeed because this may result in lush vegetation at the expense of tubers.

Try to purchase named varieties but, if you cannot find them, tubers from the greengrocer can be used. The planting time is not critical – any time in spring will do. Plant the tubers 10–13cm/4–5in deep in holes made with a trowel. They should be about 38cm/15in apart and the rows should be 90cm/3ft apart.

They need little attention apart from being kept weed free. If they are likely to be rocked by the wind, draw earth up around the stems to help stabilize them so that the tubers are not disturbed. In very windy sites, individual stems may need to be supported with canes. The stems can be cut off in summer at about 1.8m/6ft to lessen the chance of wind damage – this is necessary not so much because the

RIGHT **The top growth of Jerusalem artichokes shows its relationship with the sunflower. Unfortunately, all this lush growth is of no use except for making compost.**

plants will be flattened but because the tubers will be disturbed by the movement of the plants and not develop properly.

Harvesting

The tubers can be lifted once the leaves start to wither in autumn. The skins should be pale brown, without any soft patches.

Cut off the stems, then lift the tubers with a fork, digging right under them. Sift through the soil to check that all the pieces are removed. Any piece of tuber remaining in the soil will grow again in the following year. This is all right if you plan to plant in the same place next year, but a nuisance if you do not. They can be quite difficult to eradicate, especially in heavy soils where it is easy to miss tubers, so harvest carefully.

Storing

Jerusalem artichokes are frost hardy and are best stored in the ground and dug only as they are required. A few can be dug if frost threatens to freeze the soil, making digging impossible, and stored in trays of just-moist sand or peat (peat moss) in a frost-free shed or garage.

Pests and diseases

Jerusalem artichokes do not attract pests and diseases.

Jerusalem artichokes

Cultivation

Sowing time spring
Sowing distance 38cm/15in
Sowing depth 10–13cm/4–5in
Distance between sown rows 90cm/3ft
Harvesting summer onwards

Varieties

Often listed simply as Jerusalem artichokes.
'Boston Red'
'Dwarf Sunray'
'Fuseau'

Radishes

Raphanus sativus

Radishes are one of the easiest and quickest of all crops to grow. The rapidity with which they appear through the soil makes them suitable for children to grow, because little patience is required, and, indeed, many gardeners' first experience of growing vegetables was with this humble plant. However, the wide range of types and varieties that are available make this a vegetable that is of as much interest to the mature gardener as to the embryonic one.

The radish has a long history as far as cultivation is concerned, having been known in Ancient Egypt. Its origins are obscure, but it probably derived from native plants found growing in Mediterranean countries. At first, varieties had long, tapering roots, originally black, later white, and these larger rooted forms are still cultivated in Europe. By the 18th century, however, the more familiar round ones with red skins began to appear.

Today the small, red-skinned radishes are the most frequently grown, and these are mainly used in salads or as a decorative garnish. In China and Japan, where the large varieties are still common, they are eaten both raw and cooked, and the large-rooted types are becoming more widely grown in the West, especially new varieties imported from China. These larger varieties have the advantage that they can be left in the ground for longer and so make a valuable contribution to the selection of winter crops.

One of the advantages of the short life-cycle of the radish is that it can be grown among slower growing crops, thus making the best use of the available ground. Radishes make good markers if they are sown along with a vegetable that is slow to germinate, such as parsnips. Because

BELOW **These neat rows of radishes have been planted in abundance. You will have to consume large quantities to grow so many at once.**

ABOVE **These round radishes are suffering from slug damage (top) and from cracking due to irregular watering (middle).**

HARVESTING

Radishes are harvested simply by pulling them from the ground by hand. They should be harvested when they are large enough to eat.

Cultivation

Summer
Sowing time late winter (under cloches) to early spring onwards
Sowing distance thinly
Sowing depth 1cm/½in
Distance between sown rows 15cm/6in
Thinning distance 2.5cm/1in
Harvesting late spring onwards

Winter
Sowing time midsummer
Sowing distance thinly
Sowing depth 1cm/½in
Distance between sown rows 25cm/10in
Thinning distance 13cm/5in
Harvesting autumn onwards

radishes appear quickly they will indicate the position of the row so that the parsnip seeds are not accidentally disturbed by hoeing or weeding.

Cultivation

Ordinary summer radishes do not need either a deep or particularly rich soil. They prefer one that does not dry out or they will quickly run to seed. Slow-growing radishes also tend to be woody and over-hot to the taste. They should be grown in an open, sunny position.

Sowing can start under cloches in late winter or in early spring in the open soil. Sow in shallow drills about 1cm/½in deep, set about 15cm/6in apart. Water the soil along the row if it is dry at the time of sowing. Sow thinly so that little thinning is required, then thin to about 2.5cm/1in. Do not sow too much at once because radishes are rapidly past their best, and it is better to sow short rows every two weeks to obtain a succession of crops than one long one in which many of the roots will be wasted. Do not let them dry out.

Sow the larger winter radishes at about midsummer. Do not sow too early or they may run to seed. These should be sown in drills set 25cm/10in apart. When they are large enough to handle, thin to about 13cm/5in apart.

Varieties

Summer
'Cherry Belle' globe
'Crystal Ball' globe
'Flamboyant Sabina' cylindrical
'French Breakfast' cylindrical
'Juliette' globe
'Long White Icicle' tapering
'Prinz Rotin' globe
'Saxa' globe
'Scarlet Globe' globe
'Sparkler 3' globe

Winter
'Black Spanish Long'
'Black Spanish Round'
'China Rose'
'Mino Early'
'Minowase'
'Violet de Gournay'

Harvesting

Summer radishes should be pulled when they are large enough to eat. Discard any that have become large or old because these will be too woody as well as too hot to eat. Winter radishes can be dug up from autumn onwards.

Storage

Summer radishes quickly shrivel once they are out of the ground and should be used as soon as possible after harvesting. Long-rooted winter varieties can be left in the ground until they are required. In very cold areas or if severe frosts are threatened, which would make digging them from the ground impossible, dig the roots and store them under cover in trays of just-moist peat (peat moss) or sand.

Pests and diseases

Although they may not look like it, radishes are related to cabbages and so suffer from the same pests and diseases. Flea beetle is likely to be the worst problem, and should they appear, young plants should be dusted with derris. Slugs are also partial to radishes and can leave unsightly holes in the roots. If anything worse than this happens, scrap the plants and re-sow elsewhere in the garden.

ABOVE **A bunch of recently harvested cylindrical radishes. They should not be allowed to grow too large, or they become woody and very hot.**

radishes

Broad (Fava) Beans

Vicia faba

Unlike other forms of bean, broad (fava) beans can be an acquired taste; not everybody likes them. However, when they are cooked straight from the plant, home-grown beans have a flavour that is never found in bought ones, so if you have not enjoyed them in the past, grow some and try them again – you may be pleasantly surprised. These beans also have the advantage of being one of the first vegetables of the year to mature. While the other two main forms of garden bean come from the Americas, the broad (fava) bean is native to the Old World, probably originating in the Near East. Like the pea, it has been grown since Neolithic times, and, also like the pea, it can be eaten fresh or it can be dried and stored, which is a valuable attribute that has been appreciated right up to the advent of the freezer.

ABOVE **A row of healthy young beans at an early stage of their growth.**

Broad (fava) beans are categorized in various ways. Sometimes it is by length of pod. The long-pods have up to eight kidney-shaped beans in each pod, whereas the Windsors, the short-podded form, have only half that number of seeds, each of which is rounded. They can also be categorized by the colour of the seeds, which can be green, white (pale green, really) or mahogany-red; green seeds are better for freezing. They are also categorized as dwarf or tall forms, the former being better for the small garden. Finally, they can be divided into those that can be overwintered and those that are best sown in spring; this generally corresponds to the divisions between long-pods and Windsors, as the long-pods tend to be hardier.

PINCHING OUT

Pinching out the tops of the beans is a good practice because it discourages blackfly. The tops can then be boiled and eaten.

Cultivation

These beans need an open, sunny site, which is protected from strong winds, especially if you are growing overwintering types. A reasonably fertile soil is required, and this is best achieved by incorporating manure or compost during the autumn dig. Over-wintering varieties can be sown in late autumn. Other types should be sown in late winter or early spring. Although new varieties have extended the sowing season until early summer, most varieties need to be sown before the end of spring.

Sow in double rows in a shallow trench, 23cm/9in wide and 4cm/1½in deep. Alternatively, sow each seed individually with a dibber. In both cases, the seeds should be about 23cm/9in apart, and the rows should be 60cm/24in apart. Seeds can also be raised in pots or modules in late winter under glass and planted out in spring.

Taller varieties will need to be supported with string tied to canes that are set at intervals along each side of the double row. When the beans are in full flower, pinch out the tender top by 8cm/3in to reduce the chance of blackfly infestation and to make the pods fill out. Water during dry periods.

Harvesting

Pick the pods when the beans inside them have swollen. Some can be picked at an earlier stage for cooking whole. Do not allow the beans to become too old – that is, when they are leathery and pliable – or they will be tough and too floury. Some people like to cook and eat the young tops when they are removed.

Storage

These beans are undoubtedly best when picked straight from the plant, but any excess can be frozen for future use. They can also be dried.

Pests and diseases

The most serious problem is blackfly, but this can often be avoided by removing the tips of the plant (see left). On the whole, these beans are reasonably trouble free, although chocolate spot can be a problem. This can usually be ignored, but burn or destroy the affected plants when they are finished with rather than put them on the compost heap.

STAKING

Taller varieties of broad (fava) beans will need supporting with string tied to canes that are set at intervals along the rows.

ABOVE **This row of broad (fava) beans is being supported with canes and string.**

Varieties

'Aquadulce Claudia' long-pod, white seeds
'Bunyards Exhibition' long-pod, white seeds
'Express' pale green seeds
'Hylon' long-pod, white seeds
'Imperial Green Longpod' long-pod, green seeds
'Jade' long-pod, green
'Jubilee Hysor' white seeds
'Jumbo' large green seeds
'Masterpiece Green Longpod' long-pod, green seeds
'Meteor Vroma' green seeds
'Red Epicure' red seeds
'Relon' long-pod, green seeds
'The Sutton' dwarf, pale green seeds
'White Windsor' white seeds

broad (fava) beans

Cultivation

Sowing time late autumn, late winter to late spring
Sowing or planting distance 23cm/9in
Sowing depth 4cm/1½in
Distance between sown rows 60cm/24in
Thinning distance no need to thin
Harvesting early to late summer

MARROWS & SQUASH CROPS

Marrows and Courgettes (Zucchini)

Cucurbita pepo

Although marrows (zucchini), pumpkins and squashes are essentially the same plant, they are dealt with separately because they are usually considered differently in the garden and kitchen. First, it is important to consider the difference between marrows and courgettes (zucchini). In fact, there is no real difference: courgettes are an immature form of marrow, and, if left to grow, will turn into marrows. However, some varieties are best grown as one or the other.

ABOVE **A female flower on a developing courgette (zucchini). The male flowers are often picked before they are open and used in cooking.**

The history of the marrow (zucchini) is not really known, and although they came to Europe from North America, there are no longer any native species that correspond to the plants we grow today. The marrow reached Europe in the 16th century and has been grown ever since. The idea of eating immature marrows as courgettes (zucchini) is a relatively recent development.

There are two types of marrows (zucchini): trailing and bush. The trailing forms throw out long stems that cover a great deal of space, and can be trained over a trellis or archway. The fruits appear at intervals along the stems. Bush varieties are much more compact, and the fruits grow from the central cluster of stems. They take up less space and are far better plants for small gardens. Courgettes (zucchini) are usually only grown as bushes; marrows are grown as either type.

In recent years courgettes (zucchini) have become much more popular than marrows (zucchini), partly because many people find that marrows are watery and bland and partly because, as families have become smaller, a whole marrow is difficult to dispose of in one sitting. However, marrows still have their devotees, and there are some very tasty ways of cooking them.

Courgettes (zucchini), on the other hand, are not only a more convenient size but, being immature, they do not dissolve into pulp quite so readily when they are cooked. They also have a more positive flavour. Nearly everybody who grows courgettes accidentally leaves at least one on the plant, which develops into a marrow (zucchini), so there is every opportunity of trying both. The flowers can also be eaten, either raw or cooked.

Marrows (zucchini) were traditionally grown on compost heaps. The heaps or bins were made up during winter and spring, topped with earth and left until the following autumn before being spread. The high concentration of rich, fibrous material meant that moisture and nutrients were in abundant supply, creating the ideal conditions for these plants during the summer growing season. They can, of course, be grown in ordinary vegetable plots, but using the compost heap does save space, which can be used for other crops.

LEFT **Do not plant courgettes (zucchini) too close together; leave space to harvest the fruit.**

Cultivation

Marrows and courgettes (zucchini) like an open, sunny situation and a rich, moisture-retentive soil. As noted above, they can be grown on the compost heap or in a bed that has been heavily manured during the previous autumn. They are frost tender, so plants should not be put outside before the last frosts have passed, unless they are protected with cloches.

Plants can be raised under glass by sowing the flat seed edgeways in individual pots or in modules in late spring or sown directly in the

PLANTING OUT

This marrow (zucchini) is being planted in its fibre pot. It has been grown like this to prevent disturbing the roots.

soil in early summer. Germination is speeded up by soaking the seed in water overnight. Keep seed that has been planted in the open warm by covering the soil with a jamjar or cloche until the seed has germinated. Sow two seeds at each position and remove the weaker if both germinate. Even if you sow in the open, sow a few in pots as insurance against sudden cold weather or the ravages of slugs.

Bush types can be left to develop by themselves but trailing varieties may need to be trimmed back if they get too vigorous. They can be left to trail outwards, like the spokes of a wheel, if there is enough space or they can be trained round in a circle, if

HARVESTING

Harvest a marrow (zucchini) by cutting it off at the base with a sharp knife.

Cultivation

Bush
Sowing time late spring (under glass) to early summer
Sowing or planting distance 90cm/3ft
Sowing depth 4cm/1½in
Distance between sown rows 90cm/3ft
Thinning distance no need to thin
Harvesting midsummer onwards

Trailing
Sowing time late spring (under glass) to early summer
Sowing or planting distance 1.2–1.8m/4–6ft
Sowing depth 4cm/1½in
Distance between sown rows 1.8m/6ft
Thinning distance no need to thin
Harvesting midsummer onwards

the stems are pegged down as they grow. If they are grown up a trellis or some other support, the shoots must be tied in regularly. Towards the end of summer remove the tips of each shoot. Keep well watered.

Harvesting

Courgettes (zucchini) are best harvested while they are still young – that is, when they are about 10cm/4in long – but in practice they can be harvested at any time, and circumstances usually dictate that they are picked at any stage between being a courgette and a small marrow (zucchini). If they are left on the plant, courgettes will eventually develop into full marrows and can be cut at any time until the first frosts. Whatever the size of the crop, cut through the stem 2cm/¾in or more away from the fruit.

Storage

Courgettes (zucchini) are difficult to store for more than a few days and are best eaten fresh from the plant. They can be frozen, although they become less firm. Marrows (zucchini), in contrast, will last for several weeks after picking, especially if they have been left to mature and ripen. Pick marrows at the end of the season, before the first frosts, and then store them in a frost-free place for several weeks, on trays or hanging in net bags.

Pests and diseases

Although generally trouble free, slugs are the most severe problem, eating right through the stem if not checked.

Cucumber mosaic virus is the most common disease, causing mottled leaves and distorted fruit. The plant should be burned or destroyed. In some years powdery mildew is also a problem; rightly or wrongly gardeners tend to ignore it.

Varieties

Bush	Trailing	Courgettes (Zucchini)
'All Green Bush'	'Long Green Trailing'	'Ambassador'
'Badger Cross'	'Long White Trailing'	'Burpee Golden Zucchini'
'Green Bush'	'Table Dainty'	'Bush Champion'
'Long Green Bush'	'Tender and True'	'Defender'
'Long White Bush'		'Early Gem'
'Minipak'		'Gold Rush'
		'Greyzini'
		'Tondo di Nizza'
		'Zucchini'

Pumpkins

Cucurbita maxima

The pumpkin is a curious vegetable. In some arable areas it is treated seriously and grown for the kitchen; in other areas it is planted for fun, to see who can grow the biggest, or it is grown to be carved and hollowed out for a Hallowe'en lantern or mask. Whether for decorative or culinary use, pumpkins are definitely worth growing if you have the space.

ABOVE **The skins of pumpkins should be hardened in the sunshine.**

LEFT **A healthy crop of pumpkins.**

Originally from South America, where they have been part of the staple diet for centuries, pumpkins are extremely popular in North America, and it is from there that their recent revival in Britain has come. They are, in fact, winter squashes but are frequently separated from the other members of the family simply on grounds of their size and uses. The distinctive name of pumpkin is usually given to the large, round winter squashes.

Some people consider pumpkins rather too large for consumption, but not all pumpkins need be big. The smaller ones, no more than 30cm/12in across, have usually been bred for taste rather than appearance and there is plenty of flesh on them for most purposes. Similarly, not all are the golden colour of Hallowe'en and show-bench pumpkins. 'Crown Prince' for example, has a bluish-grey skin and is only 30cm/12in across. The dense flesh, a deep old-gold colour, tastes delicious when cooked, and 'Crown Prince' will store much better than its big brash cousins.

Although pumpkins take time and patience, they are good plants with which to encourage young gardeners. The prospect of growing a huge vegetable that will weigh several hundred pounds – so heavy that even their parents can't lift it – seems to appeal to children, although what the cook does with so much pumpkin flesh defies thought – there is a limit to the amount of pumpkin soup and pies one can consume.

Cultivation

Pumpkins need a sunny site that is open and yet protected from strong winds, which can soon tear the large leaves to shreds. The soil should be rich in well-rotted organic material, not only to feed the pumpkins but also to hold plenty of moisture in the soil. At each site, dig a pit 45cm/18in deep and 60cm/24in square and half-fill it with manure before replacing the top soil. In late spring start the pumpkins off in the greenhouse in modules or fibre pots. They do not need such a high temperature as cucumbers – a gentle heat of 15–18°C/59–64°F will be adequate. You can speed up germination by soaking the seed in water overnight.

PLANTING

Pumpkins are rich feeders and appreciate moisture near their roots, so add plenty of organic material to the soil when planting.

HARVESTING

Harvest pumpkins when they have reached their mature colour by cutting through the stem at the top with a sharp knife.

Cultivation

Sowing time late spring under glass
Sowing or planting distance 1.8m/6ft
Sowing depth 4cm/1½in
Distance between sown rows 1.8m/6ft
Thinning distance no need to thin
Harvesting autumn

RIGHT **This is a large bed of pumpkins and squashes. Such close planting makes harvesting difficult, unless they are all harvested at once.**

When the threat of frost is passed, plant in the prepared ground at distances of 1.8m/6ft or further apart for more vigorous varieties. Keep the plant within bounds by training the stems in a spiral around the plant, pinning them down with wire pegs. If you want to grow giant specimens, reduce the number of young fruit to between one and three. Water regularly and apply a high-potash liquid feed at least once every two weeks and more frequently for giant fruit. Towards the end of summer, pinch out the tips of the shoots. Stop watering and feeding once the fruit is mature.

Harvesting

Harvest the pumpkins when they have reached their mature colour: deep orange or blue-grey. A good indicator that they are ready is that the stems begin to split. Cut them with a stem of about 5cm/2in. Make sure that they are all picked before the first frosts. Place them in a sunny position for about a week so that the skins fully harden.

Storage

Orange-skinned pumpkins will store for several weeks in a frost-free position. Blue-grey ones will last much longer, sometimes up to several months.

Pests and diseases

On the whole, pumpkins are trouble free. Slugs are probably the most severe problem and will eat right through the stem if not checked.

Cucumber mosaic virus is the most troublesome disease. The leaves become mottled and the fruit distorted. Destroy the entire plant.

Varieties

'Atlantic Giant' very large, orange skin
'Crown Prince' medium-sized, grey-blue skin, stores well
'Hundred Weight' large variety, yellow skin, stores well
'Jack Be Little' very small, orange skin, stores well
'Jackpot' medium- to large-sized, mottled orange and green skin
'Janne Gros de Paris' large, rough pink skin, stores well
'Mammoth' large, orange skin
'Small Sugar' small- to medium-sized, orange skin
'Spellbound' medium-sized, orange skin, stores well
'Spirit' medium-sized, orange skin
'Tom Fox' medium-sized, orange skin

pumpkins

Cucumbers

Cucumis sativus

One of the quickest ways to prepare a meal is to pop into the garden, grab a lettuce, some tomatoes and a cucumber. Add some fresh, crusty bread – and there you are. Most gardeners grow lettuces and tomatoes, but fewer grow cucumbers, perhaps because they think they require a greenhouse or they are difficult to grow. They need not be either. Outdoor cucumbers can be grown as easily as courgettes (zucchini), which few gardeners find a problem.

Cucumbers have been used as a vegetable for the best part of 5,000 years. They were first grown and eaten in India, where they were developed from a native species, and from there they spread north-east into China and north-west into Greece and Rome.

There are several colours and shapes. In the West we are more used to long cucumbers with green skins, but they can also be oval or even round, and colours can range from white to yellow.

As far as the gardener is concerned, there are two types of cucumber: the climbing varieties with long fruit that are grown under glass and the ridge varieties that are much shorter and are grown in the open. The advantage of greenhouse varieties is that they can be started earlier and are not as dependent on the weather. Ridge varieties, on the other hand, need less looking after and are less prone to attack by pests and diseases, which thrive in the warmth of the greenhouse. From the culinary point of view, the greenhouse forms are often preferred, mainly because outdoor cucumbers have tough, often prickly, skins and do not look quite as elegant as their indoor cousins. Until recently, many outdoor varieties tended to taste bitter, but this is now no longer generally the case.

Gherkins are a form of ridge cucumber, which are used for pickling. Any immature ridge cucumber can be used, but some varieties have been specially bred for the purpose. Like courgettes and marrows (zucchini), there is no difference in cultivation technique other than the time of picking.

LEFT **A ridge or outdoor cucumber, with its attractive yellow flowers and tough, prickly skin clearly on display.**

Cultivation

Greenhouse cucumbers need a high temperature in which to germinate and a high temperature in which to grow. Using seed of all-female varieties – they are less likely to be bitter – sow two seeds, edgeways, in pots or modules and place in a propagator at 24°C/75°F. When they germinate, remove the weaker seedling and reduce the temperature to 21°C/70°F. Plant the young plants with as little root disturbance as possible into growing bags, two per bag depending on the size. Use square-meshed netting or a system of poles and horizontal wires as supports, and tie in the shoots as they grow. Pinch out the tip of the shoot when it reaches the roof. Tie the laterals to horizontal wires and pinch out the tips two leaves beyond the first fruit to form. Water to keep the soil constantly moist and throw some water on the floor of the greenhouse to keep the atmosphere humid. Keep the house shaded. Once the fruit start to develop, feed them with a high-potash liquid feed once every two weeks.

ABOVE **Ridge or outdoor cucumbers growing in the open need a sunny spot that is sheltered from the wind.**

Ridge or outdoor cucumbers need a sunny spot sheltered from the wind. Add plenty of well-rotted manure to the soil before sowing. Sow ridge cucumbers either inside in pots or outdoors where they are to grow. If sown directly, cover them with a glass jamjar or cloche to raise the temperature. Do not sow until after the threat of frost has passed and the soil has warmed up. Sow, leaving about 75cm/30in in each direction between plants. If the seed is germinated in pots, ensure that the roots are not disturbed when they are transplanted. Fibre pots can help with this,

Cultivation

Greenhouse
Sowing time late winter onwards
Sowing or planting distance 60cm/24in
Sowing depth 2.5cm/1in
Thinning distance no need to thin
Harvesting midsummer onwards
Ridge
Sowing time late spring (under glass) to early summer
Sowing or planting distance 75cm/30in
Sowing depth 2.5cm/1in
Distance between sown rows 75cm/30in
Thinning distance no need to thin
Harvesting midsummer onwards

ABOVE **This ridge or outdoor cucumber has been trained up a cane tripod. The large leaves and fruits have a pleasing architectural quality.**

because the cucumbers can be planted without removing them from the pots. Pinch out the tip of the main shoot after six leaves have formed so that the plant bushes out. Water freely. Once the fruit start to develop, feed with a high-potash liquid feed once every two weeks.

Harvesting

Cut the fruit with a short length of stalk as soon as they are large enough to eat. Pick frequently and more fruit will develop. Harvest gherkins when they are 5–8cm/2–3in long.

ABOVE **Climbing varieties of cucumber are grown under glass. They have smooth skins and are longer than ridge varieties.**

Varieties

Ridge
'Burpless Tasty Green'
'Bush Champion'
'Crystal Apple'
'Long Green Ridge'
'Masterpiece'
Greenhouse
'Birgit'
'Fenumex'
'Pepinex'
'Petita'
'Telegraph'
'Telegraph Improved'
Gherkins
'Bestal'
'Venlo Pickling'

Storage

Keep for no more more than a few days; they are best eaten fresh.

Pests and diseases

Slugs and snails can quickly eat through a stem, killing the plant; remove by your preferred method. In the greenhouse, red spider mite and whitefly may be a problem.

SHOOT CROPS

ABOVE **Harvest asparagus by cutting the stems below the ground.**

Asparagus

Asparagus officinalis

Asparagus was once the food of the wealthy – if you didn't have your own garden, you couldn't grow it. Nowadays it is much more widely available, but shoots cut straight from the garden and cooked immediately still taste best. Asparagus is not only good to eat, but the decorative foliage has a wonderful filmy quality about it. A great uncle of mine grew asparagus all his long life, not to eat it, but so that he could use the cut foliage with his sweet peas. In a potager or decorative kitchen garden, the great plumes of finely cut foliage make a fine display.

The tender shoot of asparagus is the part of the plant that is eaten. The shoot emerges from below ground in late spring and early summer. Once it gets above approximately 15–20cm/6–8in long it becomes tough-skinned and rather chewy and is then best left, the remaining shoots developing into tall foliage stems with inconspicuous flowers and, eventually, orange-red berries.

Asparagus grows wild throughout Europe and has been eaten and possibly cultivated from at least the time of the Ancient Greeks. It has long been grown in gardens, but the main disadvantage is that it takes up quite a lot of space. If you have a small garden but want to grow asparagus, try planting one or two crowns in the flower borders, picking the spikes in early summer and then leaving them in the border as a decorative foliage plant.

One of the attractive features of creating an asparagus bed is that it lasts for at least 20 years, and apart from a little maintenance, not much effort is required to produce a wonderful feast each year. Asparagus plants are either male or female. Male plants have the advantage of being more productive and not producing seed (which readily self-sows). Asparagus can be raised from seed, but the results can be disappointing if you use your own collected seed; it is better to buy named varieties on which you can rely. An increasing number of F1 hybrids is available, and these produce very good all-male plants.

APPLYING A SPRING MULCH

In the spring, before growth starts, apply a deep mulch of manure over the rows of asparagus.

Cultivation

Asparagus needs an open, sunny site, and it likes a light, preferably sandy soil, although it can be grown in any soil as long as it is free-draining and reasonably fertile. In heavy soils it can be grown by raising the level of the soil or by making a raised bed. In the autumn before planting, dig the bed, removing all traces of perennial weeds and incorporating plenty of well-rotted manure or compost. In the spring dig out a trench 20cm/8in deep with an 8cm/3in ridge running down the centre. If more than one row is required, set the trenches 90cm/3ft apart. Set each asparagus crown on the ridge, spreading out its roots around it. Each crown should be 45cm/18in apart. Cover them with soil to a depth of 8–10cm/3–4in.

If you are growing from seed, soak them overnight in water and sow in a drill 1cm/½in deep. Do this in spring. Thin to 15cm/6in and transplant the following spring in the same manner as for bought crowns above. As the plants grow, draw in more earth from the side of the trench until it is filled.

Do not cut any spears in the first year and only one or two from each plant during the next year. Each spring, cover the trench with a layer of manure or compost, leaving it slightly heaped up so that over the years the row becomes earthed (hilled) up in the

CUTTING DOWN IN AUTUMN

In the autumn, as the asparagus fronds are turning brown, cut them down to the ground.

same way you treat potatoes. Keep the ground weeded. Cut down the ferns as they begin to turn yellow and, if possible, before the berries begin to ripen; alternatively, pick all the berries. If they are left on the plants the birds will eat them and before long asparagus will be appearing all over the garden. For the same reason, avoid putting berried stems on the compost heap.

Cultivation

Sowing
Sowing time spring
Sowing depth 1cm/½in
Distance between sown rows 30cm/12in
Thinning distance 15cm/6in
Transplanting following spring
Planting
Planting time early spring
Planting distance 45cm/18in
Planting depth initially 8–10cm/3–4in
Distance between sown rows 90cm/3ft
Harvesting in late spring for six weeks (third year onwards)

Harvesting

In late spring, when the shoots that have emerged are 10–15cm/4–6in long, cut them by inserting a knife 5cm/2in below the surface of the soil. Only cut through the stem, do not thrash around below the soil level or you may damage spears that have not yet emerged. Make a slanting cut. After the third year cutting can take place over about six weeks.

Storage

Asparagus is best used fresh from the plant, but it can be stored for a couple of days if it is stood in a jug of cold water in the refrigerator.

Varieties

'Accell'	'Giant Mammoth'
'Boonlim'	'Limbras'
'Cito'	'Lucullus'
'Connover's Colossal'	'Martha Washington'
'Franklin'	

ABOVE **Once the harvesting season is over, the asparagus is left to grow to its full height.**

Pests and diseases

Asparagus is usually pest and disease free. Slugs, as usual, are likely to be the worst problem, making holes in the spears. Asparagus beetle can also be a nuisance.

asparagus

Celery

Apium graveolens

Celery is an important vegetable for the kitchen as it is used, at least in part, in many dishes, including basic recipes such as stocks. Its culinary importance is not reflected in the garden, however. At one time no vegetable garden was complete without celery, but it is seen less often today, which may be partly because it is slightly difficult to grow and partly because it needs a constantly moist soil to do well. Whatever the reason, it is a shame it is not more widely grown, because if you do grow it you will find that you are constantly using it and, as always, will find the flavour so much better than shop-bought stalks.

ABOVE **Green varieties of celery, such as the one shown here, do not need blanching.**

Celery grows wild throughout Europe and Asia, and it is rather surprising to learn that it has entered cultivation only in relatively recent times. Celery was first cultivated in Italy as recently as the 16th century but it did not arrive in Britain until the end of the 17th century.

It is the blanched leaf stalks of celery that are eaten. These can be eaten green but taste sweeter if the light has been excluded, causing the stalks to turn white. This always used to be done by heaping earth up round them, but more often these days the stems are wrapped in cardboard or felt. This type of celery is often referred to as trench celery. Breeding has produced celery with self-blanching stems, although not everybody feels that these are wholly successful and that the old-style blanched stalks taste better. There are also forms with green, pink or red stems. There is a form of celery, known as green or American celery, which does not require blanching.

As well as the stems, some people like to eat the heart, the solid part of the plant, where the stems join the root. Some recipes also call for the leaves to be included, particularly when the celery is a flavouring agent rather than a vegetable in its own right. It can be cooked or eaten raw.

Cultivation

There are two ways of growing celery, depending on what type is being grown. To grow traditional trench celery, in the preceding autumn or winter dig out a trench 45cm/18in wide and 30cm/12in deep and put in an 8cm/3in layer of rotted manure. Backfill the trench, leaving it about 10cm/4in deep. Sow the seeds under glass in modules in early spring and place them in moderate heat of 10–16°C/50–61°F. Do not check the plants by subjecting them to a sudden change of temperature or by allowing them to dry out. Once the frosts are over, harden off the plants and plant them out in the trench at 30cm/12in intervals. When the plants reach about 30cm/12in, tie the stems loosely together just below the leaves and draw up earth over part of the stems. Repeat the process three weeks later, pulling up more soil, and again three weeks after this, until the soil is up to the lower leaves. Alternatively,

BLANCHING CELERY

1 Blanching celery stems will make them taste sweeter. When the stems reach a height of about 30cm/12in, tie them loosely together just below the leaves.

2 A collar of cardboard or waterproof paper is tied around the stems of celery. The stems eventually blanch because of the lack of light.

3 Soil can be used to hold the collar in place. Although soil can also be earthed up around the stems to blanch them, a collar will stop soil from getting into the crown.

plant on flat ground and wrap cardboard or waterproof paper round the stems when they are 30cm/12in long. When the stems grow taller, wrap a second collar round them. Keep the celery well watered and do not allow the soil to dry out.

Self-blanching celery is started in the same way from seed and then planted out in blocks rather than rows, setting the plants at intervals of 23cm/9in in all directions. The dense foliage helps to blanch the stems. Place straw around the outside of the block to help keep out the light. Green celery can be grown in the same way, although there is no need for the straw.

HARVESTING

Harvest the celery by digging beneath it with a fork and levering it out of the soil. Replace any soil around the next plant if it falls away.

ABOVE **The celery planted here with some cabbages is one of the self-blanching varieties now available – 'Golden Self-blanching'.**

Harvesting

Trench celery can be lifted in autumn by digging it up with a fork. Replace soil around the next plant if it falls away. Continue to dig as required. The flavour is improved by the first frosts, but cover the plants with straw in severe weather so that penetrating frosts do not reach the stems. Self-blanching celery can also be harvested as required from the autumn onwards, but it should be lifted by the time of the first winter frosts.

Storage

Leave trench varieties where they are growing until required. In colder areas, before the weather becomes severe, lift and store in a frost-free place, where they should stay fresh for several weeks. Celery can be frozen, but it becomes mushy when it is defrosted, so it can only be used as flavouring or in cooked dishes.

Pests and diseases

Slugs are one of the worst enemies of celery, and it is important to cull them regularly by your preferred method. Other problems can include celery fly and carrot fly.

Diseases include celery heart rot and celery leaf spot. Boron deficiency, which causes the stems to crack, may also be a problem.

Cultivation

Trench
Sowing time early to mid-spring
Planting date early summer
Planting distance 30cm/12in
Distance between sown rows 60cm/24in
Harvesting autumn onwards

Self-blanching
Sowing time early to mid-spring
Planting date early summer
Planting distance in blocks 23cm/9in
Harvesting autumn

Varieties

Trench
'Giant Pink'
'Giant Red'
'Giant White'
'Hopkins Fenlander'
'Martine'
'New White Dwarf'

Self-blanching
'Celebrity'
'Golden Self-blanching'
'Ivory Tower'
'Lathom's Self-blanching'
'Victoria'

Green
'Greensnap'
'Imperial'
'Tall Utah'

trench celery

Celeriac (Celery Root)

Apium graveolens var. *rapaceum*

Although it is often thought of as a root crop, celeriac (celery root) is considered in this section partly because it fits more neatly beside celery and partly because it is not, in fact, the root but the swollen stem that forms the vegetable. Like cultivated celery, celeriac is derived from the wild celery which is a native plant found in Europe and the Middle East. It was a much later development than celery and is said to have been introduced to Britain from Alexandria in the early 18th century.

Celeriac (celery root) is the swollen area of the plant where the leaf stalks join the root. This produces a hard, round vegetable, often with knobbles and leaf scars over its dirty-looking surface. Although it looks far from appetizing, it is a useful vegetable. It is most frequently used as a flavouring, making an excellent winter substitute for celery, but it is also used as a vegetable in its own right, either cooked or grated raw in a salad.

Celeriac (celery root) is easier to grow than celery because it does not need blanching and is less prone to pests and diseases. However, like celery, it does need a moist soil in order to keep it growing.

Celeriac (celery root) should be given as long a growing season as possible or it will not develop into a large enough size that is worth harvesting and eating. This means that you will have to start off the celeriac plants early under glass.

EARTHING (HILLING) UP

Earth (hill) up the lower half of the celeriac (celery root) bulb in order to keep it white.

Cultivation

Celeriac (celery root) likes an open, sunny position, but it will tolerate a little light shade. The soil must be rich in organic material, not only to provide nutrients but also to help retain moisture around the roots.

BELOW **A row of celeriac (celery root), showing perfect spacing between the plants, and leaves trimmed from the tops of the bulbs.**

Sow celeriac (celery root) under glass in modules or fibre pots in late winter or early spring. Place them in a propagator at about 15°C/59°F. Maintain an even temperature and keep them watered so that growth is not checked. Towards the end of spring, when the plants are about 8cm/3in tall, harden them off and plant out at 30cm/12in intervals in rows set 30cm/12in apart. Plant them so that the base of the stem is level with the surface of the soil. Remember to keep them watered so that growth is not checked.

Cut off any side shoots that appear and towards late summer remove a few of the lower leaves and earth up around the swollen stem so that it stays white. In cold areas cover the plants with straw to protect from severe frosts.

ABOVE **Remove a few of the lower leaves from the bulb to let the light onto the top. This should be done in late summer.**

Harvesting

Dig celeriac (celery root) as needed from autumn onwards. They should be left to develop until they are as large as possible, although they are edible from about 8cm/3in across.

Storage

Unless the weather is particularly severe, celeriac (celery root) can be left in the ground until it is required. A covering of straw will help protect it if necessary. In colder areas it can be lifted, cleaned and placed in trays filled with just-moist sand or peat (peat moss) and kept in a frost-free place.

WATERING

The growth of celeriac (celery root) must not be checked; it must be watered during dry spells.

Pests and diseases

On the whole, celeriac (celery root) is relatively trouble free, although slugs can be a problem with young plants. Carrot fly and celery fly may also cause problems.

Cultivation

Sowing time late winter to mid-spring
Planting time late spring to early summer
Planting distance 30cm/12in
Distance between sown rows 30cm/12in
Harvesting autumn onwards

Varieties

'Alabaster'	'Marble Ball'
'Balder'	'Monarch'
'Brilliant'	'Snow White'
'Giant Prague'	'Tellus'

celeriac (celery root)

Globe Artichokes

Cynara cardunculus Scolymus Group

Globe artichokes were not much grown by the old country gardeners, who tended to concentrate on staple foods rather than "fancy ones". The artichoke was regarded as belonging on the tables of the rich. Today, however, although many people still grow their own vegetables, they are not dependent on doing so and can, therefore, afford to include a few delicacies that are not absolutely necessary to everyday life. Once you have grown and tasted globe artichokes, however, you may join the growing ranks of gardeners who consider them an essential part of their diet.

Unlike most vegetables, the part of globe artichokes that is eaten is the flower-head or, rather, the flower-bud before the flower begins to open. The whole head is boiled or steamed and then various parts consumed. First, the scale-like bracts are removed and the soft fleshy part at the base of each is eaten. As these are removed, the hairy tuft of the flower, the "choke", is revealed. This is usually removed and discarded and then the base of the flower, or the heart, is scooped out and eaten. It can then be served with lots of butter, which, needless to say, gets everywhere.

Globe artichokes were grown by the Ancient Greeks and the Romans, before spreading to the rest of Europe. They are handsome plants, looking a bit like the giant thistle, to which they are related. They are usually grown in the vegetable garden because you need several plants to give a constant supply throughout the summer, but if you decide to have only a couple of plants you could easily grow them in the flower border to save space. They have attractive silvery foliage, and if you leave a few flowers they develop large purple heads, which will usually be covered in bees.

Globe artichokes are usually grown from offsets rather than from seed, which is likely to produce variable results. If you have difficulty in getting offsets, you could initially grow them from seed and select the best plants, then continue to propagate these by division. This can be done by cutting off the young, outer growth from the old plant with a sharp knife in spring. Each shoot should be growing strongly and have some roots attached. Plant out immediately. Divisions can also be taken in autumn, when the offset can be potted up and over-wintered in a greenhouse or cold frame.

BELOW **Harvesting an artichoke by cutting the stem just below the head.**

CUTTING BACK

Cut down all stems to ground level when the plant dies back in the autumn. Replace plants after three or, at most, four years.

Cultivation

Globe artichokes need an open, sunny situation. Because they will be in the ground for several years, the soil must be thoroughly prepared. Remove all perennial weeds and incorporate plenty of organic material. In spring plant the offsets at 75cm/30in

COVERING WITH STRAW

Cover the plant with straw during autumn in colder areas.

ABOVE **A bed of globe artichokes with heads that are nearly ready for cutting.**

intervals in rows set 90cm/3ft apart. Trim off about a third of each leaf to reduce water loss while the plant is getting established. Water and keep watered in dry periods.

Seed can be sown in spring about 2.5cm/1in deep in rows 30cm/12in apart. Thin to 15cm/6in apart. Transplant the following spring. In autumn cut down the main stems and draw up soil around the crown. Cover with straw in very cold areas. Replace plants after three or, at most, four years, and aim to replant a third of your plants every year.

Cultivation
Seed
Sowing time spring
Sowing depth 2.5cm/1in
Distance between sown rows 30cm/12in
Thinning distance 15cm/6in
Transplanting following spring
Offsets
Planting time spring
Planting distance 75cm/30in
Distance between rows 90cm/3ft
Harvesting summer of second year onwards

Harvesting

Harvest from the second year onwards. Take the flower-heads before they open and while they are still green, cutting about 2.5cm/1in below the head with a sharp knife or secateurs (pruners).

Storage

Globe artichokes should be eaten straight from the plant. They can be frozen but remove the stem and choke first.

Varieties	
'Green Globe'	'Vert de Laon'
'Purple Globe'	'Violetta di Chioggia'

Pests and diseases

On the whole globe artichokes are not troubled by many problems. Blackfly can be a nuisance in bad seasons.

globe artichokes

Rhubarb

Rheum × hybridum

Gardening has many contradictions and rhubarb is one of them. It is a vegetable, but it is mainly used as a fruit – that is, it is eaten with sugar as a dessert. Tomatoes, on the other hand, are, strictly speaking, fruit but are used as a vegetable. Does it matter? These are problems only when you start classifying plants or writing books; in the garden and kitchen it doesn't matter at all.

Originally rhubarb was grown as a medicinal plant (the root was powdered and used as a laxative), and it was only much later that it was used as a vegetable. It was used in medicine nearly 5,000 years ago in Ancient China, but it was only in the 18th century that it was realized that it also made a good vegetable. Forcing to obtain an early crop was not discovered (accidentally, as all good discoveries seem to be) until early in the following century, less than 200 years ago.

Only the young stalks are eaten, and these must be cooked. The leaves are poisonous, so do not be tempted to experiment with them in an attempt to invent new dishes. The crop is normally harvested from spring to early summer, but it is possible to "force" it, by covering the dormant crown with a box, bucket or, if you can afford it, a decorative terracotta rhubarb forcer. This produces a crop of sweet-tasting stems, several weeks earlier than if the plant is left in the open.

Rhubarb is an easy crop to grow and, once planted, it is not at all demanding. It can be left where it is for 20 years or more, although some gardeners prefer to replace their plants every five years or so in order to keep them vigorous. Rhubarb does take up quite a bit of space, but a couple of plants will keep a small family well supplied. The space may be considered well used because rhubarb plants are also quite decorative, with their huge green leaves and attractive red stems. In summer they throw up large flowering stems, covered with masses of creamy flowers, which can be spectacular.

Cultivation

Seed
Sowing time spring
Sowing depth 2.5cm/1in
Distance between sown rows 30cm/12in
Thinning distance 23cm/9in
Transplanting following winter
Division
Planting time winter or (if potted) spring
Planting distance 90cm/3ft
Distance between rows 90cm/3ft
Harvesting summer of second year onwards

Cultivation

Rhubarb must have a sunny position, away from shade. The soil should be rich in organic material but it should also be reasonably free draining. Because the site will be in use over a long period of time, take care in its preparation, removing all perennial weeds and digging deeply to incorporate as much well-rotted manure as

LEFT **A decorative terracotta rhubarb forcer for producing sweet early rhubarb. Alternatively, a box or bucket can be used.**

possible. In the past new plants were bare rooted and were planted in winter, while they were dormant. This is also a good time to divide an existing plant to start a new one: dig up the old plant and remove an outer section that includes at least one bud. Plants that are purchased in pots can be planted in spring or even summer if they are kept well-watered. They should be spaced 90cm/3ft apart.

Rhubarb can also be grown from seed, but this method takes longer and the quality of the plant cannot be guaranteed in the same way as buying a named cultivar. However, the seed can be sown in 2.5cm/1in drills and thinned to 23cm/9in once they have germinated. Plant out in their final position, in the same way as for dormant crowns, during the following winter. Water well in dry weather. Apply a mulch of well-rotted, seed-free manure in autumn and again in spring.

To force a rhubarb plant, cover it with a large upturned bucket or other similar container in midwinter. Do not force the same plant for two years running or it will be weakened.

ABOVE **A bed of healthy looking rhubarb is an attractive sight. Remember that rhubarb leaves are poisonous and cannot be eaten.**

HARVESTING

Harvest by pulling on the sticks of rhubarb so that they come out of their "socket". Cut off the leaves and discard on the compost heap.

Harvesting

Rhubarb is harvested from spring to early summer unless it has been forced, when it can be pulled a few weeks earlier. It is harvested by pulling each stem vertically from close to the base – it will come out of its "socket". Cut off the leaves and discard on the compost heap.

Storage

Rhubarb is best cooked straight from the garden. Otherwise it can be stored by freezing or bottling.

Pests and diseases

There are a few pests and diseases that trouble rhubarb, but you will be unfortunate if you come across them.

Varieties

'Appleton's Forcing'	'Hawkes Champagne'
'Canada Red'	'Macdonald'
'Champagne'	'The Sutton'
'Early Victoria'	'Timperley Early'
'Glaskin's Perpetual'	'Victoria'

rhubarb

1

herbs

Herbs have been an important part of gardening for generations. Indeed, some of the first gardens were herb gardens. However, our perception of herbs has changed over the centuries. Gone are the times when it was essential to grow your own headache remedies and now few people grow medicinal herbs for their own use.

On the other hand, culinary herbs are still widely grown. There are two possible approaches to growing culinary herbs: one is simply to grow those that you actually cook with and the other is to make a comprehensive collection so that you can make a feature of the herb garden. For either type of garden, there is a tremendous range of herbs from which to choose.

Herbs can be grown in a variety of ways. For many people, the traditional herb garden remains the only way to grow them and with care it can become an attractive part of the whole garden. Herbs can also be grown in the vegetable garden or mixed with flowers in the ornamental garden. Another alternative is to grow your herbs in containers which is often the ideal solution for many gardeners because they can be sited near the kitchen for convenience.

Chives

Allium schoenoprasum

Chives, a low-growing perennial with narrow, grass-like leaves, are one of the basic kitchen herbs that few gardeners will want to be without. They provide a mild onion flavouring and garnish in a wide range of dishes.

Chives also have the advantage that they are attractive, particularly when in flower, and can be grown easily in a flower border. They are excellent for a potager or decorative kitchen garden, and make a fine edging to a path or plot.

Chives are easy to grow. Initially, you will need to buy – or be given – a plant, but once you have one you can go on dividing clumps as frequently as you like. Set the plants out in spring, planting them in a sunny position at intervals of 23cm/9in. If the pot or clump is large, split it up and plant them out as separate bulbs or in small clumps. Harvest by cutting off the leaves at the base. The flower stems are tough and should be discarded. Every two years, divide the clumps to prevent them from becoming congested. Chives are best used fresh, but the leaves can be frozen, either individually or in ice cubes, or dried.

ABOVE **A white-flowered form of chive that is usually grown for decorative purposes.**

ABOVE **Use only the leaves of chives because the flower stalks are usually too tough for culinary use.**

Cultivation

Planting time spring
Planting distance 23cm/9in
Harvesting any time the plant is in growth
Storage frozen or dried

Dill

Anethum graveolens

Dill is a tall, upright herb with feathery leaves, similar to those of fennel, and yellow flowers. It is mainly used for its seeds, although the leaves can also be used. Both are used as flavourings, especially for fish dishes and salads. The seeds can also be used in pickling.

Because dill is an annual it has to be grown from seed each year. Dill grows best in an open position and rich soil. It is advisable to avoid planting dill near fennel if you are planning to use the seeds of either plant, either for cooking or for propagation, because the two herbs can cross-pollinate easily.

Sow in shallow drills, 1cm/½in deep, in spring or early summer. Thin the resulting seedlings to 23cm/9in apart. Keep watered so that the growth is not checked, or the plants will prematurely run to seed. Start picking the leaves when the plants are 10cm/4in high and continue to do so until flowers appear. Harvest the seeds when they are ripe – that is, when they turn brown. The leaves are best used fresh but can be dried. Seeds can be dried and stored.

Cultivation

Sowing time spring to early summer
Sowing depth 1cm/½in
Thinning distance 23cm/9in
Harvesting (leaves) late spring until flowering
Harvesting (seed) when ripe
Storage (leaves) dried
Storage (seed) dried

ABOVE **The feathery leaves of dill are useful for decorating dishes as well as for enhancing flavour.**

Angelica

Angelica archangelica

A tall, hardy biennial, angelica is a statuesque plant with large, white flower-heads. It can be grown in an ornamental border, and it is also an ideal decorative plant for a potager. This is a herb that nowadays is used more for its decorative qualities than anything else, but many people still use the seeds for herb teas and crystallize the young stems. The leaves are used for flavouring fish dishes and fruit desserts, especially acidic ones.

This plant needs to be regrown every two years, but if the seedheads are left on, the chances are that there will be plenty of self-sown seedlings. Angelica prefers a lightly shaded position and rich, moist soil. Station sow in late summer, in 1cm/½in drills at intervals of 90cm/3ft. Remove the weakest seedlings, leaving one at each position. Alternatively, sow in early spring in a pan or tray and prick out the seedlings into individual pots. Plant out at intervals of 90cm/3ft in autumn. They can be either grown in a herb garden or decoratively in a flower border.

Pick angelica leaves only before flowering time. They can be dried. Cut stems while they are still young for crystallizing. The seeds should be picked when ripe and then dried.

Cultivation

Sowing time late summer
Sowing depth 1cm/½in
Planting and thinning distance 90cm/3ft
Harvesting (leaves) until flowering
Harvesting (stems) while young
Harvesting (seed) when ripe
Storage (leaves) dried
Storage (stems) crystallized
Storage (seed) dried

ABOVE **Angelica seeds can flavour drinks, although the herb is mainly grown for its leaves and stems.**

Chervil

Anthriscus cerefolium

Chervil, with its delicately cut leaves and white flowers, is increasingly being used in the kitchen for the subtle flavour of its leaves, which taste like a mixture of aniseed and parsley. Its dainty appearance as well as its flavour make it a valuable addition to a decorative herb garden.

Although a biennial, chervil is primarily used in its first year. Unlike many herbs, which prefer a sunny situation, chervil can be grown in light shade, preferably in a position where it will avoid the hot midday sun, because this may cause it to run to seed prematurely.

Sow seed successively, every three to four weeks, from spring until summer in 1cm/½in drills in a sunny position and a free-draining soil. Thin the seedlings to intervals of 20cm/8in. Chervil will happily self-sow if left to go to seed. Seed can also be sown in late summer for potting up plants to keep under glass and to provide a supply of fresh chervil leaves throughout the winter.

Keep watered, especially in hot weather or they will quickly run to seed. Harvest the leaves while they are still young – that is, before flowering – and use fresh or store after drying. Combined with parsley, chives, and tarragon, it is an essential ingredient of the classic French combination, *fines herbes*.

Cultivation

Sowing time spring to summer
Sowing depth 1cm/½in
Thinning distance 20cm/8in
Harvesting late spring onwards
Storage dried

ABOVE **Chervil leaves should be harvested when they are still young.**

Horseradish

Armoracia rusticana

It is debatable whether horseradish is a herb or a vegetable. Since it is really used only in small quantities and then mainly as a flavouring, it can be classed as a herb, but it does not really matter what you call it. It is a rather coarse plant, which looks much like a dock (*Rumex*). It is, however, grown for its roots, which are used in the celebrated horseradish sauce (which is much better made from fresh roots than bought in a jar) or grated raw on salads. Young leaves can also be used in salads.

It is best to start growing horseradish with a bought plant or with a length of root begged from a friend. One plant may be enough for most homes, but if you need more plant them 30cm/12in apart. Horseradish likes an open position and a light, rich soil, although it will grow in most soils. Remove a root when it is required. For winter use, dig several roots and store them in trays in just-moist sand. If you dig up a whole plant take care to remove it all, or any remaining pieces will reshoot. Unless this task is performed very carefully, a forest of deep-rooted horseradish will appear throughout the garden. Do not plant horseradish near a fence if you have neighbouring farm animals as the leaves can prove fatal to them if eaten.

Cultivation

Planting time spring
Planting distance 30cm/12in
Harvesting (roots) as required
Harvesting (leaves) while young
Storage (roots) in trays of sand

ABOVE **This flush of horseradish leaves shows that there is a flourishing root system below ground.**

French Tarragon

Artemisia dracunculus

A half-hardy perennial herb, French tarragon needs winter protection or to be replaced each year. It is grown for its narrow, strap-like leaves, and although it is not a particularly decorative herb, it is very valuable in the kitchen and is one of the basic herbs that should be grown. It is especially valuable in sauces and for many French dishes, particularly those containing chicken.

You have to start by buying a specimen of French tarragon, because you cannot grow it from seed. Further increases of tarragon can be made by division or by taking cuttings in midsummer. Plant the tarragon in spring in a sunny, warm position at intervals of 30cm/12in. If necessary, cover to protect against frost in winter. The leaves can be harvested at any time. Use fresh, but they can be dried or frozen.

The seed that is sold is for Russian tarragon (*Artemisia dracunculus dracunculoides*) which is much hardier but has a more bitter taste. Russian tarragon is, in fact, often grown as a substitute for French tarragon, in spite of its inferior taste. It has the added advantage of being able to tolerate much lower temperatures than the French variety which means that it can thus be left in its position in the open garden. The taste of Russian tarragon improves the longer it is left to grow.

Cultivation

Planting time spring
Planting distance 30cm/12in
Harvesting any time
Storage dried or frozen

ABOVE **For the discerning cook, tarragon is a necessity in any herb garden.**

Borage

Borago officinalis

Borage is an annual herb with rough, greyish-green leaves, which beautifully set off the sky-blue flowers. It is not much used as a herb these days except for the flowers, which are used as decoration for drinks and dishes. The young leaves may be used in salads and drinks. It is, however, worth growing both in the herb garden and the potager for its decorative qualities.

Once you have had borage in the garden, you need not worry about being without it as it self-sows copiously. Fortunately, unwanted plants are not difficult to remove and any that are required can be easily transplanted. For a more controlled approach, sow the seed in spring to early summer in 1cm/½in drills and thin the resulting seedlings to intervals of 30cm/12in. They are not particularly fussy about the soil they grow in, but they should have a sunny position. The stems and leaves are covered in bristles, which some people may find uncomfortable, and you may like to wear gloves when touching the plant. The flowers can be harvested at any time. They can be stored by freezing in ice cubes or by crystallizing. As a contrast, white-flowered varieties are also available.

Cultivation

Sowing time spring to early summer
Sowing depth 1cm/½in
Thinning distance 30cm/12in
Harvesting (flowers) any time
Harvesting (leaves) when young
Storage (flowers) frozen in ice cubes or crystallized

ABOVE **Borage is mainly grown for the decorative qualities of its beautiful blue flowers.**

Caraway

Carum carvi

Caraway is a biennial herb with feathery leaves and flat, cow-parsley-like heads of white flowers. It is grown for its seeds, which have a distinctive flavour that was first appreciated at least as far back as the Stone Age. It has an aniseed taste and is used in a wide range of dishes as well as in breads and cakes. The leaves can also be used to impart the same flavour. It is not a particularly attractive plant but is important because of its seed.

Caraway is not the most elegant of plants. For this reason, it is best grown in a herb garden rather than in a decorative border. Although it is a biennial, it will self-sow, providing a succession of plants. If you leave the seed on one or two plants, when harvesting, it will provide enough offspring for the following year. Caraway likes a sunny position and a rich, free-draining soil. It should be given a position that it can occupy for two years because it does not flower and set seed until the second. Sow in late spring to late summer in drills 1cm/½in deep. Thin the seedlings to 20cm/8in apart. Leaves should be picked while they are still young and before flowering. Seed can be gathered when it is ripe and turns brown. Dry and store the seed.

Cultivation

Sowing time late spring to late summer
Sowing depth 1cm/½in
Thinning distance 20cm/8in
Harvesting (leaves) while young
Harvesting (seed) when ripe
Storage (seed) dried

ABOVE **The delicate flower-heads of caraway soon give way to aromatic seeds.**

Rosemary

Rosmarinus officinalis

What would lamb be without its traditional accompaniment? For that matter, it is difficult to imagine many other dishes without the unique flavour that rosemary contributes. This is not only a herb for the kitchen, however, for this attractive shrub, with its bright green, needle-like leaves and blue flowers, plays a key role in the ornamental herb garden or potager. It is one of those plants that you cannot resist brushing or running your hands over every time you pass.

Rosemary is one of those herbs that should be planted next to a path or patio so that you can appreciate its lovely scent as you pass by. However, rosemary can grow quite large, so do not plant it too close to the path or it will eventually cause an obstruction. If it is established in the right position, however, rosemary will grow for many years, although it may eventually get rather straggly. It is marginally tender and may succumb to a very cold winter, especially if it is wet as well. It needs a well-drained soil and a warm, sunny position. It is best to start with a bought plant or one grown from cuttings. Plant out in spring, and if you need more than one plant set them 75cm/30in apart. Pick the leaves as required, but those that are needed for drying are best picked before the flowers appear.

Cultivation

Planting time spring or late summer
Planting distance 75cm/30in
Harvesting any time
Storage dried

ABOVE **The best time for picking rosemary is before the flowers appear.**

Sage

Salvia officinalis

Sage, that almost inevitable ingredient of stuffing, is a long-lived shrub with grey, felted leaves. Its distinctive flavour is particularly appropriate with meats and dairy produce, such as cheese. It is a good, decorative shrub for the herb garden or potager, and although the normal culinary form has grey leaves, it is also available in forms with sultry purple or bright yellow and green foliage. Spikes of blue-purple flowers are borne in late spring.

All forms of sage like a well-drained soil in a sunny position. They are best grown from cuttings or purchased as young plants, although they can also be grown from seed. They should be planted out in spring and if several plants are required, they should be planted 60cm/24in apart. The leaves can be picked at any time, but those for drying are best picked before the flowers appear.

There is an attractive purple-leaved form, *Salvia officinalis* Purpurascens Group which has striking, purple, grey and green foliage. Some of its variants produce blue flower spikes. It has a strong flavour, is often used as a culinary herb and is widely cultivated for is ornamental value. Golden sage (*S. o.* 'Icterina') does not have such a good taste, but it will add colour to salads.

Cultivation

Sowing time spring
Sowing depth 1cm/½in
Cuttings taken summer
Planting distance 60cm/24in
Harvesting any time
Storage dried

ABOVE **Sage has coarse-looking leaves that feel soft and felt-like to the touch.**

Savory

Winter savory (*Satureja montana*) and summer savory (*S. hortensis*)

Although these two herbs are among the oldest of herbs, they are not widely grown or used today. Winter savory is a low-growing, spreading, shrubby perennial; summer savory is an annual with a less tidy appearance. The leaves of both species have a spicy, peppery flavour and are used in a wide range of vegetable dishes as well as in stuffings and other recipes. Summer savory is often used in bean dishes.

Both winter and summer savories are Mediterranean herbs that need a sunny position and well-drained soil. Although both herbs can be used for culinary purposes, many people find that winter savory has a less refined taste than summer savory. Savories can be grown readily from seed, which is station sown in mid-spring in shallow 1cm/½in drills at intervals of 30cm/12in. Winter savory may need pruning in spring to keep the plant neat and compact, and in cold areas it will need winter protection. Harvest the leaves at any time, but leaves for storing are best picked just as the flower-buds are opening.

Savories can be grown as alpine plants in a rockery or in a raised bed as well as in the herb garden. This is the ideal place to grow them, in many ways, because it exploits their decorative qualities while also raising them towards the light.

Cultivation

Sowing time mid-spring
Sowing depth 1cm/½in
Thinning distance 30cm/12in
Harvesting any time
Storage dried

ABOVE **The leaves of savories are best harvested just as the flowers begin to open.**

Thyme

Thymus

There are a very large number of thymes for the gardener to grow. From a culinary point of view, there is not a great deal to choose among them, because the flavour is basically the same although the intensity varies considerably, with the broad-leaved thymes having the stronger flavours. For garden display, there is a wide range of forms with coloured leaves as well as variations in flower colour, which makes thymes especially useful in ornamental herb gardens and potagers.

Thymes are good plants for growing in the cracks and crevices between paving in the herb garden. Being robust plants, they can survive being walked on. They can also be grown in the cracks between paving slabs. However, care should be taken if people are likely to walk over the thyme in bare feet, because the herbs are usually full of bees when in flower. Thymes are easy to grow, but they do need replacing from time to time as they grow rather straggly and threadbare. They like a sunny position in a well-drained soil. They can be grown from purchased plants or from cuttings taken at any time from existing plants. Set the plants about 30cm/12in apart and keep them well weeded. Trim over the more straggly forms after flowering to keep them more compact. Harvest leaves as required.

Cultivation

Cuttings taken any time
Planting distance 30cm/12in
Harvesting any time
Storage dried

ABOVE **Thymes are colourful plants with flowers in a wide variety of pinks, purples and white.**

fruit

Fruit can be one of the most enjoyable crops that comes from the kitchen garden, and yet it is probably the most neglected area of gardening. It is difficult to know why this should be the case. In the past, it may have been that fruit was considered to take up too much space, but the modern cultivars now available even make it possible to grow apple trees in containers on a balcony.

One possible reason for people's reluctance to grow fruit is that it can take time to see results. An apple tree may take several years before it produces fruit in any quantity. However, the wait is usually worth it because fresh fruit straight from the plant is one of the great joys of life. Another reason could be that many gardeners are put off by what they see as the complicated art of pruning. But most people perform tasks that are far more complicated than this, and soon pruning becomes second nature.

One point to bear in mind if you are considering planting fruit trees or bushes is that they can be very decorative, especially trained as fans or espaliers, for example. Full-sized fruit trees also have their advantages – they are wonderful for sitting under on hot summer days.

Strawberries

Fragaria × ananassa

Strawberries are one of the best loved fruits. No matter how readily they are available in the supermarkets, there is nothing quite like wandering into the garden and picking a few to eat there and then. The taste is always better, especially if the fruit is still warm from the sun.

It is now possible to pick strawberries from early summer right through to the first frosts and even beyond, if protection is provided. Strawberries are categorized by their time of fruiting and are known as "early", "mid-season" and "late", which continue to fruit well into autumn. There are also perpetual strawberries, which produce fruit in summer, have a break and then start again in autumn. If you have space it is a good idea to plan your strawberry bed so that you have as long a productive season as possible. There are also alpine strawberries, which produce very small fruits over a long period. All strawberry plants should come from certified stock to ensure against virus diseases.

Strawberries are not very difficult to grow. If grown in beds they take up quite a bit of space, but they can also be grown in pots or in towers – a series of containers one on top of the other. They can be grown in a greenhouse, which produces earlier and later crops, but the flavour is not as good as that of crops grown outdoors.

The plants will remain productive for only about three years, and it is important to have a rolling programme to renew a third of the plants each year. Unfortunately, they really need to be planted in fresh ground, so it is not simply a question of taking out one row and replacing it with another; the new plants should ideally go elsewhere in the garden. Alternatively you can create a completely new bed in the third year, and abandon the old one immediately after the fruit has been produced.

Cultivation

Strawberries need an open, sunny site. The soil should be fertile and well drained. The plants should be set out in late summer or early autumn, at intervals of 38cm/15in, with each row 75cm/30in apart. As the plants come into fruit the following year, place clean straw under the leaves and fruiting stems to keep the fruit off the ground. Polythene (plastic) or felt mats will serve the same purpose. Deep water during dry periods.

Pruning and training

Strawberries are not pruned or trained as such, but after fruiting it is normal practice to cut off all the old leaves and burn or destroy these, together with the straw mulch, to remove any pests and diseases. Remove any runners as they are formed unless you want keep a few new plants.

Harvesting

Pick the fruit as it ripens. Pick with a short piece of stalk attached.

Storage

The fruit is best eaten straight from the plants, although it can also be frozen or bottled. Unfortunately, frozen strawberries go mushy when they defrost.

Pests and diseases

Birds and slugs are two of the worst problems. Birds can be kept at bay if the plants are netted while they are in fruit. Viruses and grey mould can also be problems. Burn or destroy any plant with viral disease.

ABOVE **After fruiting, the strawberry plant sends out a series of runners that root along their length to produce new plants.**

CARE AFTER FRUITING

After the strawberries have produced their fruit, cut off all the leaves and burn or destroy them, along with the straw mulch. This helps prevent the spread of diseases.

RUNNERS

The strawberry runners have produced a perfect new plant through layering. The layered plants can be dug up once they have rooted and used to start a new bed.

ABOVE **On this plant a succession of stages can be seen, from flowers to ripe fruit. Fruit picked straight from the plant tastes best.**

PROTECTING THE FRUIT

Place a layer of straw under the leaves of the strawberry plants in order to prevent the developing fruit from getting muddy or covered with dirt.

Varieties

Early
'Cambridge Early Pine'
'Cambridge Prizewinner'
'Cambridge Vigour'
'Honeoye'
'Maxim'

Mid-season
'Cambridge Favourite'
'Cambridge Sentry'
'Grandee'
'Hapil'
'Jamil'
'Redgauntlet'
'Tamella'
'Tenira'

Late
'Cambridge Late Pine'
'Domanil'
'Fenland Wonder'
'Merton Dawn'
'Montrose'
'Saladin'
'Le Sans Rivale'
'Symphony'
'Troubadour'

Perpetual (remontant)
'Calypso'
'Mara des Bois'
'Rabunda'
'Red Rich'
'St Claude'

Alpine
'Alexandria'
'Baron Solemacher'
'Delicious'
'Yellow Wonder'

strawberries

Raspberries

Rubus idaeus

Raspberries are an appealing fruit, although they are often overshadowed by strawberries, which come into season at the same time. They are a good fruit for eating straight from the plant or for freezing and for making into jams and preserves. Raspberries can be used in a wide range of cakes and desserts as well as sauces for both sweet and savoury dishes.

It is possible to provide a good "taste" of raspberries by growing a group of just a few canes, but it is more usual to grow the canes in a row. This may take up quite a large amount of space, but it can be used as a hedge or screen, so fulfilling a double function. The canes are tied into wires that are supported on posts, which adds to the initial cost, but once the framework has been erected it will last for a long time, as will the raspberries.

As with strawberries, new varieties of raspberry have been developed so that it is possible to have a supply of fruit from early summer right through to the first frosts, which in a mild year can mean early winter. Rather than having three separate rows, which would take up a great deal of space, it is possible to divide a single row into three or even four separate sections for early, mid-season, late and autumn fruit.

ABOVE **Ripening and immature fruit on a raspberry cane. Ripe raspberries can be obtained over a very long period if the varieties are chosen carefully.**

Cultivation

Like most fruit, raspberries like an open situation with plenty of air circulating among them, but, unlike most other fruit, they will tolerate a little partial shade. The soil should be fertile and moisture retentive, but it should not be waterlogged. Permanent supports in the form of posts and wires should be erected. The wires should be 75cm/30in, 1.1m/3ft 6in and 1.5m/5ft from the ground. Allow 1.5m/5ft between rows. Plant the canes at intervals of 38–45cm/15–18in, spreading out their roots, during late autumn or early winter. Remove any suckers that appear out of the row, and use them as new stock if required. Mulch with garden compost or manure every spring

Pruning and training

Each autumn remove all the old fruiting canes by cutting them off at the base. Tie in the new canes to the wires. In late winter cut off the tip of each cane to a bud about 15cm/6in above the top wire. If you grow autumn-fruiting varieties, cut *all* canes to the ground in late winter.

Harvesting

Pick as the fruit becomes ripe, squeezing gently with the fingers so that the fruit slides off its "plug".

LEFT **If this crop of ripening raspberries is left uncovered in this way, there will be few to eat because the birds will strip them away.**

Storage

The fruit is best eaten straight from the plant. However, it can be stored by freezing, bottling or turning into jam or other preserves. Frozen fruit becomes mushy and loses its shape and firmness, although it is still useful as fillings and sauces. You can overcome the storage problem by selecting and growing a range of varieties. This means you will have a continuous supply of fresh fruit from early summer right through to the first frost.

Pests and diseases

Birds are a nuisance unless the raspberry canes are netted or protected in a fruit cage. Raspberry beetle – the grub is found in the fruit – is often a nuisance. Spray with derris as soon as the first fruits begin to ripen, and then make a second application two weeks later. Grey mould can cause the fruit to rot and there is also the possibility of some virus diseases. Infected canes should be removed and either burned or destroyed.

ABOVE **This double row of raspberries is supported by wires that are secured on a well-constructed wooden framework.**

ABOVE LEFT **These raspberry canes are tied into wire supports by twisting a continuous piece of string around the wire in order to trap the canes.**

Varieties

Early
'Delight'
'Glen Clova'
'Glen Coe'
'Glen Moy'
'Malling Exploit'
'Malling Promise'
'Sumner'

Mid-season
'Glen Lyon'
'Glen Prosen'
'Julia'
'Malling Jewel'
'Malling Orion'

Late
'Augusta'
'Leo'
'Malling Admiral'
'Malling Joy'

Autumn
'Autumn Bliss'
'Fallgold'
'Heritage'
'Norfolk Giant'
'September'

Growing raspberries on posts and wires It is essential that raspberries have a strong supporting system of posts and wires. The plants are set at 38–45cm/15–18in intervals. Each year, new raspberry canes are thrown up. When fruiting has finished on the old canes, these are cut out and the new canes are tied to the wires in their place. This sequence is followed every year. Raspberry plants put out suckers which can become established in the gangways between the rows. These should be dug up as soon as they appear.

raspberries

Blackberries and Hybrid Berries

Rubus fruticosus

Although blackberries that are picked in the wild have a great deal to offer, there are advantages to be gained from growing cultivated forms. The first is that they are conveniently at hand. Second, the fruit is usually much larger and often sweeter. Then there is the fact that you can get thornless varieties, which makes picking much easier. A disadvantage, however, is that you do need quite a bit of space to grow them successfully, although they do not need to be a free-standing crop. They can, for example, be grown along a boundary fence, which may well be a good use of space as well as acting as a deterrent to intruders.

ABOVE **Blackberries fruit over a long season, as is shown by a sprig of ripe and immature blackberries.**

RIGHT **This vigorous stand of blackberries shows the prodigious nature of many of these plants.**

Cultivated blackberries are derived from their wild relatives; the hybrid berries are crosses between various *Rubus* species, often involving blackberries and raspberries in their parentage. Each of these berries, including loganberries, boysenberries and tayberries, has a distinctive flavour and is grown in the same manner as blackberries.

They come into fruit from late summer onwards and are, therefore, available later than most other soft fruit, which is another advantage. Like most fruit, blackberries and hybrid berries are best eaten straight from the garden, but they can also be used in a wide range of dessert dishes and sauces.

Blackberries are usually grown on post and wire supports, the wires being placed at 38cm/15in intervals up to about 1.8m/6ft. The thornless varieties are not as vigorous and take up less space. In a really large garden, blackberries could be left to grow free, like their wild cousins, but this is not recommended because cultivated varieties are often much more vigorous than wild forms.

Cultivation

Blackberries prefer a sunny spot, but will grow in a modicum of partial shade. The soil should be well prepared, with plenty of added humus. Plant the canes in late winter or early spring, placing them 3.5–4.5m/12–15ft apart (thornless varieties can be closer together), and immediately shorten them to a bud about 23–30cm/9–12in above ground. Do not plant deeply; the soil should only just cover the roots, which should be spread out in the planting hole. Mulch with manure in the spring and water in dry weather. They can be increased by bending down a vigorous shoot and planting its tip to form a layer. A new plant will quickly form and can be severed from the parent.

Pruning and training

In autumn cut out all the old fruiting stems and tie in the new growth. There are several methods of training blackberries and hybrid berries. One is to tie in all of one year's growth to one side, several canes to each wire, and the new growth to the other side. Another is to tie the fruiting growth along the wires, allowing the new growth to grow up the middle. A more formal and higher yielding method is to create a fan, with the shoots tied in a radiating pattern from the base, again leaving the centre free for new growth.

Harvesting

Pick as fruit becomes ripe, without any stalks.

Storage

Fresh blackberries last a day or so but can be frozen, bottled or used in preserves.

Pests and diseases

Blackberries are prone to the same problems as raspberries.

Alternate bay One way to train blackberries is to tie all the new growth to one side of the wirework. After fruiting, remove the previous year's growth from the other side and then use this for the next year's new growth. Repeat each year.

Rope training A second way to train blackberries is to temporarily tie in all new growth vertically to the wirework and along the top wire. The current fruiting canes are tied in groups horizontally. These are removed after fruiting and the new growth tied into their place.

Fan training The new canes are temporarily tied vertically and along the top wire, while the fruiting canes are tied in singly along the wires. Any excess canes are removed. After fruiting, these canes are taken out and the new growth tied into their place.

Varieties

Blackberries	'Merton Thornless'	Marionberry
'Ashton Cross'	'Oregon Thornless'	Sunberry
'Bedford Giant' – early	'Smoothstem'	Tayberry
'Himalayan Giant'	'Thornfree'	Tummelberry
'John Innes'	**Hybrid berries**	Vietchberry
'Loch Ness'	Boysenberry	Worcesterberry
'Merton Early'	Loganberry	

Red and White Currants

Ribes rubrum

The only difference between red and white currants is the colour of the fruit. Both types of currant have a very distinctive, slightly tart flavour, but, unlike many other types of fruit, they have a comparatively short season, around midsummer. Red currants in particular are very attractive, and the bushes can be trained into standards, cordons or fans and used as a decorative feature.

As well as being used as fruit in their own right, both are widely used as decoration on cakes and in a wide range of desserts and savoury dishes.

Cultivation

Both red and white currants prefer a sunny site and a rich, moisture-retentive soil. Plant between autumn and early spring at intervals of 1.2–1.5m/4–5ft. Cordons can be 30cm/12in apart and fans can be 1.8m/6ft apart. Mulch in spring with well-rotted organic material. Propagate from hardwood cuttings taken in early autumn.

Pruning and training

Initially, prune back all main stems to four buds. After that, prune in spring and summer, reducing the growth on the new leader by about half and that on laterals to about 8cm/3in in spring and to four or five leaves in summer. Once the bushes are established, cut back all side shoots to one bud and take the tip out of the main stems. Let new shoots from the base replace older wood. If you are growing them as cordons, in early spring remove a third of the new growth on the leader and cut back laterals to three buds. In summer cut back all laterals to five leaves.

Harvesting and storage

Pick when the currants are ripe, taking the whole cluster of fruit. They can be frozen or turned into preserves – but remove the stalks first.

Pests and diseases

Birds, which will attack both buds and fruit, are likely to be the biggest problem. Aphids and black currant gall mites may also be troublesome. Grey mould may be a problem and coral spot can affect the branches.

BELOW **These cordons of red and white currants have been tied to vertical canes which are, in turn, tied to horizontal wires.**

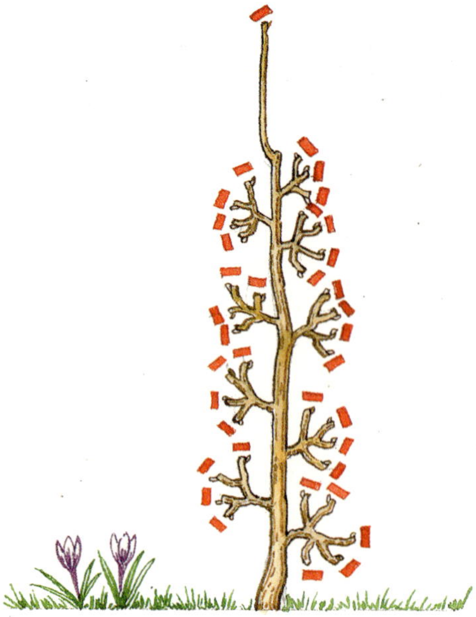

Pruning a red or white currant cordon On planting, cut back the leader by half of its new growth and cut back the side shoots to one bud. Thereafter, cut back the side shoots every summer to five leaves and, in winter, further reduce these to one bud.

Pruning a red or white currant bush After planting, cut back each shoot by about half. Subsequent pruning involves ensuring that the plant becomes an open bush. Cut back all new growth on the main shoots and reduce the new growth on all side shoots to one bud.

Varieties

Red currants	White currants
'Jonkheer van Tets'	'Versailles Blanche'
'Junifer'	'White Dutch'
'Laxton's Number 1'	'White Grape'
'Red Lake'	'White Pearl'
'Redstart'	
'Rondom'	
'Rovada'	

red currants

white currants

Blackcurrants

Ribes nigrum

Not only do blackcurrants have a unique flavour, but they are much valued for their high vitamin C content. They are used widely in desserts as well as jams and drinks. Blackcurrants, like red and white currants, tend to have a relatively short season compared with other soft fruit, but although related to red currants it is important to realize that they are pruned in a different way. Because the fruit is produced on the previous season's growth, it is important that this is not removed. Unlike red currants, blackcurrants can only be grown on bushes.

Varieties

'Baldwin'
'Ben Connan'
'Ben Lomond'
'Ben More'
'Ben Sarek'
'Boskoop Giant'
'Malling Jet'
'Mendip Cross'
'Wellington XXX'

blackcurrants

They are long-lived plants, lasting up to 15 years or more. Joostberries, a cross between blackcurrants and gooseberries, are grown in the same way.

Cultivation

Blackcurrants prefer a sunny site, although they will tolerate a little light shade. The soil should be well prepared and have plenty of well-rotted humus added to it. Plant between autumn and early spring, setting the plants at intervals of 1.5m/5ft. Mulch in spring with a layer of organic material. Water during dry spells but not when the fruit starts to ripen or it may split. Propagate from hardwood cuttings taken in autumn.

Pruning and training

After planting, reduce all shoots to one bud above the ground. The following winter remove any weak wood. After that remove any weak wood and up to a third of the older wood so that new growth is produced. Never reduce the lengths of the shoots.

Harvesting and storage

Pick the fruit as it ripens, retaining the stalks. Store by freezing or preserving, removing all stalks first.

Pests and diseases

Birds are likely to be the biggest problem. Aphids, big bud mite and gall mites may also be troublesome. Leaf spot and powdery mildew can also be a problem.

Pruning a blackcurrant bush After planting, cut blackcurrant bushes back to a single bud above the ground. The following winter, remove any weak or misplaced growth. Subsequent pruning should take place after fruiting and consists of cutting out up to a third of two-year-old or older wood in order to stimulate new growth. Also remove any weak or misplaced stems.

RIGHT **Blackcurrants and red currants are usually picked in bunches, complete with their stalks. They can be collected in a trug for convenience.**

Gooseberries

Ribes uva-crispa

Because most people think that gooseberries need cooking and so do not fit into the world of convenience foods, they are not, perhaps, as popular as they were in the past. This is a pity, partly because gooseberries have a very distinctive flavour, suitable for a range of dishes and sauces, but also because gooseberries can be eaten raw – there are some delicious dessert varieties. Unfortunately, these rarely find their way into shops, and so it is only gardeners who are likely to appreciate them – an excellent reason for growing your own.

Gooseberries are easy plants to grow, the only drawback being the thorns, which can be very sharp, but well-trained bushes and the use of cordons make it easier to get at the fruit without being torn to pieces. Typical gooseberries are green, but there are also red and yellow varieties.

Cultivation

Gooseberries require an open, sunny position, although they will take some light shade. The soil should contain plenty of well-rotted organic material. Plant the bushes at any time between autumn and early spring when the weather and soil are favourable. They should be set 1.5m/5ft apart. Mulch in spring with a good layer of manure. Avoid hoeing because the roots are only just below the surface and can be damaged. New plants can be propagated by hardwood cuttings taken in autumn.

Pruning and training

Gooseberries can be grown as bushes, cordons or standards. They are treated in the same way as red currants. Keep the centre of the bush open so that plenty of air can circulate as well as making it easier to get at the fruit.

Harvesting and storage

Start harvesting before the fruit is quite ripe. Such fruit can be cooked or frozen. Wait until fruit is fully ripe if it is for eating raw. Continue picking as the fruit ripens. Pick with a stalk, although this must be removed before storing. Store by freezing, bottling or by making jam or other preserves.

Pruning a gooseberry The basic aim when pruning gooseberries is to create an open framework. Establish a framework, first of all, by removing the basal shoots and cutting back the main shoots by about half in their first and second years. After this, cut back the new growth on the leaders in winter by about half and reduce the side shoots from these to two buds. Remove any damaged wood and any branches that cross or rub. Remove suckers and basal growth. In summer, prune the side shoots back to five leaves, but leave the main stems uncut.

Pests and diseases

One the whole, gooseberries are not prone to a great many pests and diseases. The main problem is powdery mildew, and one way to prevent this is to ensure that plenty of air can circulate around and through the bushes. Birds can also be a nuisance in spring when they strip off buds.

Varieties

'Broom Girl'	'Lancashire Lad'
'Careless'	'Leveller'
'Early Sulphur'	'Whinham's Industry'
'Greenfinch'	'White Lion'
'Invicta'	'Whitesmith'
'Jubilee'	'Yellow Champagne'

gooseberries

LEFT **Gooseberries can be grown as single cordons. This is achieved by tying them into canes which are supported by horizontal wires.**

Blueberries

Vaccinium corymbosum

The high-bush blueberry is becoming more popular in the garden. The rich, fruity flavour that is a characteristic of the berries has made it popular as a fruit to be eaten straight from the bush and for inclusion in an ever-increasing number of desserts and other dishes. Its disadvantage as a garden fruit, at least for some people, is that it must have acid conditions. In chalky or limestone (alkaline) regions bushes could be grown in large containers away from the normal garden soil, but this could become quite a chore, no matter how tasty the resulting berries.

The bushes and berries are decorative and are a useful addition in the potager or ornamental border.

Cultivation

Choose a sunny site, although a little light, partial shade will be tolerated. The soil must be acidic. Add ericaceous compost (soil mix) if your garden soil is just on the borderline. Set out the plants at any time the weather and soil conditions allow between autumn and early spring. Plant them as free-standing bushes, 1.5m/5ft apart. Mulch with manure, but only if it has not been "sweetened" with chalk or limestone. An ericaceous compost can be used or marginally acid soil. Do not allow the soil to become dry, watering regularly as necessary. Propagate from softwood cuttings taken in midsummer.

Pruning and training

Because the fruit appears on the second- or third-year wood, do not prune until cropping starts. After that, cut out any dead or weak wood and then remove up to a third of the oldest wood to promote new growth. Prune in winter or early spring.

Harvesting and storage

Pick as the fruit ripens and store, if necessary, by freezing or bottling.

Pests and diseases

Blueberries are remarkably trouble free. The worst problem will be birds, which will steal the fruit, but netting will solve this.

ABOVE **This healthy looking cluster of ripening blueberries clearly shows the distinctive powdery bloom of the fruit which most gardeners try to retain when picking.**

Pruning an established blueberry bush Blueberries fruit on older wood, so no pruning is needed for several years. Thereafter, cut out any weak or misplaced shoots as well as the old wood that has ceased fruiting in order to stimulate new growth.

BELOW **A vigorous blueberry bush, such as this, with plenty of ripening fruit, must be protected to stop birds from stripping away the fruit before it ripens.**

Varieties

'Berkeley'
'Bluecrop'
'Bluejay'
'Bluetta'
'Duke'
'Goldtraube'
'Herbert'
'Patriot'
'Spartan'

blueberries

Apples

Malus domestica

Apples are a staple fruit, grown in many countries around the world, but although there are, literally, thousands of varieties, the number available in shops can be limited. Unlike many other fruits, in which the taste is only marginally different from one variety to another, apples exhibit a great range of flavours and textures. Some are suitable for cooking, others are dessert (eating) apples, and others combine these qualities.

To help you choose among the vast range of apple varieties, visit one of the open days held by specialist apple nurseries and collectors. It is usually possible to taste several different varieties of ripe fruit and see the trees themselves, which you can often buy or order.

One aspect of apple growing that may restrict your choice is pollination. Most apples need another variety to pollinate them, and because the flowering time varies from variety to variety it is essential to choose two that flower during the same period.

Another question that will have to be addressed is what type of plant do you want. The old standard trees look best and produce a heavy crop, but they are usually too large for today's smaller garden, and ladders are needed for pruning and harvesting. Cordons take up the least space, but the crop is small. On the other hand, cordons allow you to have several different varieties in a small space. There are, however, all kinds of shapes and sizes between the two extremes, some of them very decorative. Always check the rootstock of the plants you buy to see how vigorous and large the tree will be ultimately.

Cultivation

Apple trees will be in position for years, so prepare the soil well, adding plenty of organic material. An open, sunny position is best. Plant young trees at any time of year between late autumn and early spring, as long as weather and soil conditions are favourable. The planting distances vary considerably depending on the type and size of tree. Cordons, for example, may be only 75cm/30in apart, whereas the full standards can be 10m/ 30ft or more apart, so check first with your supplier. Stake young trees, especially in a windy position. Newly planted trees should not be allowed to dry out. Mulch around the tree every spring with organic material. If necessary protect the blossom from late frosts with fleece.

Thin the apples in early and midsummer if there are too many of them – a good guide is to ensure that individual fruits should not touch each other. If branches begin to sag under the weight of fruit, the fruit may need thinning or the branches may need to be supported.

Rootstocks

The rootstock on an apple tree affects the size and rate of growth of the tree.

M27 an extreme dwarfing stock (bush, dwarf pyramid, cordon)
M9 dwarfing stock (bush, dwarf pyramid, cordon)
M26 semi-dwarfing stock (bush, dwarf pyramid, cordon)
MM106 semi-dwarfing stock (bush, spindle bush, cordon, fan espalier)
M7 semi-dwarfing stock (bush, spindle bush, cordon, fan espalier)
M4 semi-vigorous stock (bush, spindle bush)
MM4 vigorous stock (standard)
M2 vigorous stock
MM111 vigorous stock (half-standard, standard, large bush, large fans, large espaliers)
M25 vigorous stock (standard)
MM109 vigorous stock
M1 vigorous stock

BELOW **These pole apples have been grown as vertical cordons. The bottoms of the trunks have been protected against attacks by rabbits.**

Spur pruning an apple bush tree After planting, cut back the leader to about 75cm/30in above the ground. Leave any side shoots that appear just below this cut and remove any others lower down. The following year, reduce all new growth by about half. This will form the basic framework. Subsequent pruning is restricted to reducing the length of new growth by about a third and removing overcrowded growth.

ABOVE **Apples are not only delicious when they are picked straight from the tree, but they also retain their qualities when stored. This crop of ripening apples will make for a successful harvest.**

LEFT **Training cordon apples against a fence in this way is a suitable method of growing fruit if you only have a small garden.**

Pruning and training

Pruning is not difficult once you have done it the first time. Apple trees fall into two groups, depending on where the fruit is borne. On tip bearers the fruit develops near the tip of the shoots, so it is, obviously, important that you cut back shoots in spring. Trees in the other group produce fruit on spurs, which are found on older wood. Most training and pruning involves cutting out dead or weak wood and maintaining the shape and open nature of the tree. Larger trees are pruned in winter only, but those with a more controlled shape need to be pruned in both winter and summer.

Harvesting and storing

Apples should be picked when ripe, which is usually when the fruit comes away easily with a quick twist of the wrist. Some apples store better than others; in general, early apples do not store as well as later ones. If possible, store in a dark, dry, cool place, and ensure the fruits do not touch. Only store sound fruit. Freezing is appropriate for apples that have already been cooked and puréed.

Pests and diseases

A wide range of pests and diseases can affect the trees and fruit. Birds, wasps and codling moths are three of the most important pests. Canker is one of the worst diseases.

Varieties

Dessert (eating)
'Blenheim Orange'
'Cox's Orange Pippin'
'Discovery'
'Egremont Russet'
'George Cave'
'Idared'
'James Grieve'
'Jonathan'
'Laxton's Fortune'
'Laxton's Superb'
'Lord Lambourne'
'Millers Seedling'
'Ribston Pippin'
'Starking'
'Sturmer Pippin'
'Worcester Pearmain'

Cooking
'Bramley's Seedling'
'Grenadier'
'Howgate Wonder'
'Lord Darby'
'Newton Wonder'

Planting and pruning an apple cordon Cordons are planted as feather maidens at 45° to the wirework. All side shoots are cut back to three buds on planting. Subsequent summer pruning (above right) consists of cutting back any new side shoots to three leaves and new growth on existing side shoots to one leaf. Winter pruning consists of thinning out any of the older spurs if they have become congested.

apples

Pears

Pyrus communis

In the past, pears were, like apples, widely grown, partly for eating and cooking, and partly for turning into perry, a drink akin to cider. Pears for cooking and perry did not have to be the luscious juicy ones that are wanted for eating, and so many people have inherited trees in their gardens that bear pears that are as hard as bullets. This, unfortunately, has put them off growing pears altogether, which is a shame, because ripe eating pears, picked straight from tree can be mouth-watering.

ABOVE **Conference pears have a distinctive elongated shape. These healthy specimens are ripe for picking and enjoying.**

Pears can be grown as standard or dwarf trees as well as in the form of cordons, espaliers and fans. For the smaller garden, cordons are ideal as they make it possible to have several different varieties in a relatively small area. This means that you do not have a glut of one variety but can spread the harvest over a longer period. Pears need warmth to grow well, which is one reason that they are frequently grown against a wall. The warmth is needed not only during the spring at blossom time – they flower early and are particularly susceptible to frosts – but also during summer and autumn so that the fruit can ripen properly. In cold years, when the pears remain hard, they can still be cooked, often by poaching, to make them soft and edible.

Pear trees are vigorous and are, therefore, often unsuitable for small gardens and for some of the smaller forms in which the trees are grown. It is more usual to grow a pear tree that has been grafted onto a quince rootstock to curb its vigour. This means that any suckers appearing below the graft should be removed.

As with apples, pears must be grown near a different variety so that the blossom can be pollinated. Unless there happens to be a compatible tree in a neighbouring garden, you will have to plant at least two trees. Unfortunately, you cannot use any variety – the trees must be compatible. Consult your supplier about suitable pairs.

LEFT **These pears have been grown in a cordon against trellis, a method suitable for small gardens.**

Cultivation

Pear trees must have a sheltered, warm site and fertile, free-draining, but moisture-retentive, soil. Add plenty of organic material while preparing the ground. Set out new plants at any time between late autumn and spring with favourable weather and soil conditions. Planting distances vary according to the type of plant. Bush trees can be up to 4.5m/15ft apart, dwarf pyramids 1.5m/5ft apart, cordons 75cm/30in apart, and espaliers and fans 4.5m/15ft apart. Stake free-standing trees to prevent wind-rock. Mulch with manure in the spring. Thoroughly water during dry spells. If the crop is heavy, thin out young fruit in early to midsummer so that they do not touch.

Pruning and training

Most varieties of pears are spur-bearers, which means that they produce fruit on spurs that grow on two-year-old or older wood. The leader's new growth can, therefore, be safely cut back in winter by about a third of its length, and laterals can be pruned to three or four buds. Spurs are readily produced and should be thinned once the tree is established. Before starting to prune and shape a tree, always remove any dead, dying or weak growth and then work with what is left.

Harvesting and storage

The picking time for pears is crucial. The fruit should be just ripe; any that is left on the tree beyond this stage will soon become overripe. Pick as soon as the fruit comes away readily to a twisting motion of the hand. Early varieties can be picked just before they ripen, but mid-season and late varieties should be left until they are ripe. Pears can be stored in slatted trays in a cool room. Only store sound fruit and position them so that they do not touch each other.

Rootstocks

As with apples, the rootstock on which a pear tree grows affects the size and rate of growth of the tree.
Quince C moderately dwarfing stock (bush, cordon, dwarf pyramid, espalier, fan)
Quince A semi-vigorous stock (bush, cordon, dwarf pyramid, espalier, fan)
Pear vigorous stock (standards, half-standards)

RIGHT **A pear tree trained in the shape of a cone.**

Pruning an espaliered pear After planting, cut back to two buds above the bottom wire. In the first summer, tie the central growth to a vertical cane and the next two shoots to canes at 45°. Cut back all other shoots to two leaves. In autumn, lower the two side shoots to the horizontal and tie the cane to the bottom wire. In winter, cut back the leader to two buds above the second wire and repeat the above until the espalier covers all the wires. When established, cut back all new shoots to three leaves each summer.

Pruning a dwarf pyramid pear After planting, cut back the leader by about a third. Cut side shoots back to about 15cm/6in. In the first summer, cut back the new growth on the main side shoots to about five leaves and on the secondary shoots to three leaves. Thereafter, cut back new growth on the main stems to five leaves and reduce other new growth to one leaf. During the winter, thin out any congested spurs.

Pests and diseases

Pears are prone to a number of problems, including aphids, codling moth and pear midge. Diseases include fireblight, canker, scab and brown rot. Fireblight will probably mean the removal of the entire tree; it must then be burned or destroyed. For other pests and diseases, check on the latest controls with your local nursery or garden centre.

Varieties

'Beth'
'Beurré Hardy'
'Black Worcester'
'Concorde'
'Conference'
'Doyenné du Comice'
'Durondeau'
'Glou Morceau'
'Jargonelle'
'Joséphine de Malines'
'Louise Bonne of Jersey'
'Merton Pride'
'Onward'
'Williams' Bon Chrétien'

pears

Cherries

Prunus species

Although cherries are a really delicious fruit, they are not widely grown in gardens. One reason for this is that until relatively recently cherries could be grown only on large trees. This was a problem in small gardens as well as creating a problem in trying to prevent birds from stealing the whole crop since it is virtually impossible to net a large tree. Now that dwarfing stock are available, much smaller trees can be grown and it is worth finding the space to grow them.

There are two types of cherry: sweet cherries (*Prunus avium*) and sour or acid cherries (*P. cerasus*). Sweet cherries are perfect for eating, while the sour varieties, typified by "Morello" cherries, are cooked or bottled. Most people prefer sweet cherries, but the sour forms are easier to grow in a small garden. This is because they are less vigorous, and when they are on "Colt" dwarfing stock they do not make very large trees. They are also self-fertile, so one tree is sufficient.

If you do not have room for a big tree, sweet cherries are best trained as fans on a warm wall, where their size can be controlled and they can be easily covered against marauding birds. Improvements are being made in the development of dwarfing stock for cherries, and it may soon be possible to grow them as small trees, smaller than the current 4m/13ft. Sweet cherries generally need two varieties in order for pollination to be effective, except for 'Stella', Sunburst' and a few other self-fertile varieties.

Cultivation

Cherries need a warm, sunny position – a south-facing wall is ideal. The soil should be well-drained so that it is not waterlogged but it must be sufficiently moist to provide the precise conditions that cherries like. Plant full-sized trees 9m/30ft apart. Smaller trees and fan-trained cherries can be 4.5–5.5m/15–18ft apart. Stake young trees firmly so that the lower part of the trunk and the rootball are not rocked by the wind. If possible, mulch with manure or other organic material to help retain moisture. Water cherries in dry spells but keep the level of moisture even, because a sudden glut of water during a dry spell is likely to crack the fruit, which ruins it. There is no need to thin cherries.

ABOVE **The delicate blossom that appears in early spring is an attractive feature of cherry trees and a welcome bonus.**

Pruning and training

Sweet cherry trees need little pruning, apart from removing dead or damaged growth, unless they are trained as fans, when new growth is cut back to five leaves every summer. In early spring remove all new side growth. Sour cherries grow

Sour cherry fan Once established, there are two purposes to pruning a cherry fan: to keep the fan shape and to ensure that there is a constant supply of new wood. To keep the shape completely, remove any shoots that are pointing in the wrong direction. For renewal, cut back in summer all shoots that have fruited, preferably as far back as the next new shoot. Tie these new shoots to the cane and wire framework.

Sour cherry bush or tree Once established, bush and full-sized sour cherry trees need little pruning other than to remove a third of the old fruiting wood, cutting back to a new growth. Also remove any crossing branches.

on year-old wood, and so some of the older wood is removed each year so that new growth is produced. After picking the fruit in summer, cut back existing, one-year-old shoots on which the fruit was borne to the first new growth. In early summer reduce the number of new side shoots to about one every 8cm/3in. Remove all shoots that face towards or away from the wall. Remove any "water" shoots that appear from the bottom of the tree. Bush and full-size trees need little pruning.

Harvesting and storage

Pick sweet cherries as they become ripe. If you have a lot of cherries to pick, early in the morning is the best time because the leaves are crisp and stand up, revealing the fruit. Later in the day, especially if it is hot, the leaves tend to be limp and hang over the fruit, hiding it. Pick the fruit with the stalks on. The stalks of sour cherries should be cut rather than pulled to avoid tearing, which would allow disease to enter. Cherries can be frozen or bottled. They should be stoned (pitted) first.

Pests and diseases

Birds are the worst problem – given the chance, they will eat every cherry long before the gardener can get to them. Aphids can also be a problem. Canker, silver leaf and brown rot are the most likely diseases.

Varieties

Sweet
'Colney'
'Early Rivers'
'Governor Wood'
'Greenstem Black'
'Kent Biggarreau'
'Merton Bigarreau'
'Merton Favourite'
'Merton Glory'
'Napoleon Bigarreau'
'Noir de Guben'
'Stella'
'Sunburst'
'Waterloo'

Sour or acid
'Kentish Red'
'May Duke'
'Montmorency'
'Morello'
'Nabella'
'Reine Hortense'
'The Flemish'

ABOVE **This fan-trained cherry has been netted to protect it against marauding birds. Here, it is trained against wires, but it could also be trained against a wall or fence.**

sweet cherries

Plums

Prunus domestica

Plums are one of the great unexplored parts of the fruit world. In the past there were many different varieties, all with different flavours and textures, but now all knowledge of such fruit seems to have been lost. At most, one or two varieties surface occasionally in shops, but few people seem to know of the treasury of delights that could be available. Fortunately, many of the old varieties are available from specialist nurseries, and anyone who takes the trouble to search them out is really in for a treat.

ABOVE **A cluster of plums that would have benefited from thinning out – they are growing too close together and could have filled out more.**

The name "plum" actually encompasses a great diversity of fruit, including damsons, bullaces and the gages. Plums come in all shapes and sizes as well as a range of colours, from red to black and from yellow to green. The flesh, too, varies from red to yellow. As with the other main tree fruits, distinctive cultivars have been developed for dessert (eating uncooked) purposes and for cooking. The former are succulent and mouthwatering; the latter are firmer and less sweet.

In general, plums like a sunny situation, but there are plums for all sorts of climates and you may well find that some are better suited to local conditions than others.

Pruning a plum fan in spring and summer The main aim when pruning a plum fan is to maintain the fan shape. In spring, cut out any new side shoots that are pointing to or away from the wall. If necessary, reduce the number of new shoots to about one every 15cm/6in. In summer, cut back all new shoots to about six leaves, leaving any that are needed to fill in gaps in the main framework. In autumn, after cropping, further cut back the shoots to three leaves.

Check to see what varieties are still grown in your neighbourhood area and what may have been grown in the past when they were more widely grown.

Plums are mainly grown as trees, varying from full-sized standards to spindle bushes and pyramids. They can also be trained as fans. Unfortunately, they cannot be grown as cordons. Plums trees are not usually large and can be accommodated, even in small gardens.

Damsons were traditionally grown as hedgerow trees and can be planted in a hedge, saving a lot of space and yet producing a good crop of fruit. Plums vary in fertility, some being self-fertile, but they all do better for having a pollinator in the area.

Cultivation

Plums must have a sunny position; in cooler areas, a position against a wall will be ideal. They flower early and so should not be planted in frost pockets, where the blossom will be lost. The soil should be

Rootstocks

The rootstock on which a plum tree grows affects the size and rate of growth.

Pixy dwarfing stock (bush, pyramid)
Damas C moderately vigorous stock
St Julien A semi-vigorous stock (bush, fan, pyramid)
Brompton A vigorous stock (half-standards, standards)
Myrobalan B vigorous stock (half-standards, standards)

Varieties

Dessert	
'Ariel'	'Merton Gem'
'Cambridge Gage'	'Oullin's Gage'
'Coe's Golden Drop'	'Victoria'
'Early Laxton	**Cooking**
'Greengage'	'Belle de Louvain'
'Jefferson'	'Czar'
'Kirke's Blue'	'Early Rivers'
'Marjorie's Seedling'	'Laxton's Cropper'
	'Pershore Yellow'

fertile and moisture retentive, although they will tolerate drier soil than many other tree fruits. Plant the trees at any time between autumn and early spring, as long as weather and soil conditions allow. Planting distance will vary from 3m/10ft to 7.5m/25ft, depending on the size of tree. Fan-trained trees will need to be 3–4.5m/10–15ft apart. Smaller trees and fan-trained varieties should be covered if frost threatens while they are in blossom. Mulch in early spring with a good layer of organic material. If the crop is heavy, thin the fruit as soon as the stones begin to form. Thin so that they are 5–8cm/2–3in apart.

Pruning and training

Any pruning should be carried out in summer to reduce the chances of the tree being infected with silver leaf. Once the initial shape has been determined, larger trees do not need any pruning apart from the removal of dead or damaged wood. On fans, remove all new shoots that face towards or away from the wall. Shorten any retained new growth to six leaves.

Harvesting and storage

Pick the plums as they ripen. For cooking and preserving pick a little earlier, just before the fruit is ripe. Keep the stalk on the fruit as you pick them. They can be frozen or bottled for storage, but it is best to remove the stones first.

Pests and diseases

Wasps and birds can cause problems as can larger animals such as rabbits and hares. Other insect pests include aphids and winter moths. The main diseases are silver leaf, canker and brown rot. Trees that are affected with silver leaf and canker should be burnt or destroyed at once.

ABOVE **Ripening damsons are suitable for cooking once they have coloured. Eat fresh when fully ripe.**

Peaches and Nectarines

Prunus persica and *P. p.* var. *nectarina*

Peaches and nectarines are closely related, the main difference between the two is that peaches have a downy skin, while nectarines are smooth skinned. They are treated similarly in the garden, although nectarines do better in warmer conditions and are less hardy.

Both fruits can be grown as free-standing trees, but in cooler climates both are better grown as fans against a warm, south-facing wall or even a solid fence.

Cultivation

Peaches and nectarines need a warm, sunny site. The soil should be free draining, but it is also important that it is moisture retentive, so plenty of organic material should be added to the soil. Plant the trees or fans in autumn or early winter, with both at a distance of 4.5m/15ft. Trees should be staked to avoid wind-rock. Mulch in the spring with a good layer of manure or garden compost. If frosts are forecast when they are in blossom, cover the plants with fleece or polythene (plastic) frames. Water during dry periods.

It may be necessary to assist pollination by hand pollinating. Use a soft brush to transfer pollen from the anthers of one flower to the stigmas of another. The flowers should be fully open and the weather dry and warm. With a good fruit set it will be necessary to thin them, removing the excess fruits so that they are 15cm/6in apart.

Pruning and training

Mature trees do not require much pruning apart from the removal of dead or damaged wood and the cutting out of some of the older wood to promote new, vigorous growth. Remove all the shoots that face towards or away from the wall. Initially, thin other shoots to intervals of about 15cm/6in, tying them to the wires and removing the tips if they are longer than about 45cm/18in. Once the plant is established, allow a new bud to form at the base of each lateral in spring, but remove all other buds.

After fruiting, remove the fruiting wood and tie in the new lateral to replace it. Remove the tip if it is too long.

Harvesting and storing

Pick the fruit as it ripens. They are best eaten straight from the tree but can be kept for a few days in a cool place. They can be stored for longer periods by freezing or bottling.

Varieties

Peaches
'Amsden June'
'Bellegarde'
'Duke of York'
'Dymond'
'Peregrine'
'Rochester'
'Red Haven'
'Royal George'

Nectarines
'Independence'
'John Rivers'
'Lord Napier'
'Pineapple'

Pests and diseases

Birds and aphids can be a common problem with peaches and nectarines as can earwigs and red spider mites. Diseases include peach leaf curl, powdery mildew and canker.

Peach bush tree Not a great deal of pruning is required for a peach bush tree. In spring, cut back some of the older barren wood as far as a replacement new shoot. Also remove any awkwardly placed branches and keep the bush open and airy. Avoid making large cuts, as this is likely to allow canker to infect the tree.

LEFT **Fan-trained peaches such as this healthy specimen provide a decorative feature for a wall.**

Rootstocks

The rootstock will affect the size and rate of growth of the tree.

St Julien A semi-vigorous stock (bush, fan)
Brompton A vigorous stock (bush)

Apricots

Prunus armeniaca

Apricots are not grown as frequently as most other fruit, partly because they are not very easy to grow and partly because, with limited space, most gardeners prefer to grow the more luscious peaches. Home-grown apricots may well be a revelation, however, because they taste much better than shop-bought fruit ever does.

One of the problems with apricots is that they flower very early and are susceptible to frosts. They are, therefore, suitable only for warm areas. Their need for warmth means that they are best grown as fans against a south-facing wall, which will help to protect them from the cold. They are self-fertile, so there is no need for different varieties and only one tree need be grown if space is limited.

Cultivation

A warm, sunny, frost-free site is required to grow apricots successfully. The soil should be free draining but moisture retentive. You will have to incorporate plenty of organic material before planting. Plant in autumn or early winter, placing fans about 4.5m/15ft apart. The blossom will need to be protected if there is the possibility of frost. Mulch the ground with a good layer of manure and keep the ground watered during dry spells. If there is a potentially heavy crop, thin out the fruits to about 8cm/3in apart.

Varieties

'Alfred'	'Luizet'
'Bergeron'	'Moorpark'
'Breda'	'New Large Early'
'Early Moorpark'	'Polonais'
'Hemskerk'	

apricots

Apricot fan Once the fan has been established, the object of most subsequent pruning is to maintain the shape. Cut out any shoots that are pointing in the wrong direction, especially those that point towards or away from the wall. Thin new shoots, leaving one every 15cm/6in. Prune the remaining shoots to five leaves in the spring and then again, after fruiting, back to three leaves.

Pruning and training

On mature fans pinch out the laterals in summer to about 8cm/3in. Remove any laterals that face towards or away from the wall. Later, in summer, remove any more laterals that have developed. Apart from that, little pruning is required because most apricot fruit is borne on old wood. Every few years, remove some of the older wood and allow new laterals to develop in order to replace it.

Harvesting and storage

Pick the fruit once it has fully ripened and can be removed easily from the stalk. Apricots do not store well, although they can be frozen or dried.

Pests and diseases

Protect fruit from birds by netting. Aphids may also be a problem. The most likely diseases are silver leaf, canker, brown rot and die back.

LEFT **An elegant fan-trained apricot spread out across a large wall. The canes, supported by wires, help to maintain the fan shape.**

Rootstocks

The rootstock will affect the size and rate of growth of the tree.

St Julien A semi-vigorous stock (bush, fan)

Brompton A vigorous stock (bush)

Grapes

Vitis vinifera

Grapes have long been appreciated, not only as fresh fruit, but also for making wine. Varieties of white or black grapes are specially selected for their purpose, and growing grapes for wine-making in particular is a very specialized business. Soil and weather conditions as well as choice of variety or varieties can make all the difference. If there ever was a case for checking what other gardeners in your area are doing, this is it.

Grapes need a great deal of sun, and in cooler areas it is easier to grow them under glass, especially if they are for eating. Outside they can be grown in the open if they are trained onto wires, but they may well do better if they are grown against a warm, south-facing wall. From a decorative point of view they make excellent climbers to cover a pergola or arbour, when they provide a dappled shade that is perfect for sitting under. However, with vines climbing over such large structures it is not easy to protect the ripening fruit from the birds.

Patience is required because it will be at least three years before grapes in any quantity are produced, but once they are established the vines may live up to 50 years, so investment in thorough initial work will be well repaid.

There are several methods of training grapevines. They can be grown against a wall as single, double or multiple cordons; in the open on wirework the double guyot is a good method. Although pruning and training are not complicated, the formative work takes place over several seasons and it is worth consulting specialist publications to check on the best methods and techniques.

Cultivation

Grapes must have a warm, sunny situation. The soil must be very free draining, and if your soil is heavy it will need a lot of work before it can be used. South-facing hillsides, with a gravelly, lightish soil are perfect. Plant the new vines in spring at intervals of 1.5m/5ft. Apply a mulch of manure in spring. Water during dry spells.

Dessert grapes need to be thinned to produce large grapes. Bunches should be thinned to 30cm/12in intervals and then the grapes themselves thinned to allow them to swell and the air to circulate. Use long-pointed scissors for the thinning. Net to prevent fruit loss to birds.

Varieties

Outdoor

'Brant' black, wine
'Chardonnay' white, wine
'Chasselas' ('Royal Muscadine') white, dessert
'Léon Millot' black, wine
'Madeleine Angevine' pale green, dual-purpose
'Madeleine Silvaner' white, wine
'Müller-Thurgau' white, wine
'Noir Hatif de Marseilles' black, wine
'Perlette' black, dual-purpose
'Pirovano 14' red-black, wine
'Précoce de Malingre' white, wine
'Riesling' white, wine
'Siegerrebe' golden, dual-purpose
'Triomphe d'Alsace' black, wine

Greenhouse

'Alicante' black, dessert
'Buckland Sweetwater' white, dessert
'Foster's Seedling' white, dessert
'Gros Maroc' black, dessert
'Reine Olga' red-black, dessert
'Schiava Grossa' ('Black Hamburgh') black, dessert
'Seyval Blanc' white, wine

Pruning and training

Whether they are grown under glass or outside, against a wall or as free-standing plants, vines need wire supports. Immediately after planting reduce the leader to 45cm/18in. From this the various basic shapes will be grown. Specialist books should be consulted for formative and established training and pruning methods for vines grown under glass. The guyot system of training and pruning may be used for outdoor vines, the double guyot system is illustrated opposite.

Harvesting and storing

Pick the grapes when they are ripe by cutting the entire bunch from the vine. It is usual practice to cut a little of the

LEFT **These bunches of wine grapes are growing on vines that are supported on wirework.**

RIGHT **Small quantities of grapes can be grown over trellis and archways as long as they have a warm, sunny situation. Grown in this way, they provide a highly decorative feature which is ideal for a small garden.**

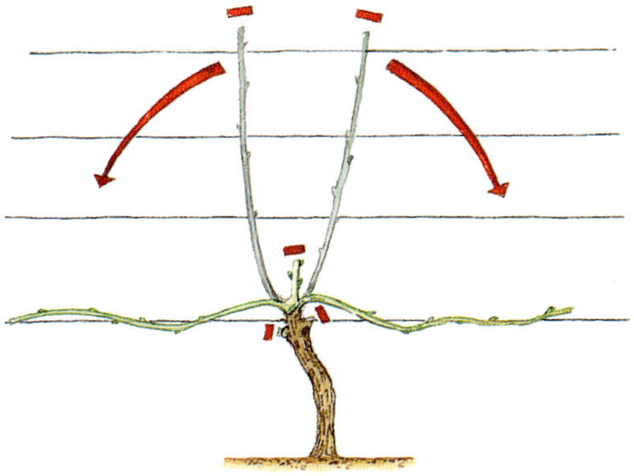

Established double guyot, winter pruning Each year remove the horizontal branches that carry fruiting stems, leaving three vertical central shoots. Pull two of these down on each side of the central shoot, so they are horizontal, and tie in place on the wire. The third shoot should be cut back to leave three strong buds which will form the three verticals for the following year.

Established double guyot, summer pruning In the summer, train the new shoots from these buds vertically, removing any side shoots that develop on them to one leaf. Allow the vertical fruiting shoots to grow on the horizontal branches, removing any side shoots that appear. Cut back above the top wire to three leaves. After fruiting, completely remove the horizontal branches and train the remaining three central shoots as described above.

woody vine stems on each side of the bunch in order to form a useful "handle". A mature vine should provide about 7kg/15lb of grapes. It is advisable to store the grapes in a container with a soft lining so that the delicate fruits are not bruised or damaged. Grapes are best eaten straight away, but they can be kept for a couple of weeks if a longer handle is cut and placed in a tall container of water so that the fruit hangs down outside the container.

Pests and diseases

Wasps and birds are two common nuisances, but scale insects, mealy bugs and red spider mite can also be a problem. Grey mould and powdery mildew are among the diseases.

Melons

Cucumis melo

It is debatable whether melons should be regarded as a fruit, which they strictly are, or as a vegetable together with marrows (zucchini) and cucumbers, to which they are closely related. However, since they are grown to be eaten as fruit, they have been treated separately from their relatives.

Melons are tropical fruit and therefore need plenty of warmth, both during germination and for their subsequent growth. In temperate climates, therefore, they are really suited only to greenhouse culture, unless they can be grown in a particularly warm position. It is possible to grow them in cold frames in the same way as in a greenhouse, except that they are grown horizontally over framework (or even on the ground) rather than vertically up canes and wires.

There are several types of melon. The cantaloupes are often considered the sweetest and best flavoured, but the honey-dew, or winter, melons are popular with some growers because they can be kept for up to a month after harvesting.

Cultivation

Seed is sown in individual pots in a propagator at about 18°C/64°F. When the plants are large enough to handle, plant them in the greenhouse border or into containers, such as growing bags. Grow them as single cordons, when they should be 38cm/15in apart, or as double cordons, when they should be 60cm/24in apart. The temperature in the greenhouse should be 30°C/86°F during the day, dropping to 24°C/75°F at night. A framework of canes and wires or plastic netting should be erected to provide support. Pinch out the top of single cordons when the plant reaches 1.8m/6ft. Pinch out the leader for a double cordon low down and allow two shoots to develop. As the fruit develops support each in a net.

Harvesting and storage

Harvest melons when the fruit is ripe. A good indication of this is that the stems will start to crack and the fruit has a sweet smell. All types of melon can be stored for a few days, but honeydew melons can be kept for up to a month.

ABOVE **These melons have been grown vertically under glass. The plants are supported on a wire frame and the ripening fruit is held in a net.**

Pests and diseases

Aphids, whitefly, red spider mite and powdery mildew are likely to be the worst problems.

Varieties

'Alaska'	'No Name'
'Amber Nectar'	'Ogen'
'Blenheim Orange'	'Ring Leader'
'Charentais'	'Romeo'
'Classic'	'Superlative'
'Galia'	'Sweet Dream'
'Hero of Lockinge'	'Sweetheart'
'Honeydew'	'Sweet 'n' Early'
	'Venus'

melons

LEFT **Melons can be grown horizontally in a cold frame. The fruit can be kept clear of the soil by resting it on straw or saucers.**

Cobnuts and Filberts

Corylus avellana and *C. maxima*

Cobnuts or hazelnuts are not very large nuts, but they are sweet, tasty and easy to crack. The trees are easy to grow and have the advantage of producing catkins or tassels of male flowers from midwinter to early spring. The female flowers are inconspicuous red tufts. Fortunately, both types are wind pollinated, which compensates for the lack of pollinating insects so early in the year. There are several self-fertile varieties, so it is not necessary to grow more than one if you are short on space. They are perfect for providing shade in which to sit plants as well as to grow shade-loving plants. They are really a large bush, rather than a tree, growing to no more than about 4m/13ft high, which makes them suitable for a small garden, unlike many of the other nut trees.

ABOVE **The bracts and shells will eventually go brown as the nuts ripen on this typical cluster of cobnuts.**

The main visual difference between cobnuts and filberts is that the husk surrounding the shell does not completely cover the cobnut – you can still see the tip of the nut – whereas on the filbert the husk completely encloses it. The trees produce better crops if they are pruned and maintained, but they can be planted in a wilder part of the garden and left to their own devices if you prefer.

Cultivation

Unlike most fruit, cobnuts like a partially shaded spot that is sheltered from strong winds. The soil should be free draining but moisture retentive, and it should not be too rich. Plant the young bushes in autumn or early winter at distances of about 4.5m/15ft. Mulch with manure to help retain moisture around the roots.

Pruning and training

Both can be grown in two main ways. They are either grown as a tree with a short "trunk" about 45cm/18in high with up to a dozen branches or as a stool, in which all the main stems come directly from the ground, more in the manner of a bush. Whichever way you choose, train the plants to be open centred. Heavier crops can be obtained by "brutting" which opens up the bush so more female flowers can form. This involves the curious practice of part-breaking some of the outer side shoots and letting them hang down.

Harvesting and storage

Pick the fruit as the husks are beginning to turn yellow. The nuts are borne after three to four years. They can be eaten fresh or dried and then stored until you need them.

Pests and diseases

These plants have few problems with the exception of squirrels that steal the nuts.

BELOW **A hazel bush can be used for decorative as well as nut-producing purposes. For larger crops, the bushes should be trained.**

Varieties

Cobnuts	Filberts
'Cosford Cob'	'Butler'
'Fuscorubra'	'Ennis'
'Pearson's Prolific'	'Gunslehert'
'Webb's Prize Cob'	'Kentish Cob'
	'Red Filbert'
	'White Filbert'

GARDENING CALENDAR

Winter

AW *all winter* **EW** *early winter* **MW** *midwinter* **LW** *late winter*

General

Clean and maintain tools and equipment **AW**
Plan next year's crops **AW**
Order seed and plants **AW**
Order sowing and potting composts (soil mixes) **AW**
Order manure **AW**
Continue digging soil when conditions allow **AW**
Avoid treading or working on waterlogged soil **AW**
Clean and prepare pots and propagators **AW**
Compost any organic waste **AW**

Vegetables

Sow early vegetables under glass for planting under protection **MW–LW**
Sow early vegetables for planting out **LW**
Check stored vegetables **AW**
Plant rhubarb **MW–LW**
Sow broad (fava) beans **MW–LW**
Sow parsnips if conditions allow **LW**
Plant early potatoes if conditions allow **LW**
Protect overwintering crops such as peas and broad (fava) beans with cloches **AW**
Protect brassicas from birds **AW**
Force rhubarb **LW**

Herbs

Continue to remove dead stems from herbaceous material **AW**
Continue to prepare ground when conditions allow **AW**
Use cloches for protection or to promote winter growth **AW**

Fruit

Prune fruit bushes **AW**
Prune apple and pear trees **AW**
Heel in bare-rooted trees and bushes when they arrive **AW**
Plant bushes and trees when conditions allow **AW**
Prevent birds stripping buds from fruit bushes **AW–LW**
Check stored fruit **AW**
Check supports and ties on supported trees and bushes **AW**
Take hardwood cuttings **EW**

Spring

AS *all spring* **ES** *early spring* **MS** *mid-spring* **LS** *late spring*

General

Prepare seed beds **AS**
Finish winter digging and ground preparation **ES**
Keep weeds under control **AS**
Water in dry weather **LS**

Vegetables

Mulch permanent beds with manure **ES–MS**
Begin main sowing and planting of hardy vegetables **AS**
Continue successional sowings **MS–LS**
Sow tender vegetables like runner beans under glass **LS**
Plant tomatoes, aubergines (eggplants), cucumbers and peppers in heated greenhouses **ES–MS**
Plant tomatoes, aubergines (eggplants), cucumbers and peppers in unheated greenhouses **MS–LS**
Plant Jerusalem artichokes, potatoes and onions **ES–MS**
Plant permanent crops such as globe artichokes and asparagus **ES**
Plant out tender vegetables after last frosts **LS**
Protect vulnerable new growth from frosts **AS**
Erect supports for peas and beans **MS–LS**
Force rhubarb **ES**
Mulch vegetables **LS**

Herbs

Finish removing last year's dead growth **ES**
Sow seed for annuals and perennials **ES**
Sow tender herbs ready for planting out after frosts **MS–LS**
Plant out hardy herbs **AS**
Prune shrubby herbs **ES**
Plant out tender herbs after last frosts **LS**
Take basal cuttings **ES–MS**
Divide herbaceous herbs **ES–MS**

Fruit

Mulch bushes and trees with manure **ES–MS**
Finish winter pruning **ES**
Remove any winter-damaged branches **ES**
Finish planting bushes and trees **ES**
Hand-pollinate early fruit trees **ES**
Protect blossom from frosts **AS**
Prune plum trees **LS**
Thin gooseberries **LS**
Mulch strawberries with straw **LS**

Summer

AS *all summer* **ES** *early summer* **MS** *midsummer* **LS** *late summer*

General

Keep weeds under control **AS**
Water when necessary **AS**
Keep an eye out for pests and diseases **AS**
Take soft and semi-ripe cuttings **MS–LS**

Vegetables

Plant out greenhouse-sown tender vegetables **ES**
Sow tender vegetables **ES**
Sow winter crops **MS–LS**
Continue successional sowings **ES–MS**
Harvest early vegetables as required **AS**
Shade and ventilate greenhouse vegetables **AS**
Dampen greenhouse floor to maintain humidity **AS**
Pick greenhouse vegetables as they ripen **AS**
Pinch out side shoots from tomatoes **AS**
Earth up vegetables that require it **AS**
Lift and dry onions, shallots and garlic **LS**

Herbs

Harvest herbs as required **AS**
Harvest herbs for storing before they flower **ES–MS**
Plant out tender herbs **ES**
Deadhead as necessary unless seed is required **AS**
Cut back herbaceous plant to stimulate new growth **AS**

Fruit

Pick early soft fruit **ES–MS**
Continue to pick soft fruit **MS–LS**
Pick cherries and early tree fruits **MS**
Net soft fruit against birds **AS**
Tie in new growth on cane fruit **AS**
Summer prune tree fruit **AS**
Thin tree fruit if necessary **ES–MS**
Remove spent raspberry canes and tie in new growth **LS**
Remove foliage and mulch from spent strawberries **LS**
Pot up or transplant strawberry runners **LS**
Tip-layer briar fruit **LS**

Autumn

AA *all autumn* **EA** *early autumn* **MA** *mid-autumn*
LA *late autumn*

General

- Continue weeding **AA**
- Compost all waste vegetation **AA**
- Water if necessary **EA**
- Start autumn digging on heavy soils **MA–LA**
- Clean and oil tools before putting away for winter **LA**

Vegetables

- Lift and store potatoes **EA–MA**
- Lift and store root crops in cold areas **LA**
- Remove and compost finished crops **AA**
- Plant garlic **LA**
- Plant spring cabbage **EA**
- Sow broad (fava) beans **LA**
- Sow salad crops under glass **EA**
- Protect globe artichokes, celeriac (celery root) and celery with straw in cold areas **LA**
- Protect brassicas from birds **AA**
- Check stored vegetables **LA**

Herbs

- Harvest seed as it ripens **AA**
- Tidy away dead material as necessary **AA**
- Protect tender herbs **MA–LA**
- Plant perennial and shrubby herbs **AA**
- Move container herbs under protection **MA–LA**
- Divide herbaceous herbs **EA**

Fruit

- Pick tree fruit as it ripens **AA**
- Store apples and pears **AA**
- Pick late crops of strawberries and raspberries **AA**
- Plant new strawberry beds **EA, MA**
- Remove old fruiting canes from briar fruit and tie in the new **MA**
- Finish removing old raspberry canes and tying in the new **EA**
- Take hardwood cuttings **LA**
- Plant new fruit trees and bushes **MA–LA**
- Check stored fruit **LA**
- Check all supports and ties **EA–MA**

WINTER It is advisable to protect permanent plants, such as globe artichokes, from winter cold and frost. A straw-filled box is a good source of insulation.

SPRING Leeks can be harvested between early autumn and late spring by simply digging them out with a fork. Autumn varieties are not as hardy and should be harvested before midwinter.

SUMMER Harvest globe artichokes, in summer, from the second year onwards. Take off the flower-heads before they open and while they are still green, cutting 2.5cm/1in below the head with a sharp knife or secateurs (pruners).

AUTUMN Potatoes can be harvested from early summer to autumn, depending on whether they are first earlies, second earlies or maincrop potatoes.

INDEX

The page numbers in *italics* refer to illustrations

CAPA: CARA A CARA

FOTOGRAFÍAS DE ROBERT CAPA
SOBRE LA GUERRA CIVIL ESPAÑOLA

Museo
Nacional
Centro
de Arte
Reina
Sofía

MINISTERIO DE EDUCACIÓN Y CULTURA

Barcelona, agosto–septiembre, 1936

CAPA: CARA A CARA

FOTOGRAFÍAS DE ROBERT CAPA SOBRE LA GUERRA CIVIL ESPAÑOLA

DE LA COLECCIÓN DEL
MUSEO NACIONAL CENTRO DE ARTE REINA SOFÍA

PRESENTACIONES POR ESPERANZA AGUIRRE GIL DE BIEDMA,
JOSÉ GUIRAO CABRERA, Y CORNELL CAPA

ENSAYOS HISTÓRICOS POR JUAN P. FUSI AIZPÚRUA,
RICHARD WHELAN, Y CATHERINE COLEMAN

APERTURE

MUSEO NACIONAL CENTRO DE ARTE REINA SOFÍA, MINISTERIO DE EDUCACIÓN Y CULTURA

ÍNDICE

Teruel, frente de Aragón, 3 de enero, 1938

La cubierta de uno de los cuadernos de Robert Capa, Archives Nationales, París

En primer lugar, queremos expresar nuestro más sincero agradecimiento a Cornell Capa, que tan generosamente ha donado al Museo Nacional Centro de Arte Reina Sofía las fotografías más significativas que su hermano, Robert Capa, reportero gráfico de prestigio internacional, tomó durante la Guerra Civil española.

La fotografía, junto con el cine, quizás una de las manifestaciones artísticas más claramente identificadoras de la cultura de nuestro siglo, se ha convertido en uno de los instrumentos fundamentales de nuestra memoria colectiva y en fuente importante de nuestra historia. La fotografía ha cambiado la percepción del mundo del hombre moderno. Robert Capa no se limitaba a documentar las grandes batallas, captaba el impacto que esta invención exclusivamente humana—la guerra—producía en la población civil. Las fotografías de Capa han constituido un símbolo de los estragos que la Guerra Civil produjo en todos los españoles, creando un icono universal, *Muerte de un miliciano* (Cerro Muriano, septiembre de 1936), que junto con el *Guernica* de Picasso continúa siendo la imagen más cruda de una contienda felizmente lejana.

Acogemos con enorme gratitud la donación de Capa, porque su presencia en una colección estatal española implica que este legado contribuirá a mantener vivo el recuerdo de los acontecimientos que se desencadenaron hace ya más de cincuenta años, unos acontecimientos que no deben caer en el olvido pero que se encuentran ya felizmente superados a través de ese instrumento de concordia que es nuestra Constitución y de la pujante realidad española de nuestros días, basada en la convivencia pacífica de todos los españoles y en la confianza en nuestro propio futuro.

Mariano Rajoy Brey
Ministro de Educación y Cultura

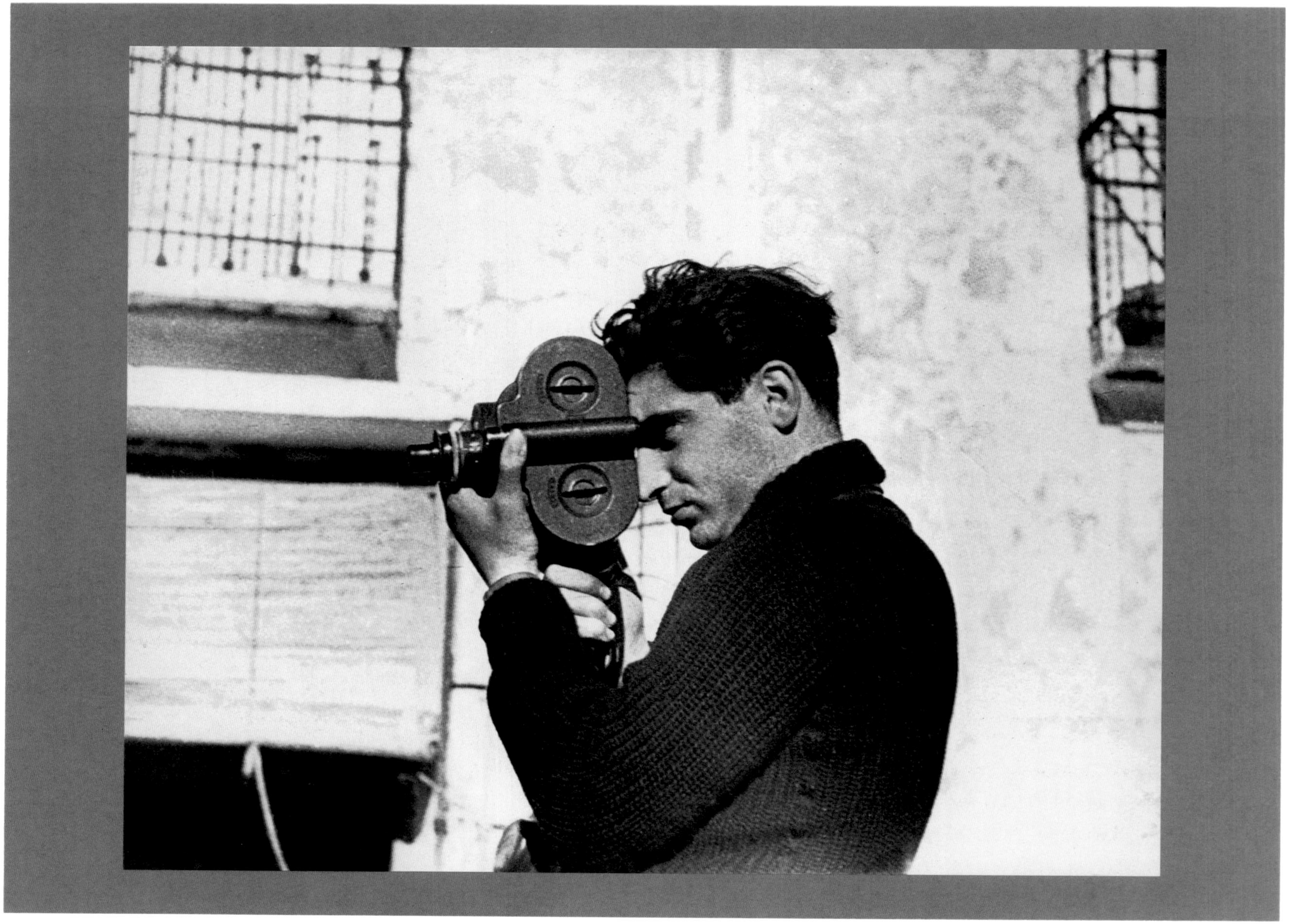

Robert Capa en España, 1936. Foto atribuida a Gerda Taro

Las fotografías que Robert Capa tomó durante la Guerra Civil española son de una belleza innegable. Son reflejo de las relaciones humanas y de su nobleza; captan momentos de alegría y de tragedia, tanto en el frente como en la vida cotidiana. Sin embargo, la donación de Cornell Capa al Museo Nacional Centro de Arte Reina Sofía es importante además por otra razón: ha otorgado al museo un corpus de fotografías de la década de 1930 que constituirán la base de futuras investigaciones y estudios comparativos.

Dicha década tiene una especial relevancia en la Colección Permanente del museo: el *Guernica* de Picasso y sus bocetos constituyen el eje en torno al cual se articulan no sólo el resto de las obras que integran la vanguardia española anterior a la Guerra Civil, sino además la totalidad de la Colección Permanente, actuando así este emblemático lienzo a manera de gozne, de elemento de unión entre las mencionadas vanguardias y las creaciones surgidas tras el final de la contienda. Las fotografías de Capa en blanco y negro documentan la destrucción causada por el bombardeo nacional en las zonas urbanas republicanas y el sufrimiento de la población civil, acto que provoca e inspira la génesis de la gran pintura de Picasso realizada en 1937. Los dos artistas plasman en la figura humana la esperanza perdida de un pueblo. La mayor parte de la obra de Capa se dedica al reportaje de guerra; Picasso lleva a cabo la misma denuncia en la pintura llamada *Guernica*. De ahí nuestra calurosa acogida a las 205 fotografías de Robert Capa que constituyen una importante aportación a nuestra colección, en constante crecimiento.

Hemos incluido en la exposición fotografías de Capa pertenecientes al Archivo Histórico Nacional, sección Guerra Civil, de Salamanca, probablemente entregadas por Capa mismo al Dr. Juan Negrín durante la Guerra Civil. Algunas de estas imágenes son únicas.

El Museo Nacional Centro de Arte Reina Sofía ha expuesto la obra de algunos grandes fotógrafos del siglo XX como Brassaï, Paul Strand, Manuel Álvarez Bravo y László Moholy-Nagy, y, evidentemente, no podía faltar Robert Capa. Su hermano, Cornell Capa, nos anunció su deseo de que España pudiera disfrutar de la historia completa de la implicación de Robert Capa en la Guerra Civil española. De ahí que ahora tengamos el privilegio de disfrutar de esta espléndida donación, que colma un vacío en las colecciones de fotografía del museo, y que queramos manifestarle nuestro más sincero agradecimiento por ello.

José Guirao Cabrera
Director, Museo Nacional Centro de Arte Reina Sofía

Gerda Taro y Robert Capa, París, otoño 1935. Fotografía de Fred Stein

Mi hermano Bob fue a España por la misma razón por la que lo hicieron todos los voluntarios procedentes de todo el mundo que fueron a luchar por la República. Todos sabían que ésa era su lucha y no únicamente la del pueblo español. Creían y albergaban la esperanza de que una victoria republicana provocaría el derrumbamiento del fascismo en toda Europa y que, de este modo, se impediría la guerra mundial que cada día que pasaba parecía más inevitable. ¡Ay!, pero esos nobles sueños se iban a ver frustrados, al menos temporalmente.

Bob fue a España con una refugiada alemana que se llamaba Gerda Taro. Eran jóvenes, idealistas y estaban enamorados. Sus cámaras eran sus armas, y las utilizaban para obtener el apoyo internacional para la causa republicana. Gerda murió trágicamente en Brunete en julio de 1937 y Bob nunca logró recuperarse totalmente de su dolor. Aunque al principio no podía soportar la idea de volver a la guerra que había matado a la mujer que amaba, su gran amor por los españoles pronto le empujó a volver para documentar la lucha del pueblo español hasta el final amargo.

Me produce un inmenso placer y una gran satisfacción donar, en memoria de mi hermano, 205 excelentes fotografías que tomó de la Guerra Civil española al Museo Nacional Centro de Arte Reina Sofía y, por tanto, a los españoles. Siempre he deseado ofrecer a España este extraordinario documento visual de uno de los capítulos más dolorosos de la historia de esta nación. Espero que este poderoso testimonio trágico ayude a curar viejas heridas y a evitar contiendas futuras.

CORNELL CAPA

Montblanc, Tarragona,
25 de octubre, 1938

Recuerdo que en España, durante la guerra, tuve la revelación de "otro hombre" y de otra clase de soledad: ni cerrada ni maquinal, sino abierta a la trascendencia. Sin duda la cercanía de la muerte y la fraternidad de las armas producen, en todos los tiempos y en todos los países, una atmósfera propicia a lo extraordinario, a todo aquello que sobrepasa la condición humana y rompe el círculo de soledad que rodea a cada hombre. Pero en aquellos rostros —rostros obtusos y obstinados, brutales y groseros, semejantes a los que, sin complacencia y con un realismo, acaso encarnizado, nos ha dejado la pintura española— había algo como una desesperación esperanzada, algo muy concreto y al mismo tiempo muy universal. No he visto después rostros parecidos.

OCTAVIO PAZ
Laberinto de soledad

Las fronteras que dividen a los pueblos
las romperemos pronto.
Las masas hablan mil lenguas
pero tienen un solo corazón.

Para los obreros no hay patria ufana
sólo libertad y paz.
Para que por la paz y la libertad
todos hablen solaz.

Los hombres cantan mientras trabajan.
Las mujeres cantan en sus tareas.
Todo el mundo canta
cuando por fin el pueblo libre.

Pero que calle ahora la guitarra
y la jota aragonesa.
Primero viene la Internacional
y luego la Marsellesa.

Rojas con la sangre del pueblo
y de las bombas del enemigo
nuestras banderas brotan como flores
sobre las barricadas de la libertad.

Muchacha del Frente Popular
no tengas celos de mí
si a mi corazón uno
a la libertad y a ti.

ANÓNIMO
Canción popular de la guerra

Barcelona, agosto, 1936

Montblanc, Tarragona, 25 de octubre, 1938

LA CULTURA DEL ANTIFASCISMO

JUAN P. FUSI AIZPÚRUA

El antifascismo fue la gran causa moral de la izquierda europea en los años treinta. Como dijo el poeta británico Stephen Spender, "los años treinta fueron la década en que los jóvenes escritores se politizaron": "la política de esta generación—añadió—fue casi exclusivamente de izquierdas".[1]

Spender se refería ante todo a la llamada *generación de Auden*, esto es, a los poetas W.H. Auden, Day Lewis, Louis Mac Niece y al novelista Christopher Isherwood (y a sí mismo). Todos ellos, en efecto, se aproximaron a la izquierda, simpatizaron con el partido comunista, trataron de escribir literatura de alguna forma *comprometida* y, en el caso que aquí nos interesa, apoyaron a la República en la Guerra Civil española. Pero el giro intelectual a la izquierda era mucho más amplio. Incluso en las universidades de Oxford y Cambridge pudo apreciarse un cierto interés por el marxismo. Uno de los mayores éxitos editoriales de toda la década fue *The Coming Struggle for Power* (*La inminente lucha por el poder*), el libro del aristócrata pro-comunista John Strachey publicado en 1932. La iniciativa, por ejemplo, del Club del Libro de Izquierda, creado en 1936 por el editor Victor Gollancz, tuvo un extraordinario éxito: llegó en poco tiempo a los 60.000 miembros y algunos de sus folletos llegaron a vender hasta 750.000 ejemplares. Dos jóvenes escritores, John Cornford y Julian Bell, los dos militantes comunistas, educados en Cambridge y miembros de familias de la alta burguesía intelectual británica, morirían en la guerra de España combatiendo por los republicanos; George Orwell resultaría gravemente herido en ella.[2]

También en los Estados Unidos, país sin gran tradición política socialista y/o izquierdizante, una mayoría de intelectuales (O'Neill, Dos Passos, Steinbeck, Edmund Wilson, Dashiell Hammett, Lillian Hellman, Richard Wright, Clifford Odets...) se identificó ahora, en los años treinta, con la izquierda e intentó dar a su obra un explícito contenido político. Revistas como *The New Masses* y *Partisan Review*, creada en 1934 y dirigida por Philip Rhav y William Phillips, y centros de debate como los clubs *John Reed*, creados en varias ciudades americanas a partir de octubre de 1929 (que tomaron su nombre de John Reed, el periodista radical creador del Partido Comunista norteamericano y muerto en Rusia en 1920), realizaron una amplia labor de discusión, análisis y divulgación de las ideas y planteamientos de la izquierda. La Guerra Civil española tendría un enorme impacto en el país (entre otras razones, por las fotografías de Capa, que aparecieron en *Life*, la revista de mayor difusión). Dos Passos, Hemingway, Martha Gellhorn, Waldo Frank, asumieron abiertamente la defensa de la causa republicana: 2.800 voluntarios norteamericanos se alistaron en el Batallón Lincoln de las Brigadas Internacionales.[3]

En Francia, algunos de los más significados escritores asociados al surrealismo (André Breton, Louis Aragon, Paul Eluard, Georges Pérec, Pierre Unik) se adhirieron en 1927 al Partido Comunista Francés (último paso de un proceso de politización desencadenado por su oposición a la creciente implicación del Ejército francés en la guerra de Marruecos contra la insurrección anticolonial en el Riff): el surrealismo estuvo hasta 1933—en que se produciría la ruptura—*al servicio de la revolución*, de acuerdo con el título de una de sus revistas. Muchos otros escritores franceses—Malraux, Gide, Rolland, Barbusse, Alain, Benda, Tzara, Guéhenno, Nizan, Cassou y un larguísimo etcétera—se adhirieron a la Asociación de Escritores y Artistas Revolucionarios creada en 1932 y participaron en iniciativas como el movimiento Amsterdam-Pleyel (1932–1933), la Liga de los Derechos del Hombre, el Comité de Vigilancia de Intelectuales Antifascistas (1934) y tomaron parte, igualmente, en los Congresos Internacionales de Escritores para la Defensa de la Cultura celebrados el primero en París en 1935, y el segundo en España en 1937, en plena Guerra Civil, por tanto, y en Valencia, en ese momento capital de la República española, como un acto evidente de adhesión a ésta.[4]

En Alemania, el teatro de Brecht, que evolucionó hacia el marxismo en los años veinte, y de Piscator, películas como *El Ángel Azul* (1930) de Sternberg, o *Hampa* (1931) de Jutzi, la pintura cruel y esperpéntica de Otto Dix y Georg Grosz, o la más alegórica de Max Beckmann, novelas como *Sin novedad en el frente* (1928) de Remarque, y *Berlin Alexanderplatz* (1929) de Döblin, habían reflejado en su momento el pesimismo de los intelectuales y artistas ante la evolución de la nueva democracia alemana—la República de Weimar, establecida en 1918, tras la derrota en la I Guerra Mundial—y ante el auge de las fuerzas de la derecha y en especial, del nacional-socialismo (atmósfera que reflejaría muy bien Christopher Isherwood en sus novelas *Mr. Norris Changes Trains*, 1935, y *Goodbye to Berlin*, 1939). La *Bauhaus*, la escuela de diseño, artes y oficios creada en 1919 y en la que colaboraron, entre otros, Walter Gropius, Mies van der Rohe, Kandinsky, Paul Klee y Moholy-Nagy, había nacido con el propósito último de aplicar los principios del arte de vanguardia a la vida cotidiana de las clases trabajadoras (fábricas, viviendas obreras) para crear así entornos revolucionarios de gran simplicidad y belleza. La llamada Escuela de Frankfurt (el Instituto de Investigaciones Sociales de la Universidad de esa ciudad creado en 1923)—Max Horkheimer, Theodor Adorno, Walter Benjamin—se centró precisamente en la elaboración de una teoría crítica del marxismo. La llegada de Hitler al poder en 1933 puso fin a todo ello: la casi totalidad de los nombres citados, y centenares de intelectuales alemanes, tuvieron que exiliarse. La vida intelectual alemana quedó así desarticulada y dispersa. Con todo, también el exilio alemán y la guerra española quedaron de alguna forma, bien siniestra, unidos: el suicidio, el 26 de septiembre de 1940, de Walter Benjamin, refugiado en París desde 1933, en la localidad de Port Bou, en la frontera franco-española—hacia donde había huido, tras la ocupación de Francia por los nazis, con la esperanza de cruzar a España—cuando el nuevo régimen español le denegó el permiso de entrada, adquirió el valor de una trágica metáfora.[5]

Desde luego, no faltaron intelectuales de derechas. Lo fueron algunos tan notables como Spengler y Heidegger, Ezra Pound, T.S. Eliot, Evelyn Waugh, Ernst Jünger—el autor de *Tempestades de acero* (1920), uno de los libros más vendidos de la posguerra, una exaltación de los ideales caballerescos de honor, riesgo y valor—como Céline y Drieu La Rochelle—cuya gran novela *Gilles* (1939) ambientada en la I Guerra Mundial contraponía la virilidad y autenticidad de la guerra y de la vida en el frente con la mediocridad e hipocresía de la vida de la retaguardia—y como los italianos Gentile, Malaparte y Mario Sironi, todos ellos adheridos al fascismo. En la misma España, donde una mayoría de intelectuales habían apoyado la República en 1931 y la seguirían apoyando en 1936 (Lorca sería fusilado; Miguel Hernández moriría en la cárcel; Alberti, Guillén, Bergamín, Luis Cernuda, Pedro Salinas, Pau Casals, Miró, Buñuel, Juan Ramón Jiménez, Madariaga y tantos otros se exiliarían), otros como Ramiro de Maeztu, Manuel Bueno, Pedro Muñoz Seca—los tres, fusilados en la guerra—D'Ors, Pemán, José Mª Salaverría, Foxá, Sainz Rodríguez, o como los intelectuales fascistas y falangistas (Giménez Caballero, Ledesma Ramos, Sánchez Mazas, Ridruejo, Eugenio Montes, Luis Rosales, Panero, etcétera) y muchos más militaron en la derecha y apoyaron, en 1936, el levantamiento militar.[6]

Pero Spender llevaba razón: la izquierda, incluso el comunismo, fue la gran tentación de los intelectuales de los años treinta. Eso tuvo su precio: lo más grave, el silencio de muchos intelectuales ante el estalinismo—incluso su complicidad con él—las críticas agresivas contra los pocos que se atrevieron a denunciar el régimen soviético y la política comunista, como ocurrió con Gide al publicar en 1936 *Retorno de la URSS* y con Orwell en 1938 por su *Homenaje a Cataluña*, el libro en el que narraba su experiencia en la Guerra Civil española. Pero la politización de los intelectuales hizo que legitimaran con su apoyo causas evidentemente populares y progresivas: la más clamorosa, la causa republicana en la Guerra Civil española. En efecto, la Guerra Civil española, que estalló cuando el 18 de julio de 1936 parte del Ejército español se sublevó contra la II República—el régimen democrático instaurado por decisión popular en abril de 1931—devino una esperanza y un símbolo: galvanizó las ilusiones democráticas y revolucionarias de la opinión internacional.

LA GUERRA CIVIL: LA SUBLEVACIÓN MILITAR

En todo caso, desde aquella fecha y hasta el 1 de abril de 1939, España se vio envuelta en una larga y enconada guerra civil que, por su violencia y por sus connotaciones ideológicas y políticas, conmocionó la conciencia del mundo occidental.[7] La derecha vio la Guerra Civil como una cruzada contra el comunismo: la izquierda la idealizó como la resistencia romántica del pueblo y del proletariado contra el fascismo. Manuel Azaña (1880-1940), el líder republicano, jefe del Gobierno entre 1931 y 1933 y presidente de la República desde la primavera de 1936, un intelectual angustiado por la tragedia de su país, la vio de otra forma: como una "alucinación colectiva", donde coexistieron el heroísmo y las atrocidades, la intolerancia y el fanatismo, el odio y el miedo.[8]

La Guerra Civil española alcanzó dimensiones internacionales. Alemania e Italia, las potencias fascistas, apoyaron abiertamente, con armas y soldados, la sublevación militar. La Unión Soviética auxilió a la República, y un importante contingente de voluntarios en su mayoría de ideología comunista, las Brigadas Internacionales, combatió a su lado. Pero la Guerra Civil fue un hecho español. Azaña mismo señaló que la discordia interna de la clase media y, en general, de la burguesía española —profundamente dividida por razones religiosas y sociales— fue el origen último de la guerra.

Estaba en lo cierto. La caída de la Monarquía y la proclamación de la República en abril de 1931 no fueron solamente un cambio de régimen. La coalición republicano-socialista que, bajo el liderazgo de Azaña, gobernó entre 1931 y 1933, inició un ambicioso programa de reformas de los que, desde su perspectiva, eran los grandes problemas de España. Quiso, para ello, expropiar los latifundios y distribuir la tierra entre los campesinos; crear un nuevo Ejército que fuera, ante todo, profesional y neutral en política. La coalición buscó limitar la influencia de la Iglesia católica, secularizar la vida social y promover una educación liberal y laica; y quiso finalmente rectificar la organización centralista del Estado y conceder la autonomía a las regiones con lenguas y culturas diferenciadas —Cataluña, País Vasco, Galicia—en las que habían surgido, desde finales del siglo XIX, importantes movimientos nacionalistas.

Los planes del Gobierno polarizaron la vida política y social. Las reformas provocaron la oposición y el rechazo de la opinión católica, de la Iglesia, de los terratenientes y de muchos militares. Algunas de las iniciativas gubernamentales —como la reforma agraria— estuvieron técnicamente mal concebidas; en otros casos, como en la disolución de los jesuítas o en la prohibición de la enseñanza a las órdenes religiosas, la República actuó con excesivo e innecesario sectarismo; se alienó así el apoyo de núcleos muy importantes de las clases medias urbanas y rurales. Sus medidas, por otra parte, no fueron suficientes para satisfacer la revolución de expectativas que el cambio de régimen había producido en amplios sectores de las clases trabajadoras y del campesinado. Algunos no le dieron tiempo: los sindicatos anarco-sindicalistas de la Confederación General del Trabajo (CNT) desencadenaron una verdadera ofensiva revolucionaria contra el Gobierno prácticamente desde el verano de 1931.

Por todo ello, el proceso político hacia la estabilidad democrática entró pronto en crisis. Las elecciones de 1933 marcaron un significativo giro a la derecha. Un partido católico, divorciado del espíritu de la República —la Confederación Española de Derechas Autónomas (CEDA)— se convirtió en la clave del poder en los años 1934 y 1935, un "bienio negro" en el que una buena parte de la legislación aprobada en 1931–1933 fue rectificada en sentido conservador. Ante el temor de un fascismo a la española, el Partido Socialista Obrero Español, la principal fuerza de la izquierda, optó por la insurrección. La revolución socialista, desencadenada en octubre de 1934 —que fracasó y provocó cientos de muertos y dejó a varios miles de personas en la cárcel— lesionó seriamente la legitimidad del régimen republicano. Por eso, cuando en febrero de 1936, la izquierda, unida en un Frente Popular encabezado por Azaña, ganó las elecciones, un grupo de militares derechistas fue a la conspiración y promovió el golpe de Estado que estalló de forma general el 18 de julio de 1936 (aunque algunos oficiales se habían sublevado en el norte de África el día anterior).

Sólo una parte del Ejército se levantó. Los militares, dirigidos por los generales Franco, Sanjurjo, Mola y Queipo de Llano, se sublevaron por varias razones: porque aducían que la República era un régimen sin legitimidad política; porque entendían que la concesión de autonomía a las regiones (de hecho, en julio de 1936 sólo se había concedido la autonomía a Cataluña) era una amenaza a la unidad de España; porque pensaban que las huelgas y los desórdenes revelaban la falta de autoridad de la democracia; porque consideraban que la legislación republicana atacaba la esencia católica de España. Los militares sublevados creyeron que el golpe de Estado triunfaría de forma inmediata. Se equivocaron: desencadenaron una devastadora guerra civil de tres años.

La sublevación militar triunfó sólo en una parte de España: en Galicia, Navarra, Álava, Castilla la Vieja, en las capitales de Aragón, en algunas ciudades de Andalucía, en las islas Canarias y Baleares

Farmacia del Globo, Madrid, 1937. Por gentileza del Archivo Histórico Nacional, Sección Guerra Civil, Salamanca. A finales de la década de 1970 se descubrió en los archivos del Ministerio de Asuntos Exteriores sueco una pequeña maleta que contenía 97 fotografías de Robert Capa y diversos documentos, perteneciente a Juan Negrín, primer ministro de la República española. Todos los documentos y fotografías de dicha maleta se hallan ahora en la Sección Guerra Civil, del Archivo Histórico Nacional de Salamanca. La fotografía de arriba es una de ellas.

(salvo en Menorca) y en las colonias del norte de África. Fracasó en Madrid, en Cataluña, en Levante, en las provincias marítimas del norte, en el centro-sur del país, en gran parte de Andalucía y de Aragón. De los 31.000 oficiales que el Ejército español tenía en 1935, se sublevaron unos 14.000; unos 8.500 permanecieron leales a la República; el resto sufrió distinta suerte. La República contó en teoría con unos 160.000 soldados, más gran parte de la aviación y de la marina; los sublevados, que adoptaron el nombre de "nacionales", retuvieron unos 150.000 soldados, entre ellos, el cuerpo de elite del Ejército español, el Ejército de África —unos 47.000 hombres—que Franco pudo trasladar muy pronto a la Península mediante un puente aéreo posible por la ayuda alemana e italiana.

El aparente equilibrio de fuerzas ocultaba, sin embargo, un hecho esencial: que la República careció inicialmente, durante varios meses, de unidad en la dirección política y militar de la guerra. Ello se debió a la naturaleza misma de la respuesta popular al golpe de Estado: la sublevación militar desencadenó un proceso revolucionario de la clase trabajadora que, bajo la dirección de los partidos obreros y de los sindicatos, rompió la estructura misma del Estado republicano. Fue eso lo que dio a la Guerra Civil española la significación que conmocionó la imaginación romántica de la izquierda europea, lo que hizo de aquélla la épica idealizada de la resistencia popular y proletaria contra la agresión del fascismo. Desde un punto de vista militar, el resultado fue desastroso: la revolución deshizo el Ejército republicano, sustituido por una fuerzas irregulares y poco disciplinadas, basadas en milicias de partidos y sindicatos, mandadas por oficiales improvisados. El entusiasmo de los milicianos impidió ciertamente el triunfo de la sublevación. Pero hasta la primavera de 1937, la República no pudo disponer de un ejército verdaderamente operativo: ésa fue la primera razón de su derrota.

EL AVANCE SOBRE MADRID

Inicialmente, el objetivo de las tropas rebeldes era Madrid. Para finales de septiembre de 1936, las tropas del Ejército de África mandadas por Franco estaban a las puertas de la capital por el sur, tras haber avanzado más de 500 kilómetros, ocupado gran parte del sur y del oeste de España y tomado ciudades importantes como Badajoz y Toledo. En el norte, las tropas de Mola habían, a su vez, conquistado San Sebastián y la línea de la frontera vasco-francesa, y amenazaban Madrid desde las sierras situadas al norte de la ciudad (Somosierra, Los Leones). La guerra era todavía una guerra "menor". Era básicamente una guerra de columnas, en la que ambos mandos empleaban pocos efectivos. La infantería era el arma principal, y aviación, artillería y marina jugaban un papel secundario. Pero la guerra había mostrado ya uno de sus aspectos más siniestros y crueles: ambos bandos desencadenaron desde el primer momento la represión a gran escala en sus respectivas retaguardias. Los militares rebeldes fusilaron a afiliados a los partidos de izquierda y sindicatos, a cientos de maestros—símbolo del laicismo republicano—a algunos intelectuales republicanos (el más conocido, Federico García Lorca), incluso a 16 sacerdotes próximos al nacionalismo vasco; los republicanos—casi siempre, simples patrullas de asesinos incontrolados, esto es, no las autoridades republicanas—ejecutaron a personas conocidas por sus opiniones conservadoras y católicas, a militantes de los partidos de la derecha, a militares sospechosos, a numerosísimos sacerdotes y religiosos (un total de 6.500 a lo largo de toda la guerra). Badajoz, donde los nacionales fusilaron a 2.000–4.000 personas en agosto de 1936, y las alocuciones del general Queipo de Llano desde Sevilla, quedaron como símbolos de la violencia franquista; los asaltos a las cárceles de Madrid y Bilbao y los fusilamientos de Paracuellos del Jarama, localidad próxima a Madrid, fueron la expresión del terror republicano. En total, unas 60.000 personas serían ejecutadas en la zona de Franco—en los años de la guerra—y unas 30.000 como mínimo en la zona republicana.

La ofensiva sobre Madrid comenzó en octubre de 1936 y tuvo varias fases, todas ya de gran intensidad militar, pues Franco no abandonó el asalto hasta febrero de 1937, cuando sus tropas fueron contenidas en la batalla en torno al río Jarama. La resistencia de Madrid, dirigida por una Junta de Defensa presidida por el general Miaja, reforzó la leyenda del antifascismo español. Probó, además, otras dos cosas: que la República empezaba a organizar sus ejércitos y que la guerra se internacionalizaba. Lo primero fue posible a partir de la formación, a principios de septiembre, de un Gobierno de coalición presidido por el socialista Francisco Largo Caballero (1869–1946), en el que los comunistas tenían dos puestos y al que poco después se incorporaron cuatro ministros anarquistas. En la defensa de Madrid, Miaja dispuso, entre otros efectivos, de ocho brigadas de nueva creación, dos de ellas integradas por miembros de las Brigadas Internacionales; y pudo usar también carros y aviones soviéticos. Franco empleó, a su vez, tanquetas y aviones alemanes e italianos.

Los esfuerzos (no demasiado consistentes) de Gran Bretaña y Francia por imponer la no-intervención internacional en España y localizar así el conflicto, habían, por tanto, fracasado. Alemania e Italia reconocieron a Franco en noviembre de 1936. Alemania envió ese mismo mes la Legión Cóndor, compuesta por un centenar de aviones con pilotos y mandos alemanes, y enviaría, además, unos 5.000 asesores a lo largo de toda la guerra. Italia mandó unos 70.000 soldados, que entraron en combate a partir de enero de 1937. La Unión Soviética puso al servicio de la República unos 2.000 asesores (instructores, aviadores, artilleros, etcétera); el total de alistados en las Brigadas Internacionales fue de unos 60.000 hombres. Franco recibió unos 1.200 aviones alemanes e italianos, y unos 350 tanques; la República, 1.300 aviones (aunque por la disposición de sus aeropuertos y la distancia entre éstos y los frentes no pudo hacer pleno uso de ellos) y 900 tanques, casi todos de la Unión Soviética. La guerra de columnas del verano de 1936 iba a convertirse en una guerra total entre dos ejércitos cada vez mejor equipados y más numerosos; unos 500.000 soldados por cada bando en la primavera de 1937; la artillería y la aviación—con bombardeos sobre poblaciones civiles—cobrarían desde entonces, según los frentes, la misma importancia que la infantería.

LA PROGRESIÓN DE FRANCO

Tras una última y también fallida ofensiva sobre Madrid, desde Guadalajara, en marzo de 1937, llevada principalmente por las tropas italianas—4 divisiones, 35.000 hombres, aviones, carros de combate, etcétera—Franco llevó la guerra al norte. El 31 de marzo de ese año, tras bombardeos masivos de la aviación y de la artillería, desencadenó un gran ataque contra el País Vasco, región autónoma (desde octubre de 1936) bajo un Gobierno encabezado por el Partido Nacionalista Vasco. El 26 de abril, aviones alemanes destruyeron Guernica, capital espiritual de los vascos, un hecho que conmocionó a la opinión internacional; Bilbao, la principal ciudad de la región, centro de la industria siderúrgica y del sector naval españoles y el primer puerto del país, se rindió el 19 de junio tras durísimos combates. Días después, Franco conseguía otro gran éxito, esta vez moral y psicológico: el 1 de julio, 48 obispos hicieron público un documento en apoyo del levantamiento militar; la guerra se legitimaba así como una cruzada en defensa de la religión. Pese a un brillante contrataque republicano cerca de Madrid—en Brunete—diseñado por el nuevo jefe del Estado Mayor Central republicano, el general Vicente Rojo (1894–1966), Franco, que supo reaccionar a tiempo y detener la contra-ofensiva, se apoderó de Santander en agosto, y de Asturias en octubre, por lo que dominaba ya toda la cornisa cantábrica y los principales centros mineros y siderúrgicos del país, hecho determinante para la victoria final.

Además, el 1 de octubre de 1936, la plana mayor de la sublevación había nombrado al general Franco jefe del Gobierno y del Estado de la España nacional, y Generalísimo de sus ejércitos. Franco pensaba crear un Estado nuevo basado, según dijera, en principios totalitarios y de autoridad, un Estado unitario y fuerte, sin autonomías regionales; una dictadura militar, sin partidos políticos ni sindicatos libres, e inspirada en las doctrinas sociales de la Iglesia católica. En abril de 1937, ordenó la unificación en un movimiento o partido único (Falange Española Tradicionalista y de las J.O.N.S., siglas de algunos pequeños partidos fascistas) de todas las fuerzas políticas que habían apoyado el levantamiento del 18 de julio del 36 (falangistas, católicos, monárquicos, tradicionalistas). En enero de 1938, creó su primer Gobierno y en abril, promulgó el Fuero del Trabajo, especie de carta fundacional del nuevo Estado, que era definido como un régimen "nacional-sindicalista", bajo doble inspiración católica y fascista.

Franco había impuesto una completa unidad de mando en su zona, factor de importancia decisiva para el resultado de la guerra. El contraste con la evolución política de la zona republicana era revelador. En Aragón mandaba desde julio de 1936 un Consejo o Gobierno anarquista. En Cataluña, existía desde entonces un verdadero dualismo de poder: de una parte, la Generalitat, el gobierno autónomo regional integrado por catalanistas de izquierda, anarquistas y comunistas; de otro, el poderoso Comité Central de Milicias Antifascistas de Cataluña, bajo el liderazgo de la CNT, la sindical anarco-sindicalista, que controlaba fábricas, suministros y las milicias armadas. La autoridad del Gobierno central republicano era allí inexistente. En mayo de 1937, estalló una guerra civil dentro de la Guerra Civil, cuando milicias de la CNT y del POUM (Partido Obrero de Unificación Marxista), un pequeño partido filotrotskista, se enfrentaron con las fuerzas de orden público de la Generalitat por el control de determinados enclaves de la capital catalana. La insurrección fue dominada, pero a un precio político y moral muy alto. El jefe del Gobierno central, el socialista Largo Caballero, dimitió—no quiso ilegalizar al POUM, como le exigían los comunistas y los asesores soviéticos—y fue reemplazado por un nuevo Gobierno presidido por otro socialista, el doctor Juan Negrín (1892–1952), en el que los comunistas eran ya la pieza clave del poder, tal vez porque fueron quienes más claramente comprendieron que la lógica de la guerra exigía la total unificación política y militar de la zona republicana. La autoridad del Gobierno central fue reafirmada en Cataluña y poco después, en Aragón. Por debajo de la visión romántica de la resistencia antifascista de la España republicana, aparecía otra realidad: la progresiva penetración de los comunistas (liderados por José Díaz y Dolores Ibárruri) en el aparato del poder político y militar del bando republicano, con una política que anteponía la victoria en la guerra a cualquier otra consideración, incluida la revolución.[9] Para quienes, como George Orwell, voluntario en las milicias del POUM, habían idealizado el carácter proletario de la lucha española, la revolución había sido traicionada: Orwell, como otros miembros del POUM acusados de agentes provocadores del fascismo, tuvo que huir perseguido por la policía bajo control del partido comunista (detenido, el líder del POUM Andrés Nín murió torturado).

LA VICTORIA FINAL

Otra fuerte contra-ofensiva de sus ejércitos, desencadenada en diciembre de 1937, permitió a la República recuperar Teruel, una de las capitales aragonesas. Pero los nacionales retomaron la ciudad el 22 de febrero del año siguiente—tras durísimos y prolongados combates, librados bajo terribles condiciones atmosféricas—y luego, ya en marzo de 1938, lanzaron una gran ofensiva por el valle del Ebro hacia el Mediterráneo, cuyas playas alcanzaron el 15 de abril, cortando en dos el territorio republicano. Franco cometió entonces el error estratégico de dirigir sus ejércitos hacia el sur, hacia Valencia, por un terreno excepcionalmente difícil—las sierras del Maestrazgo—circunstancia que facilitó la defensa republicana. Fue una operación que pudo traerle graves complicaciones militares, a pesar de que para entonces, primavera-verano de 1938, había logrado ya la superioridad aérea y la superioridad naval sobre sus enemigos. La flota republicana se vio obligada a permanecer prácticamente refugiada en sus puertos; el suministro de armamento y material bélico desde la Unión Soviética a la República a través del Mediterráneo quedó seriamente dañado.

Pero la República no estaba aún vencida. El Gobierno del enérgico Negrín había reforzado la disciplina del Ejército Popular y reorganizado eficazmente sus efectivos militares. Rojo volvió a sorprender militarmente a Franco. El 25 de julio de 1938, el Ejército republicano cruzó el río Ebro por varios puntos y avanzó en profundidad amenazando con romper la línea de las tropas nacionales. Pero, otra vez, Franco supo reaccionar a tiempo y mover sus ejércitos para detener el avance republicano. Luego, a partir del 11 de agosto, inició una agotadora guerra de desgaste contra las posiciones enemigas, mediante sucesivos ataques frontales, cuyo objetivo era la destrucción definitiva del Ejército Popular. La batalla del Ebro fue la más áspera y demoledora de la guerra: murieron en ella unos 20.000 soldados, y las bajas totales sumaron cerca de los 60.000 hombres por cada bando. Aunque la República aún retenía Cataluña, Madrid, gran parte de La Mancha, Valencia y el sureste español, y disponía de un ejército integrado por cuatro grandes cuerpos y un total de 49 divisiones (ocho menos que Franco), la suerte de la guerra estaba decidida: la batalla del Ebro había destrozado la moral y la capacidad operativa del Ejército Popular.

El 10 de diciembre, Franco inició la ofensiva sobre Cataluña, sobre el papel una de las operaciones mejor diseñadas por sus estados mayores en toda la guerra. En realidad, lo que ocurrió fue el hundimiento fulminante de Cataluña sin apenas resistencia, un hecho que indignaría al presidente Azaña que siempre pensó que Cataluña no había contribuido suficientemente al esfuerzo militar (lo que en parte era cierto, y en parte injusto: Barcelona, por ejemplo, sufrió unos 500 ataques aéreos a lo largo de la contienda). Barcelona cayó el 26 de enero de 1939, y las tropas de Franco llegaron días después a la frontera con Francia. 500.000 personas salieron penosamente (huyendo de cualquier forma) hacia el exilio (temporal o permanente), entre ellas el propio presidente de la República, Azaña, y el general Vicente Rojo.

Sólo Negrín y sus asesores comunistas creían posible prolongar la resistencia, lo que dado el estado de ambos ejércitos y la situación internacional—definida por la voluntad de las democracias occidentales de apaciguar a Hitler y Mussolini, los principales valedores de Franco—resultaba probablemente imposible. En cualquier caso, el 4 de marzo de 1939, el teniente coronel Casado, jefe del Ejército del Centro y cabeza visible del sector abandonista y no-comunista de la República, se sublevó contra Negrín y formó un Consejo Nacional de Defensa para negociar la paz con Franco. Madrid fue durante varios días escenario de violentos enfrentamientos entre las tropas de Casado y las tropas de Negrín, en los que murieron unas 2.000 personas. Franco, además, no quiso negociación alguna. Exigió la rendición incondicional. Sus tropas entraron en Madrid el 28 de marzo de 1939; el día 30, ocuparon Alicante, la última ciudad libre republicana en cuyo puerto unas 15.000 personas aguardaban inútilmente poder huir por mar. El 1 de abril, Franco proclamó la victoria: la guerra había terminado. Habían muerto unas 300.000 personas, de ellas unas 140.000 en el frente y el resto, en las retaguardias de ambas zonas. Otras 300.000 marcharon, para no regresar, al exilio, y un número similar—300.000—sufrió penas de prisión en las cárceles de Franco entre 1939 y 1945 (las cifras de ejecutados en esos años pueden estimarse entre un mínimo de 28.000—cifra admitida por el régimen de Franco—y un máximo de 200.000, cifra manejada por la oposición al mismo, y probablemente exagerada). Las destrucciones de edificios, puentes, ferrocarriles, carreteras, barcos, cultivos y ganado fueron incalculables. Los años de 1939 a 1942 fueron años de hambre en España.

La República de 1931 había sido el esfuerzo más serio que se había hecho en la historia de España para modernizar el país desde una perspectiva democrática. Franco (1892–1975), un militar conservador y católico, de pequeña estatura, prudente e inexpresivo, que creía que el liberalismo y los partidos políticos habían sido la causa de los males de España, creó un régimen autoritario y de poder personal que duró hasta su muerte en 1975.[10] Tres influen-

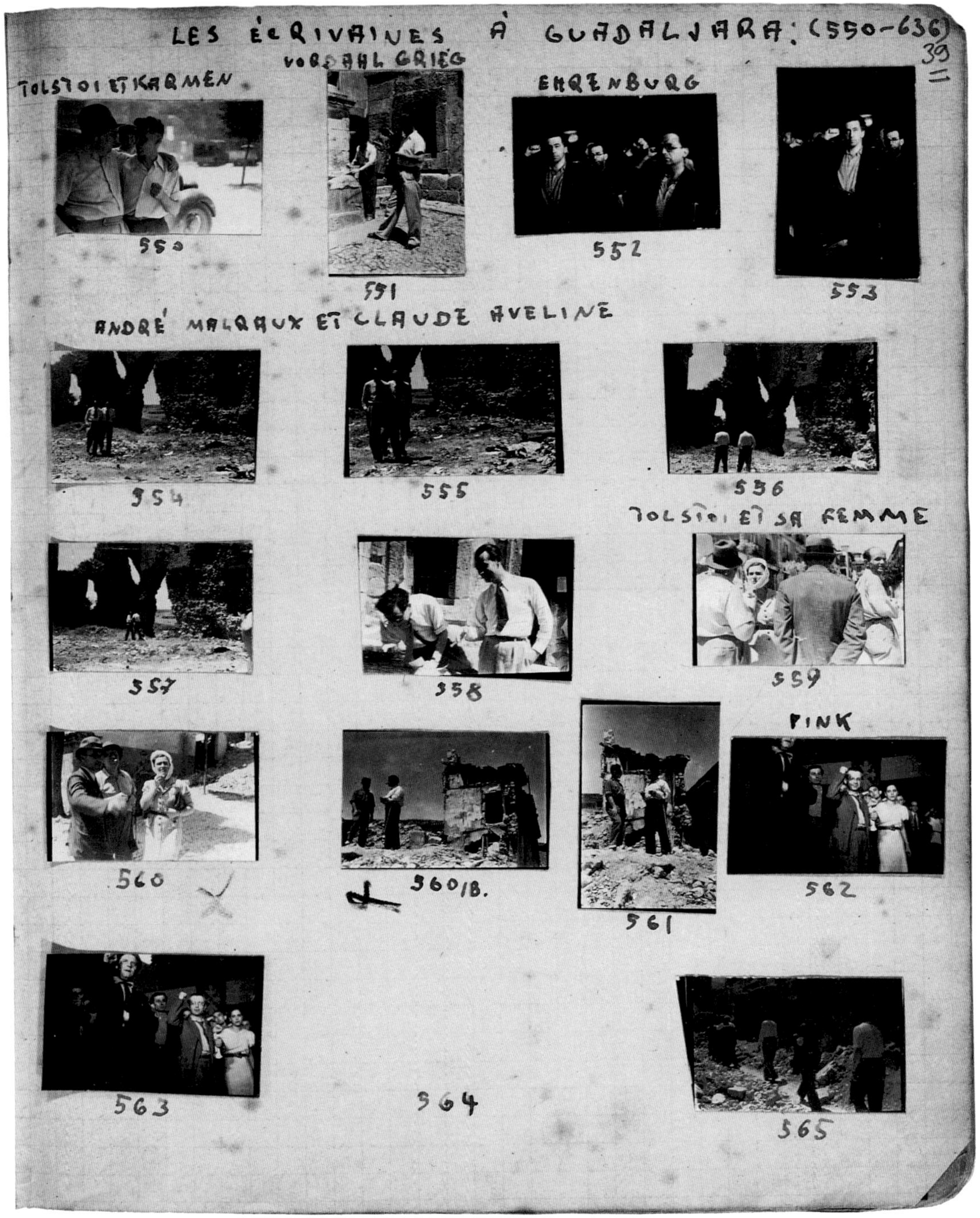

Fotografías del Congreso Internacional de Escritores por la Defensa de la Cultura, Valencia, julio de 1937. De los cuadernos de Robert Capa. Fotografías de Gerda Taro cias definieron el nuevo régimen: las ideas fascistas de la Falange, el pensamiento social-conservador de la Iglesia católica y los principios de orden, unidad nacional y autoridad de los militares. El régimen de Franco fue inicialmente un régimen totalitario, claramente alineado con la Alemania de Hitler y la Italia de Mussolini. Desde 1945 se definió como una monarquía social y católica (aunque el rey no fue restaurado). Sólo desde 1957–1961, después de dos décadas de economía nacionalista que casi llevaron al país a la bancarrota, el régimen de Franco liberalizó la economía y pudo comenzar la transformación que haría de España un país urbano, industrial y moderno.

Precisamente porque fue un gran momento de la humanidad (parafraseando lo que Péguy dijo en su día del *affaire* Dreyfus), la guerra española dejó una huella indeleble en la memoria histórica: el recuerdo de la guerra y de sus terribles consecuencias, el deseo de evitar la repetición de un fracaso colectivo como aquél, fue, por ejemplo, uno de los factores que favorecieron el espíritu de consenso y reconciliación que hizo posible la transición de España a la democracia a la muerte de Franco. La guerra produjo, desde luego, miles de libros, ensayos y artículos, centenares de novelas, numerosas películas y obras de teatro (seguía produciéndolos sesenta-setenta años después), muchos de ellos convertidos en seguida en clásicos: obras de arte como la fotografía de Capa *Muerte de un miliciano* (tomada en septiembre de 1936, en Cerro Muriano, Córdoba) y el *Guernica* de Picasso; testimonios personales como *Testamento español* de Koestler, *Homenaje a Cataluña* de Orwell, o *Los grandes cementerios bajo la luna* de Bernanos; novelas como *Por quién doblan las campanas* de Hemingway y *La esperanza* de Malraux (o el ciclo de novelas de Max Aub titulado *El laberinto mágico* o *La velada en Benicarló*, la novela dialogada escrita por el propio presidente republicano Azaña en 1937).

Buena parte de la memoria de la guerra reforzó inevitablemente la visión de España como un país trágico, violento, romántico, al tiempo generoso e idealista (antifascismo), al tiempo sangriento y brutal. Incluso, como el escritor Jorge Semprún haría decir al protagonista de su obra *La guerre est finie* (1965), la guerra terminaría convirtiéndose en un mito para antiguos combatientes y hasta en la buena conciencia lírica de la izquierda. Pero otra parte de ella, la más sustantiva—la contenida, por ejemplo, en los muchos y buenos libros de historia generados por la guerra, como los escritos por historiadores como Hugh Thomas, Gabriel Jackson, Raymond Carr y Edward Malefakis—haría posible entender la guerra en su verdadera perspectiva. Ello ayudaría a comprender por lo menos dos extremos: *primero*, que la guerra tuvo profundas connotaciones ideológicas y políticas (que, en otras palabras, no fue primariamente un conflicto de clases) y que la causa última de la Guerra Civil—como en el caso de otras guerras civiles—fue la división moral del país; *segundo*, que el proceso desencadenante de la Guerra Civil (la conspiración militar, la sublevación misma) se articuló a través de decisiones en última instancia individuales, que—por el mero hecho de serlo—pudieron, por tanto, o no haberse producido o haber sido de otra forma.

Por sus características, por sus implicaciones nacionales e internacionales, por el clima moral existente cuando estalló, por el resultado final (triunfo de Franco, ejecuciones, dictadura), la Guerra Civil española no dejó—como dejó, por ejemplo, la Guerra Civil norteamericana—una memoria épica y admirable. La memoria de la Guerra Civil española iba a ser una memoria trágica, el recuerdo de un horror incomprensible y probablemente innecesario e inútil. El historiador Jover Zamora la definiría como una verdadera crisis de civilización. Pensando en España, Orwell le comentó en cierta ocasión a Koestler que "la historia se paró en 1936".[11]

ESPAÑA
Gijón
Santander
Bilbao
Hendaye
Perpignan
Portbou
Burgos
R. EBRO
Huesca
Grañen
Zaragoza
Belchite
Barcelona
Segovia
Brunete
MADRID
Teruel
Toledo
Uclés
Benicasim
R. TAGUS
Valencia
Albacete
Alicante
Córdoba
Murcia
Sevilla
Málaga
Almería
Gibraltar

 Muerte de un miliciano. Cerro Muriano, frente de Córdoba, 5 de septiembre, 1936

ROBERT CAPA EN ESPAÑA

RICHARD WHELAN

I

En diciembre de 1938 la prestigiosa revista británica *Picture Post* publicó un reportaje fotográfico de once páginas sobre la Guerra Civil española con las fotos del joven de veinticinco años, Robert Capa, y le proclamó "el mejor fotógrafo de guerra del mundo".[1] Más de cuarenta años después de su muerte, nadie ha superado la fuerza extraordinaria y conmovedora de sus reportajes de cinco conflictos bélicos.

Además de documentar la Guerra Civil española, Capa pasó seis meses en China durante 1938 para fotografiar el movimiento de resistencia a la invasión japonesa, y posteriormente cubrió el escenario europeo de la Segunda Guerra Mundial (1941–45), la Primera Guerra Árabe-Israelí (1948), y la Guerra Franco-Indochina (1954). El 25 de mayo de 1954, mientras fotografiaba las maniobras francesas en el delta del río Rojo, Capa murió al pisar una mina anti-persona. Tenía cuarenta años.

Nació en 1913 con el nombre de André Friedmann en Budapest, donde sus padres tenían un elegante salón de alta costura. Ya de adolescente sintió un precoz interés por la reforma social y política. Su mentor, poeta y pintor, Lajos Kassak, dirigía un grupo socialista y de arte *avant-garde*. Entre los trabajos publicados en *Munka* (trabajo), la revista de dicho grupo, se hallaban las fotografías de los grandes reformistas americanos Jacob Riis y Lewis W. Hine, cuyas imágenes cargadas de sensibilidad hacia la inmigración, la pobreza y la explotación infantil sin duda influyeron en las fotografías de Capa de los refugiados, de la vida entre ruinas, de los niños soportando las dificultades y los horrores de la guerra.

Durante su etapa de estudiante de secundaria, André aún no había ni tan siquiera pensado en convertirse en fotógrafo. Aspiraba a ser periodista, ya que esa profesión le permitiría combinar su amor por la política y la literatura. Sin embargo, aún siendo brillante, sus perspectivas de ingresar en la Universidad húngara no eran prometedoras, ya que la dictadura proto-fascista y anti-semita limitaba estrictamente el número de estudiantes judíos que podían acceder a dicha institución. Como resultado de su participación en las manifestaciones y las protestas contra el régimen represor, André hubo de exiliarse de Hungría en julio de 1931, a los diecisiete años de edad.

Viajó a Berlín para estudiar periodismo en la *Deutsche Hochschule für Politik*. En Berlín participó en algunos grupos populares de discusión y asistió a las conferencias que organizaba Karl Korsch, que entonces era un alto cargo del Partido Comunista Alemán, antes de que lo expulsaran por defender una postura crítica frente a la política de Stalin. Korsch defendía una sociedad anarquista ideal, y estaba convencido de que España era la nación en la que podría generarse una sociedad de esas características.

El 12 de abril de 1931, el pueblo español había elegido un Gobierno republicano en las urnas. Dos días más tarde, el rey Alfonso XIII abdicaba, y se proclamaba la República en España. En junio de ese mismo año, Korsch asistió en Madrid como invitado a un congreso de la Confederación Nacional del Trabajo (CNT), la fuerte organización sindical anarquista (anarco-sindicalista). Lo que allí vio le llenó de entusiasmo y, a su regreso a Berlín, publicó un artículo optimista sobre la posibilidad de que en España pudiera desarrollarse una alternativa al comunismo estalinista.

Cuando Capa visitó España por primera vez para hacer un reportaje fotográfico sobre la Guerra Civil en 1936, se creyó en la obligación de buscar a las divisiones anarco-sindicalistas que luchaban en los alrededores de Córdoba. El hombre de su famosa fotografía del miliciano recién abatido llevaba una gorra con las iniciales de la CNT bordadas.

En Berlín, el ascenso del partido nazi intensificó el compromiso político de André Friedmann. La depresión económica mundial afectó seriamente al negocio familiar, y dejó sus estudios cuando sus padres ya no pudieron seguir mandándole dinero; consiguió un trabajo como chico de los recados y ayudante de la destacada agencia de fotografía Dephot. Fue allí donde se inició en la fotografía

Picture Post, 3 de diciembre de 1938. La página que presentaba a Capa como "el mejor fotógrafo de guerra del mundo". El texto dice: "los lectores habituales de *Picture Post* saben que no alabamos a la ligera las obras que publicamos. Estas son sencillamente las mejores fotografías de acción en el frente jamás sacadas. Son obra de Robert Capa... Le gusta trabajar en España más que en ningún otro lugar del mundo. Es un apasionado demócrata y vive para hacer fotografías".

Vu, 23 de septiembre de 1936. "La Guerre Civile en Espagne..." (La Guerra Civil española: cómo cayeron, cómo huyeron). Primera publicación de la foto *Muerte de un miliciano*.

periodística. Su primer encargo importante resultó muy apropiado: a finales de 1932, el joven admirador de Trotsky cubrió una conferencia que daba en Copenhague el revolucionario ruso en el exilio.

Con la llegada de Hitler al poder a principios de 1933, André se vio obligado a trasladarse a París, donde halló enormes dificultades para encontrar trabajo durante casi dos años. Se enamoró de una joven refugiada alemana, Gerta Pohorylle, a quien enseñó los rudimentos de la fotografía. Ella, a su vez, tuvo la idea de vender las fotografías de André bajo el nombre de un americano imaginario: Robert Capa, el cual, siempre según Gerda, había obtenido un gran éxito en Estados Unidos. El ardid funcionó pero pronto fue descubierto, y André no tuvo más remedio que convertirse en Robert Capa. Posteriormente, Gerta cambiaría su nombre y pasaría a llamarse Gerda Taro, tomando su nuevo apellido de Taro Okamoto, escultor japonés, amigo de ella y de Capa en París.

En la primavera de 1935, el anterior jefe de André/Capa en Dephot le organizó un viaje a España para trabajar en varios encargos para unas revistas alemanas. Primero fue a San Sebastián donde trabajó en la historia de la vida cotidiana del boxeador Paulino Uzcudun, quien tenía programado su tercer combate con el campeón alemán Max Schmeling el 7 de julio en Berlín. Seguidamente, Capa se dirigió a Madrid para fotografiar a Juan de la Cierva quien, en 1923, inventó un artefacto precursor del helicóptero. Desgraciadamente, se negó a enseñárselo a Capa alegando que lo único que le motivaba ya era la lingüística, un tema con poco interés fotográfico. Sin embargo, en Madrid, Capa consiguió fotografiar al teniente coronel Emilio Herrera, uno de los pilotos más famosos de España que se preparaba para un ascenso en globo hasta una altitud de 25.000 metros y esperaba con ello batir el récord mundial.[2] Después de cubrir en Madrid el 14 de abril el gran desfile conmemorativo del cuarto aniversario de la República española, Capa se dirigió a Sevilla para fotografiar la feria y la Semana Santa.[3]

Se sentía muy afín a la cordialidad, exuberancia y generosidad del pueblo español, y las cartas que enviaba a su familia, repletas de anécdotas en las que narraba los contratiempos con los que se había topado, se asemejaban a la novela picaresca española. De hecho, España y Hungría tienen mucho en común: ambas son naciones ganaderas, amantes del pimentón, tienen una fuerte tradición gitana, y han vivido largos periodos de dominación islámica y de gobierno de los Habsburgo.

En París, durante la primavera de 1936, Capa fotografió los tumultuosos desfiles y mítines políticos que precedieron y sucedieron a la elección de la coalición antifascista y prosoviética de liberales, socialistas y comunistas conocida como el Frente Popular y liderada por el socialista Léon Blum. Aunque por aquel entonces la Unión Soviética había adoptado por fin una posición firme contra Hitler y Mussolini, la Liga de Naciones favorecía una política de pacificación, y Estados Unidos se mantenía apartada en su política de neutralidad aislacionista.

El estallido de la Guerra Civil española en julio de 1936 brindó finalmente a los antifascistas la oportunidad de enfrentarse militarmente al fascismo. Tanto Capa como Taro creían que era absolutamente vital utilizar sus cámaras como medio para obtener el apoyo mundial a la República española y a la causa antifascista.

Ambos tuvieron su primera oportunidad apenas dos semanas

después del estallido de la guerra. Gracias a que Capa había realizado recientemente varios reportajes muy impactantes que se publicaron en la prestigiosa revista francesa de fotografía *Vu*, Lucien Vogel, el propietario de dicha publicación, invitó a Capa y a Taro a unirse a un grupo de periodistas que volaría rumbo a Barcelona.[4]

Ese 5 de agosto, al volver a la capital catalana, Capa se encontró con una ciudad radicalmente distinta a la que conociera en la primavera de 1935. La ciudad acomodada y burguesa había sufrido una revolución proletaria tras lograr reprimir rápidamente el alzamiento militar. Los trabajadores se habían apropiado de las fábricas, las tiendas y los restaurantes, y miles de ellos engrosaban las filas de las milicias que se habían organizado a toda velocidad.

En la estación de ferrocarril de Barcelona, Capa y Taro fotografiaron a los soldados destinados al frente de Aragón despidiéndose de sus mujeres y novias. Posteriormente, tras pasar en la ciudad una semana o unos diez días, los fotógrafos se dirigieron a ese frente donde, a mediados de agosto, la situación había llegado a un punto muerto, y así permanecería durante más de un año. El combate se limitaba a poco más que escaramuzas esporádicas, en su mayoría durante la noche, por lo que, obviamente, de poco les servían a los fotógrafos.

Capa y Taro fotografiaron en los alrededores del frente de Huesca a los milicianos acampando en refugios improvisados, guarneciendo los puestos de ametralladora y artillería, e incluso ayudando a los agricultores de las granjas colectivizadas cercanas a recoger y trillar el trigo. Poco después, los fotógrafos se dirigieron hacia el sudoeste por una razón más que importante: el idioma en el que ambos se manejaban mejor era el alemán, y había muchos emigrados alemanes sirviendo en las milicias entre Huesca y Zaragoza. Muchos de ellos habían asistido en Barcelona a las Olimpiadas de los Trabajadores organizadas desde la izquierda en respuesta a las Olimpiadas Oficiales celebradas en el Berlín de Hitler aquel verano.

Capa y Taro visitaron el pueblo de Tardienta, cuartel general de la Centuria Comunista Thälmann alemana, pero pasaron la mayor parte del tiempo con la columna del POUM que había establecido su base militar en Leciñena, a unos dieciocho kilómetros al nordeste de Zaragoza, (la misma milicia del POUM a la que se incorporaría George Orwell ese invierno). Al igual que los anarco-sindicalistas, el Partido Obrero de Unificación Marxista (POUM), de orientación trotskista, apoyaban al Gobierno durante la Guerra Civil tan sólo porque la victoria republicana era un prerrequisito indispensable para la revolución.

Capa y Taro se encontraron con que en Leciñena apenas había actividad, lo mismo que en los frentes de Madrid, Guadarrama y Toledo, como no tardarían en descubrir. Sin embargo, había un frente del que llegaban noticias muy alentadoras. Durante la segunda mitad de agosto, el Gobierno de Madrid había iniciado una ofensiva para recuperar Córdoba. Día tras día el Gobierno comunicaba nuevos avances, e incluso llegó a declarar—falsamente—que las tropas habían entrado en la ciudad. Si lo que uno quería era fotografiar victorias republicanas, aparentemente, tenía que estar en el frente de Córdoba. También allí actuaban las milicias más idealistas de la CNT.

II

Fue en el frente de Córdoba donde Capa hizo su fotografía más conocida, quizá la mejor fotografía de guerra realizada jamás: la del miliciano republicano español recién alcanzado por las balas. Es la foto de Capa más controvertida, y durante los años setenta, se levantó la polémica sobre el lugar en el que había sido tomada y sobre si se trataba de un documento gráfico preparado o no. Sin embargo, recientemente, la controversia ha llegado definitivamente a su fin a favor de Capa al descubrirse la identidad del hombre de la imagen: Federico Borrell García, muerto en Cerro Muriano, a doce kilómetros al norte de Córdoba, el 5 de septiembre de 1936.

Logré cerciorarme de que Capa y Taro estaban en Cerro Muriano ese mismo día gracias a algunos datos circunstanciales que pude averiguar mientras trabajaba en mi biografía sobre Capa. En su libro *The Spanish Cockpit* (El campo de batalla español) (1937) el periodista suizo Franz Borkenau narra que presenció esa tarde con dos fotógrafos de la revista francesa *Vu* una batalla en Cerro Muriano.[5] Eran Hans Namuth, que había conocido a Capa en París antes del estallido de la Guerra Civil española, y su amigo Georg Reisner. Namuth y Reisner fotografiaron a los habitantes aterrorizados del pueblo mientras huían de un ataque aéreo fascista. Cuando entrevisté a Namuth, me dijo que no había visto a Capa y a Taro en Cerro Muriano. Pero, unas semanas más tarde, cuando vio el número de la revista francesa *Vu* del 23 de septiembre de 1936 en la que aparecían (en la página opuesta a la del soldado abatido de Capa) las fotos de Capa de algunas de las personas que también fotografiaran Namuth y Reisner en la misma carretera de las afueras de Cerro Muriano, Namuth advirtió que Capa sí había estado ese mismo día.[6]

Este dato proporcionaba la clave esencial para determinar con precisión el lugar en el que Capa había disparado la fotografía *Muerte de un miliciano*. En las copias originales conservadas en los archivos de la herencia de Capa con la numeración cronológica original, los números en la secuencia de fotos a la que pertenece la de la *Muerte de un miliciano* preceden inmediatamente a la serie de los refugiados de Cerro Muriano. (Desgraciadamente, la mayor parte de las películas de España fueron reducidas a imágenes individuales por su ayudante de París, y se han perdido buena parte de los negativos originales de la secuencia de la *Muerte de un miliciano*, entre los cuales estaba el de la famosa fotografía). La numeración de las copias originales sugiere claramente que Capa sacó la foto del soldado en Cerro Muriano el 5 de septiembre de 1936. Capa confirmó repetidas veces a lo largo de su vida que había hecho la foto en el frente de Córdoba.

La polémica en torno a que Capa preparara o no la foto fue iniciada a mediados de los años setenta por el anciano periodista británico O'Dowd Gallagher, quien afirmaba haber compartido con Capa la habitación de un hotel en la frontera oeste de España y Francia en el momento en que se sacó la famosa foto. Pero, casi cuarenta años después de los acontecimientos, parecía evidente que la memoria le había tendido una trampa a Gallagher. Sin duda de buena fe, había confundido a Capa con otra persona con quien compartió habitación en ese lugar en 1936. Estoy convencido de que Capa y Gallagher no coincidieron hasta enero de 1939 cuando compartieron el mismo hotel en Barcelona. La posibilidad de que en efecto pueda ocurrir un fallo de memoria de estas características me quedó clarísimamente demostrado mientras realizaba las entrevistas para mi biografía sobre Capa. Al entrevistar al dibujante de viñetas Bill Mauldin, merecedor de toda mi confianza tras su detallada narración de recuerdos, me dijo que había coincidido con Capa en el frente del río Roer en la primavera de 1945. Me sorprendió, ya que estaba bastante convencido de que Capa estaba en otro lugar por esas fechas. Sin embargo, Mauldin me aseguraba que recordaba con claridad haber estado con Capa y, para probarlo, describió las fotos que allí se sacaron y que publicó la revista *Life*. Sus descripciones eran tan precisas que pude reconocer las fotos inmediatamente en cuanto las vi en la revista. No obstante, las había hecho George Silk y no Capa, que en ese momento realizaba un reportaje sobre los paracaidistas que aterrizaron al este del Rin.

Gallagher narró la misma historia a tres entrevistadores distintos a lo largo de varios años, pero las evidentes contradicciones que surgían en sus tres relatos desacreditaban en efecto su testimonio. En primer lugar, Gallagher le contó a Phillip Knightley—escritor británico que publicó la historia en su libro *The First Casualty: From the Crimea to Vietnam; The War Correspondent as Hero, Propagandist, and Myth Maker* (1975)—que "durante varios días no había habido mucha acción y Capa y otros se quejaron a los oficiales republicanos porque no podían tomar fotos. Al final... un oficial republicano les dijo que movilizaría un destacamento hasta unas trincheras cercanas para que simularan una serie de maniobras con el objeto de que las fotografiaran."[7]

En 1978, Jorge Lewinski publicó en su libro *The Camera at War* su entrevista con Gallagher, en la que el periodista afirmaba que fueron las tropas de Franco, y no las republicanas, las que escenificaron las maniobras:

> *En España empecé por Hendaya en Francia, en la frontera española próxima a San Sebastián. La mayoría de los reporteros y fotógrafos nos hospedábamos en un pequeño hotel destartalado. Nos introdujimos en la España de Franco a través del río Irún, una vez que nos dieron permiso los oficiales de prensa de Franco en Burgos... En una ocasión, sólo invitaron a los fotógrafos... y Capa me lo contó. Les simularon escenas de batalla. Las tropas de Franco vestían de "uniforme" y estaban armadas, y simulaban situaciones de ataque y de defensa. Utilizaron bombas de humo para ambientar la escena.*[8]

Sin embargo, es imposible que Capa hubiera tenido nunca algo que ver con las tropas de Franco. El fotógrafo, judío y profundamente anti-fascista, cubrió la Guerra Civil española absolutamente comprometido con el bando republicano. Es más, en el verano de 1936 era ya un fotógrafo conocido por su afiliación a varias publicaciones francesas de izquierda, por lo que difícilmente podría ser bienvenido en territorio franquista, de no ser para arrestarlo.

En cualquier caso, es posible documentar los viajes de Capa por

España entre el estallido de la Guerra Civil y la primera publicación de su fotografía; nunca estuvo a menos de varios cientos de kilómetros de San Sebastián.

Como ya se ha comentado anteriormente, una reciente y dramática revelación ha disipado toda duda sobre la autenticidad de la fotografía. Se ha identificado, sin ningún género de dudas, al hombre de la fotografía como Federico Borrell García, un miliciano de 24 años de edad, natural de Alcoy, cerca de la ciudad de Alicante, en el sureste de España. El responsable de rastrear su identidad fue Mario Brotóns Jordà, un español que falleció recientemente en Alicante. También natural de Alcoy, Brotóns se unió a la milicia republicana de la zona cuando tenía catorce años y estuvo en la batalla de Cerro Muriano el 5 de septiembre de 1936.[9]

Cuando un amigo de Brotóns, Ricardo Bañó, joven historiador de Alcoy, le mencionó que había leído que la fotografía de Capa pudiera haber sido tomada en Cerro Muriano el 5 de septiembre de 1936, Brotóns emprendió la búsqueda. Sabía que el hombre de la fotografía debía haber pertenecido al regimiento miliciano de Alcoy, ya que las cartucheras que llevaba el hombre eran como las que diseñara el comandante de la guarnición de Alcoy y fabricaran los artesanos del cuero de la zona.

Brotóns entonces descubrió en los archivos del Gobierno español en Salamanca y Madrid que sólo hubo una baja en la milicia de Alcoy en Cerro Muriano el 5 de septiembre de 1936: Federico Borrell García. Brotóns volvió a Alcoy con una reproducción de la famosa foto y se la enseñó a Evaristo, el hermano pequeño de Federico que estuvo también en Cerro Muriano aquel fatal día. En realidad Evaristo no presenció la muerte de su hermano pero confirmó que la fotografía coincidía exactamente con la descripción verbal que le habían hecho de aquellas circunstancias, y que el hombre de la fotografía era efectivamente su hermano. La identificación se confirmó una vez examinadas las fotos de familia de Federico.

La imagen de la *Muerte de un miliciano* pertenece a una secuencia que muestra al hombre en cuestión entre un grupo de soldados saltando un barranco y disparando hacia el otro lado. La revista *Vu* publicó la fotografía justo encima de otra de un hombre que caía a su vez exactamente en el mismo lugar. Aunque algunos autores han afirmado que las dos fotos retratan al mismo hombre, tras un minucioso análisis, no hay duda de que son dos hombres distintos. En una de las fotografías de la serie aparecen los dos hombres alineados junto a otros camaradas agitando los rifles. El hombre de la famosa fotografía aparece en el extremo izquierdo; el otro es el tercero desde la izquierda. Éste lleva unas cartucheras en unas correas que cruzan su pecho en forma de X, en contraste con las correas en verticales paralelas típicas del diseño de Alcoy.

En la serie de las fotos de Capa parece que el fotógrafo corría junto a los soldados cuando éstos iniciaban su ataque al saltar el barranco. Tras tirarse de frente al suelo para disparar un par de veces, los soldados inician su ataque descendiendo una ladera expuesta, en la que por lo menos dos hombres resultaron abatidos al entrar en el radio de las balas enemigas. Es obvio que Capa estaba muy cerca del suelo y que apuntó con la cámara hacia arriba cuando captó la imagen de la *Muerte de un miliciano* y permaneció en esa posición relativamente segura al menos el tiempo suficiente como para fotografiar la caída del otro hombre.

Cerro Muriano, frente de Córdoba, 5 de septiembre, 1936.

Francisco José de Goya y Lucientes, *Los fusilamientos del 3 de mayo, 1808*, 1814.

Aparentemente, el primero en caer fue Federico Borrell García. En la otra fotografía no vemos su cuerpo derribado sobre el terreno ya que presumiblemente el impacto lo impulsó unos metros hacia delante, fuera del campo visual de la segunda fotografía de Capa, antes de caer definitivamente. En la otra fotografía, el hombre ha caído a tal distancia que parece probable que su cuerpo quedara ya en el sitio.

En 1938 Capa publicó un libro con sus fotografías (y las de Gerda Taro) de la Guerra Civil española que tituló *Death in the Making*.[10] Hace algunos años, un crítico escribió que el hecho de que Capa no reprodujera en él la imagen justificaba las dudas sobre su autenticidad. Sin embargo, evidentemente, el crítico no había visto el ejemplar con la sobrecubierta en la que Capa reprodujo la *Muerte de un miliciano*. Lejos de omitir la imagen, le reservó un lugar privilegiado.

Cuando la fotografía de Capa se publicó por primera vez, en septiembre de 1936, los lectores quedaron impactados ya que nadie había visto nada parecido hasta entonces. Las anteriores fotografías de guerra habían sido necesariamente estáticas y tomadas a distancia. En la Primera Guerra Mundial, no tan lejana de aquella época, la cámara habitual era la Graflex mediana, con un fuelle y placas de cuatro a cinco pulgadas. Además de resultar muy llamativa, impedía prácticamente obtener fotos espontáneas, era muy pesada y dificultaba el margen de maniobra del fotógrafo en situaciones de peligro. Por el contrario, la Leica de 35 mm de Capa era discreta y le permitía la máxima movilidad. Con ella se lanzó al torbellino de la guerra, como nadie antes que él se había atrevido a hacerlo.

Cuando, en una ocasión, alguien le preguntó por su fotografía, conocida ya entonces en 1937, Capa respondió: "No hace falta servirse de trucos para sacar fotos en España. No hay que colocar la cámara (es decir, no hay que colocar a los objetos). Las fotos están ahí, y basta con sacarlas. La verdad es la mejor imagen, la mejor propaganda."[11]

Lo grandioso de la fotografía de Capa radica, en último término, en sus implicaciones simbólicas, y no en la exactitud literal con la que se documenta la muerte de un hombre en concreto. Podría decirse que la fotografía aglutina en una sola imagen todo el dramatismo del gran cuadro de Goya de los fusilamientos de los patriotas españoles a manos de las tropas de Napoleón. Es más, la postura del miliciano recuerda a las pinturas de la crucifixión de Cristo. Es la constatación abrumadora del dilema existencial del ser humano, representado por el hombre solitario abatido por un enemigo oculto, como si del mismo Destino se tratara.

Finalmente, aun ahora que conocemos la identidad del miliciano, la fotografía sigue siendo símbolo terrible de todos los soldados republicanos que murieron en la guerra y de la propia España republicana, lanzándose con valentía hacia delante para resultar finalmente derrotada.

III

El 6 de noviembre el ejército de Franco ocupó definitivamente los alrededores de Madrid. Se habían realizado muy pocos preparativos para la defensa, y la guarnición republicana era escasa y estaba mal equipada. La caída de la ciudad parecía inevitable. Cuando el 7 de noviembre comenzó la batalla, tanto soldados como civiles republicanos respondieron al fuego de las metralletas alemanas más avanzadas con las ráfagas de simples fusiles.

Sin embargo, a la mañana siguiente, como por milagro—así lo creyeron los madrileños asediados—apareció la primera Brigada Internacional, integrada por voluntarios de todos los países de Europa (sólo habían llegado unos cuantos americanos). Puesto que Franco recibía el apoyo de Alemania e Italia, muchos hombres y mujeres de Europa y América creían que alistándose como voluntarios para

Cerro Muriano, frente de Córdoba,
5 de septiembre, 1936

apoyar al bando republicano, al menos tendrían la oportunidad de luchar contra el fascismo e infligir una derrota tan decisiva que el movimiento fascista internacional quedaría desacreditado a escala mundial y, por tanto, se impediría la guerra mundial que, por otra parte, parecía cada vez más inevitable. Estos guerrilleros proclamaban desafiantes: "¡Madrid será la tumba del fascismo!"

Se encontraban en pleno entrenamiento en Albacete pero corrieron a ayudar a las tropas republicanas en cuanto fue evidente que todo hombre disponible, independientemente de lo mal entrenado o equipado que estuviera, era necesario para defender Madrid. La llegada de estos refuerzos de aproximadamente 2.000 hombres levantó extraordinariamente la moral de los republicanos y les permitió detener el avance nacional en la Ciudad Universitaria, donde la batalla quedó paralizada.

Capa llegó a Madrid el 18 de noviembre. Durante su primera semana de estancia pasó gran parte del tiempo con la XII Brigada Internacional, cuyo comandante—un hombre enérgico y carismático que se hacía llamar General Lukács—era húngaro y a cuyo comisario político, Gustav Regler, Capa conoció en una asociación de escritores alemanes emigrados en París.[12]

Durante la consiguiente batalla que tuvo lugar en los edificios agrícolas y alrededor de la casa solariega fortificada conocida como el Palacete de la Moncloa y en las granjas prefabricadas vecinas pertenecientes a la Escuela de Agrónomos de la Universidad, Capa se unió al Batallón Thälmann de la XII Brigada, el núcleo formado por comunistas alemanes de la Centuria Thälmann que Capa y Gerda habían visitado en el frente de Aragón en el mes de agosto. Capa también acudió a los mataderos, situados al oeste en tierra de nadie entre los dos frentes, y allí fotografió a los dinamiteros asturianos mientras utilizaban una pequeña catapulta para lanzar granadas a través de los viejos recintos para animales y alcanzar así las líneas enemigas. La idea de que los antiguos mataderos de animales eran ahora mataderos de hombres atrajo enormemente a Capa, que vio reflejada en ella su visión acerca de la ironía grotesca de la guerra.

Probablemente Capa no realizó una visita exhaustiva a la Ciudad Universitaria hasta una semana después de su llegada a Madrid; allí encontró a la XII Brigada Internacional en plena acción de resistencia. Pasó la mayor parte del tiempo con una compañía del Batallón de la Commune de París en la Escuela de Medicina, un edificio inmenso y laberíntico situado en un terreno alto de la zona este del *campus*. Allí tuvieron lugar algunas de las peores batallas, y aunque las escaramuzas continuaban, la mayor parte de las fotografías de Capa sólo mostraban la vigilancia, la camaradería y el valor de los voluntarios franceses y belgas que se habían instalado para defender el edificio.

Las fotografías que Capa realizó de Madrid dejan patente que comenzaba a comprender que la verdad acerca de la guerra se hallaba no sólo en el corazón de la batalla, en el espectáculo oficial, sino también en el límite de las cosas, en los rostros de los soldados soportando el frío, la fatiga y el tedio en el frente, y en los de los civiles desfigurados por el miedo, el sufrimiento y la pérdida. A lo largo de toda su carrera Capa siempre fue ante todo un fotógrafo de personas, y muchas de sus fotografías de guerra no son tanto la crónica de sucesos como el estudio extraordinariamente comprensivo y solidario de las personas que se hallan en situaciones extremas. Raras veces fotografiaba a los muertos o a los heridos graves; por el contrario, se centraba en los supervivientes sobrellevando sus vidas a pesar del dolor provocado por las pérdidas y la destrucción hasta límites insospechados: el triunfo del espíritu humano indómito.

Ya muestren soldados o civiles, las fotografías de Capa se caracterizan por la intimidad y la inmediatez, por la solidaridad y la empatía. Lo terrible de la guerra moderna es que tiende a la deshumanización. Los soldados pueden utilizar sus devastadoras armas de destrucción masiva sólo por el hecho de haber aprendido a conceptuar a sus víctimas no como individuos sino como una categoría: el enemigo. La estrategia de Capa consistía en humanizar la guerra *de nuevo*, en poner de relieve que los que sufren los efectos de la guerra son individuos y que quien contempla las fotografías no puede ayudarles pero se puede identificar con ellos. Si se comparan con la visión general de una batalla o del traslado masivo de los refugiados, uno se puede sentir simplemente abrumado y paralizado. Pero el impulso natural de cualquiera que contempla la fotografía de un individuo que sufre el dolor o la necesidad es el de tender la mano y ofrecer ayuda.

Capa pasó la mayor parte del tiempo en el barrio obrero de Vallecas, que sufrió muchos bombardeos. Allí fotografió mujeres vestidas de negro con la cara macilenta y que se las apañaban para reír entre ellas mientras permanecían en fila entre las ruinas esperando su ración de comida diaria. Sin embargo, los que se habían quedado sin hogar y que se refugiaron en los andenes del metro de Madrid no encontraban motivo para reír. Las fotografías de Capa, en las que los vemos tumbados en colchones o sentados en los bancos de la estación de Gran Vía sólo muestran miedo, tristeza, resignación y aburrimiento.

Había, no obstante, un motivo de alegría ya que el 5 de diciembre, cuando Capa dejó Madrid, parecía seguro que la ciudad no caería. Cuando volvió a París sus fotografías fueron todo un éxito. *Regards* les dedicó gran parte de sus cuatro números siguientes.[13] A pesar de que en esa época las publicaciones francesas no tenían a menudo en cuenta a los fotógrafos, en la portada del número de *Regards* del 10 de diciembre se leía el siguiente titular:

LA CAPITAL CRUCIFICADA:
las prodigiosas fotografías
de
CAPA
NUESTRO ENVIADO ESPECIAL EN MADRID.

En el interior de la revista, el editorial decía: "*Regards*, con el deseo de ofrecer a sus lectores una imagen verídica e irrefutable de la tragedia que viven los habitantes de Madrid, bombardeados por los fascistas, ha enviado a la capital española a uno de sus fotógrafos más cualificados y audaces."

Regards, 10 de diciembre, 1936. "La Capitale Crucifiée" (La capital crucificada).

En pleno mes de febrero de 1937, Capa y Taro se dirigieron al sur de España. Primero fueron a Almería, a un pueblo encalado de la costa andaluza al que habían huido miles de refugiados procedentes de Málaga. La gran mayoría había realizado el trayecto a pie; y habían hecho 270 agotadores kilómetros caminando y bajo los constantes ataques de los aviones nacionales. En la ciudad de Almería, al igual que en Murcia, adonde habían trasladado a algunos refugiados, Capa y Gerda se concentraron en escenas muy similares a las de las estaciones de metro de Madrid, e incluso más desgarradoras aún. Aquí, la gente acampaba en el pavimento a la intemperie. Ancianas y niños se amontonaban sobre pilas de ropa y sábanas. Las cabezas y los pies de muchos estaban vendadas. Incluso los rostros de los niños más pequeños, normalmente ajenos a la tragedia, mostraban desesperación.

Tras una semana en las montañas entre Almería y Málaga, en las que no presenciaron ninguna batalla, los fotógrafos se dirigieron al frente del Jarama, en el que los nacionales trataban de cortar la carretera vital Madrid-Valencia. Sin embargo, cuando Capa y Taro llegaron, los republicanos mantenían la carretera a salvo, al menos de momento. Tampoco vieron ninguna batalla cuando volvieron a Madrid y visitaron el elaborado sistema de trincheras, túneles y cuevas que habían cavado los republicanos alrededor del Hospital Clínico en la Ciudad Universitaria y que controlaban los nacionales.

A comienzos del mes de marzo, Capa aceptó un trabajo como fotógrafo de plantilla para *Ce soir*, un periódico del Frente Popular, de reciente creación, cuyo redactor jefe, Louis Aragon, era un afamado comunista. El periódico publicaría muchos de los reportajes más importantes de Capa en España.

Tras cerca de una semana de visitas a los frentes de las afueras de la ciudad, que una vez más estaban paralizados, Capa vio claro que las noticias realmente interesantes procederían de Bilbao y no de Madrid. Después del revés nacional en el frente de Guadalajara, al noreste de Madrid, Franco—ávido de ganar el control del mineral de hierro, carbón y la industria del norte—había decidi-

Regards, 16 de diciembre, 1936. "Nos Envoyés Spéciaux..." (Nuestros enviados franceses en el frente con los voluntarios de la libertad).

do trasladar el grueso de sus fuerzas de los alrededores de la ciudad y enviarlas a luchar contra las provincias vascas.

Cuando Capa llegó a comienzos de mayo, las tropas nacionales se estaban acercando a la ciudad desde el este por un amplio frente. Después de tomar las poblaciones indefensas de Durango y Guernica tras despiadados bombardeos, alcanzaron la sierra de bajas montañas que servía como última línea de defensa natural de Bilbao. El 7 de mayo atacaron el monte Sollube, una de las montañas más importantes desde el punto de vista estratégico, y Capa cubrió la batalla desde las trincheras vascas.[14]

Pasó los diez días siguientes documentando la vida de la ciudad sitiada, donde las sirenas que advertían de los ataques aéreos a menudo sonaban quince o veinte veces en una mañana. Mientras el pueblo corría hacia los refugios desesperadamente, Capa permanecía tranquilamente en las calles tomando fotografías hasta que se quedaban vacías. La mejor fotografía de esa época muestra a una madre y a su hija cogidas de la mano y corriendo; presa del pánico, la niña se ha abrochado mal el abrigo. Capa tenía la virtud de capturar ese tipo de detalles impactantes y reveladores.

A finales del mes de mayo, Capa y Taro volvieron a Madrid y se hospedaron en el hotel Florida, el preferido por los periodistas por su proximidad a la oficina de prensa de Telefónica, que por entonces era el edificio más alto de la ciudad. Esta proximidad también tenía, sin embargo, un inconveniente desagradable ya que, de vez en cuando, una bomba nacional dirigida contra Telefónica aterrizaba en el hotel, causando pequeños daños aparte de romper ventanas y reventar el sistema de agua caliente, y, en cualquier caso, conmocionando a los residentes.

Entre los periodistas que se hospedaban en el Florida se encontraba Ernest Hemingway, quien había llegado a Madrid a finales de marzo para colaborar con John Dos Passos y el realizador de documentales alemán Joris Ivens en una película que, finalmente, se llamó *The Spanish Earth* (La tierra española).

El 31 de mayo, Capa y Taro estaban en el Paso de Navacerrada, cerca de Segovia, para cubrir la ofensiva republicana frustrada que Hemingway describió en *Por quién doblan las campanas*. El primer día de la batalla, los dos fotógrafos se turnaron una cámara de cine Eyemo para rodar la serie de noticiarios *The March of Time* de Time Inc. y una Leica para las imágenes estáticas. Hemingway no estuvo presente, y la mayoría de las descripciones de su novela se basaron en las fotografías y en los informes de Capa como testigo ocular.

De vuelta en Madrid, que estaba soportando uno de los bombardeos más duros de todo el asedio, Capa y Taro fotografiaron y filmaron dinamiteros que utilizaban tácticas de guerrilla luchando de una casa a otra en el sector sudoeste del barrio de Carabanchel, y también cubrieron el funeral de estado del general Lukács, que había muerto en un ataque contra Huesca el 12 de junio, cuando su coche fue alcanzado por una bomba enemiga.[15]

Lo más importante que había tenido lugar en Madrid y aledaños había sido la resistencia republicana frente a una ofensiva nacional sobre la rica región minera alrededor de Peñarroya, Pozoblanco y Almadén, por lo que los fotógrafos se dirigieron hacia el sur y el 24 de junio llegaron al cuartel general del Batallón Chapaiev, situado cerca de Peñarroya. El primer día, Capa y Gerda fotografiaron y filmaron una reconstrucción del victorioso ataque del batallón sobre la población de La Granjuela que había tenido lugar el 5 de abril.[16]

Después, Capa volvió a París, pero Taro permaneció en España para cubrir el congreso de la Asociación Internacional de Escritores en Defensa de la Cultura. Sin embargo, Gerda pronto decidió que era mucho más importante cubrir la gran ofensiva republicana recién iniciada contra Brunete, al oeste de Madrid. Día tras día conducía desde Madrid para documentar la batalla, que fue, con diferencia, la más sangrienta que hasta ese momento había tenido lugar en toda la Guerra Civil.[17]

A última hora de la tarde del domingo 25 de julio, durante una confusa retirada, Taro saltó sobre el estribo del coche en marcha de un general para huir del peligro. ¡Ay!, el coche fue embestido por un tanque fuera de control y Taro resultó gravemente aplastada. Murió a primera hora de la mañana siguiente. Se la admiró mundialmente por tratarse de la primera mujer fotógrafo muerta en combate, y se convirtió en una heroína para miles de mujeres jóvenes.

Cuando Capa se enteró de la terrible noticia quedó desconsolado. Tras el espléndido funeral que el Partido Comunista Francés tributó a Taro y tras su entierro en el cementerio del Père-Lachaise, Capa fue a Nueva York, donde vivían su madre y su hermano. Incapaz de soportar la mera idea de volver a España, hizo planes para acompañar a Joris Ivens a China y realizar un documental sobre la resistencia China a la invasión japonesa que había comenzado el año anterior. Como Japón era aliada de Alemania, China era considerada por todos como el frente oriental de la guerra antifascista en España.

Poco antes de partir para China, Capa se sintió atraído por la idea de volver a España para cubrir una batalla que consideraba demasiado importante para ignorarla a pesar de su dolor personal. La mañana del 15 de diciembre de 1937, los republicanos iniciaron un ataque masivo sobre la ciudad amurallada de Teruel, un bastión nacional en las montañas yermas del sur de Aragón. Era evidente que los nacionales planeaban usar Teruel como punto de partida de la campaña que pretendía crear un corredor hacia el Mediterráneo para, de este modo, separar Barcelona de Valencia y Madrid. Los republicanos albergaban la esperanza de que su ofensiva no sólo detendría el empuje nacional hacia el mar, sino que también proporcionaría la victoria psicológica decisiva que la ofensiva de Brunete no había logrado.

Capa llegó a Teruel el día 21, y acompañó a un destacamento de dinamiteros que encabezaban un ataque directo contra la ciudad y que culminaron abriéndose camino con granadas. Tras acompañar a las primeras tropas republicanas que entraron en la ciudad, y con la victoria republicana aparentemente asegurada, Capa volvió de inmediato a Valencia esa misma noche para enviar su exclusiva.

Durante los tres días siguientes condujo con Hemingway y otros dos periodistas para presenciar el duro asedio, volviendo cada noche a la relativa comodidad de Valencia.

Más tarde, el día de Año Nuevo, los periódicos y las emisoras de radio nacionales proclamaron que su bando había recuperado Teruel. Debido a que las líneas de comunicación alrededor de Teruel habían sido destruidas, ni siquiera los oficiales militares de Barcelona podían refutar estas proclamas con certeza. Capa y Herbert Matthews, reportero del *New York Herald Tribune*, salieron a investigar. Después de una dura jornada a través de carreteras obstruidas por la nieve, averiguaron que, a pesar de que los nacionales habían ganado una gran cantidad de terreno, la mayor parte de Teruel permanecía aún en manos republicanas. Capa y Matthews cubrieron un ataque republicano contra la mayor concentración de nacionales en las ruinas carbonizadas del palacio del Gobernador Civil; después de volar la fachada, los republicanos se amontonaban sobre los escombros y en el interior del edificio donde, escribió Capa, que se mezcló entre ellos, tuvo lugar "una despiadada lucha con granadas".[18]

Cuando aquella noche Capa dejaba Teruel para volver a París, los republicanos conservaban el palacio y al final de la semana, de nuevo, toda la ciudad estaba en sus manos. Pero no pudieron conservarla durante mucho tiempo. Hacia finales de febrero, los nacionales volverían a tomar Teruel, y el Viernes Santo Franco alcanzaría el mar.

Capa pasó la mayor parte de los primeros nueve meses de 1938 en China. Cuando finalmente regresó a España en octubre, las noticias eran malas. En un intento por granjearse la amistad de Hitler, Stalin había ordenado la desintegración de las Brigadas Internacionales, más o menos garantizando, de este modo, la victoria de Franco, aliado de Hitler. El 16 de octubre, en las colinas cercanas a Falset, algunos kilómetros al este del río Ebro, Capa fotografió la marcha de los hombres de las brigadas cuando pasaban su última revista.

El 25 de octubre, Capa condujo hasta el Montblanch, donde el Gobierno y los jefes militares habían ido a despedir a una amplia delegación de voluntarios de todas las nacionalidades. Capa se concentró en los rostros enérgicos de los hombres, cuyos semblantes

Regards, 27 de mayo, 1937. "Bilbao Sous le Feu" (Bilbao bajo el fuego).

reflejaban la certeza de que la partida de las brigadas significaría la derrota de la República. Cuatro días más tarde, Capa y Chim cubrieron el desfile de despedida dedicado a los voluntarios, entusiasta pero agridulce.[19]

El 5 de noviembre, Capa y Hemingway condujeron a Mora de Ebro y cruzaron el traicionero río Ebro en un pequeño bote para pasar un día con el general Líster y su 5° Cuerpo de Ejército, que a duras penas resistía una tremenda ofensiva nacional.[20]

La noche siguiente, en un intento por distraer a los nacionales de la batalla de Mora de Ebro, tropas republicanas vadearon el río Segre, afluente del Ebro, unos sesenta y cinco kilómetros al norte. Cuando en la madrugada del día 7 llegaron noticias de la ofensiva a Barcelona, Capa se dirigió al frente sin dilación. Lo encontró al sudoeste de Urida, cerca de la ciudad de Fraga, donde la lucha era especialmente cruenta. En este terreno estéril, rocoso y montañoso, mientras miles de hombres hacían un último y fútil intento por frustrar la inminente victoria nacional en el Ebro, Capa sacó algunas de las fotografías de primera línea de fuego más dramáticas de toda su carrera. Mirándolas, casi podríamos creer percibir el olor acre de la pólvora y sentir temblar la tierra por la explosión cercana de una bomba.[21]

Life dedicó dos páginas al relato; *Regards* le dedicó cinco páginas y la contraportada; y la nueva revista británica de Stefan Lorant, *Picture Post*, dedicó once páginas a las fotografías, y a una de ellas (varios hombres refugiándose bajo una roca saliente mientras las bombas explotaban junto a ellos) la llamó "la más asombrosa imagen de guerra jamás captada". La revista prologó el reportaje con una fotografía de Capa a toda página, cuyo pie decía "el mejor fotógrafo de guerra del mundo: Robert Capa".
Cuando volvió a España, hacia el 10 de enero de 1939, se dirigió primero al frente de Cataluña para fotografiar al general Líster y a sus hombres, pero se estableció una tregua y, por lo tanto, permaneció en Barcelona.

A pesar de que algunos esperaban que la ciudad siguiera el heroico ejemplo de autodefensa de Madrid, los más realistas supusieron correctamente que la ciudad hambrienta, exhausta y escasamente armada, terriblemente bombardeada en aquel momento, ofrecería poca resistencia.

Durante la noche del 12 de enero, Barcelona se cubrió de carteles anunciando la movilización general de todos los hombres menores de cincuenta años para la defensa de Cataluña, y a mediodía del día 13, los centros de movilización estaban llenos hasta rebosar. Aquella tarde, Capa se dirigió a uno de dichos centros, un estadio a las afueras de la ciudad. En su impactante serie de fotografías de los hombres con sus familias, captó el miedo, el pesar y la resignación de las despedidas.

Dos días después, el 15 de enero, Capa se encontraba en la carretera de la costa sur de Barcelona para fotografiar a los refugiados que habían esperado hasta el último minuto para abandonar Tarragona. Algunos habían apilado tantas posesiones en sus carros que tenían que ayudar a las demacradas mulas empujando desde atrás. De repente, se precipitaban aviones sobre la carretera para ametrallar a los refugiados indefensos. Las fotografías más desgarradoras que Capa tomó aquel día pertenecen a una serie que muestra a una anciana que milagrosamente salió ilesa de un ataque que acabó con el resto de su grupo, así como con su perro y sus dos mulas. Capa la encontró dando vueltas sin descanso alrededor de su carro en estado de conmoción y desconcierto.[22]

Para acompañar su reportaje, Capa escribió:

He visto a cientos de miles de personas huir así en dos países, España y China. Y me aterroriza pensar que cientos de miles de otros que aún viven en paz en otros países, algún día encontrarán el mismo destino. Porque durante estos últimos tres años el mundo en el que queríamos vivir ha tomado esta dirección.[23]

Unos días más tarde, tras describir a una hermosa jovencita de ojos oscuros que había fotografiado mientras estaba sentada desanimada en una pila de sacos frente a un centro de refugiados de Barcelona, escribió: "No siempre es fácil estar presente y ser incapaz de hacer nada excepto documentar el sufrimiento que te rodea."[24]

El 21 de enero, los bombarderos Heinkel se habían convertido en una visión más cotidiana y temible que nunca sobre los cielos de Barcelona. A menudo, un respiro de no más de quince minutos separaba los ataques, día y noche. Después, alrededor de la una de la madrugada del miércoles 25 de enero, llegaron noticias alarmantes de que los nacionales habían cruzado ya el río Llobregat, a menos de quince kilómetros al oeste. Capa y algunos otros corresponsales se amontonaron en sus coches y condujeron hacia el norte por la carretera de la costa hasta Figueras, la última ciudad importante antes de llegar a la frontera con Francia. Uno de los compañeros de Capa escribió que ellos "adelantaron a miles y miles de refugiados, en carros, en mulas, a pie, suplicando un sitio en camiones y coches, y siempre luchando cansinamente por tratar de alcanzar la inhóspita frontera que aún permanecía inexorablemente cerrada para ellos", pues los franceses aún no permitían el acceso de los refugiados en Francia.[25]

A continuación, Capa pasó varios días en Figueras, fotografiando refugiados en la ciudad y en las carreteras circundantes. El 28 de enero, junto con algunos de los primeros 400.000 hombres, mujeres y niños que finalmente cruzaron la frontera, abandonó España para no volver jamás. Cuando estaba en Londres, en febrero de 1939, le llegaron noticias de que el Gobierno francés (que hasta entonces sólo había admitido civiles españoles) por fin había permitido que el ejército de 200.000 soldados republicanos en retirada atravesara la frontera, aunque deberían permanecer en centros de recogida de refugiados cerca de Perpiñán. Lorant encargó

Picture Post, 3 de diciembre de 1938. "This is War!" (¡Esto es la guerra!).

inmediatamente a Capa un reportaje en los campos, pero el fotógrafo no soportaba aún la idea de enfrentarse a la humillación que sus camaradas españoles estaban sufriendo a manos de los franceses, los cuales, como escribiría después, "recibieron a los exhaustos refugiados españoles con la cruel indiferencia de un pueblo bien abrigado y bien comido".

Hasta mediados de marzo no realizó el viaje al enorme campo de la playa de Argelès-sur-Mer, donde estaban internados cerca de 75.000 hombres. El campo, rodeado de alambre espinoso y patrullado por soldados senegaleses montados, que eran una reminiscencia hiriente de los moros de Franco, era, como escribió Capa "un infierno en la arena". La mayoría de los hombres vivían aún en tiendas de campaña improvisadas y en cabañas de paja que ofrecían escasa protección contra la abrasiva arena levantada por el viento. Para hacerlo aún más difícil, no había agua corriente, sólo agua salobre extraída de hoyos excavados en la arena.[26]

Cuando llegó Capa se había construido un campo algo más confortable en Le Barcarès, treinta kilómetros al norte. Una gran serie de fotografías muestra una fila de hombres, aparentemente infinita, encabezada por gendarmes, que caminaba por la costa hacia el nuevo campo.

Durante la primera semana de mayo, Capa fue a Biarritz para fotografiar los cómodos orfanatos que el Plan de Padres Adoptivos para Niños Españoles había establecido en cinco fincas próximas. Cada niño tenía su correspondiente padrino o madrina, como por ejemplo Eleanor Roosevelt, Helen Hayes, Tallulah Bankhead, Archibald MacLeish, Rockwell Kent, y el reparto del éxito de Broadway, *The American Way*, y aquellos que habían sido "adoptados" por una persona famosa se enorgullecían especialmente de ello. Capa tomó varias fotografías de Lorenzo Murias, un niño de doce años apodado "Rooseveltito" en honor a su "madre adoptiva".[27]

IV

A comienzos de noviembre de 1944, Capa condujo desde un París liberado hasta Toulouse para asistir a una reunión de tres días de la Unión Nacional Española. Toulouse, que se había convertido en el centro de las actividades de los republicanos españoles en Francia, estaba lleno de españoles que creían que por el hecho de haber ayudado a liberar Francia, los Aliados ahora tenían la responsabilidad de ayudarles a liberar España. En efecto, los Aliados, en secreto, habían planeado una estrategia similar, pero abandonaron la idea.

Durante el mes de octubre, de hecho, varios grupos de exiliados españoles trataron de hacerse cargo de la situación por su cuenta. El 22 de octubre, un grupo de unos 150 hombres (los informes del Gobierno español hablaban de millares de un modo exagerado) cruzó la frontera al sudeste de Bagnères-de-Luchon y, por poco tiempo, tuvieron bajo su control varias poblaciones del valle de Arán. Las tropas gubernamentales entraron rápidamente; asesinaron, hirieron y capturaron a muchos, y provocaron la huida del resto de nuevo hacia las montañas. Desde Toulouse, Capa subió a las montañas para ver por dónde cruzaban la frontera, y después se dirigió a un hospital para visitar a algunos de los supervivientes, muchos de los cuales tenían heridas leves y los pies congelados. Las fotografías que tomó de sus rostros revelan que, incluso tras años de exilio y lucha, estos hombres conservaban el valor, la determinación y el humor cálido que le habían atraído tanto durante la Guerra Civil española.[28]

Capa nunca volvió a España.

NOTA TÉCNICA

Entre 1990 y 1992, Cornell Capa y yo volvimos a examinar todos los contactos de Robert Capa. De los aproximadamente setenta mil negativos que expuso en vida, escogimos 937 imágenes para realizar un estudio exhaustivo—aunque ciertamente no completo—de su mejor obra. De esas 937 imágenes, muchas de las cuales nunca se habían publicado o exhibido, 205 eran de la Guerra Civil española. Bajo nuestra estrecha supervisión, los expertos impresores Igor Bakht y Teresa Engle Moreno realizaron una edición estrictamente limitada de tres series de 937 copias en papel de 40 x 50 cm. Este proyecto se hizo posible gracias a la generosa ayuda del Tokyo Fuji Art Museum, que adquirió la primera serie. Cornell Capa donó la segunda serie a la colección permanente del International Center of Photography de Nueva York. Debido al origen europeo de Robert Capa, la tercera se destinará a un museo europeo.

Para su donación al Museo Nacional Centro de Arte Reina Sofía de Madrid, Cornell Capa ha encargado a Teresa Engle Moreno la realización de una nueva serie de 205 copias de las fotografías de la Guerra Civil española en papel de 38,8 x 48,8 cm con el objeto de evitar cualquier confusión entre estas copias y las de las tres series de 937 copias.

Sería imposible reunir una serie en verdad definitiva de las mejores fotografías que Robert Capa tomara durante la Guerra Civil española pues, de vez en cuando, se descubren imágenes desconocidas anteriormente, y muchas de ellas resultan ser realmente brillantes.

Uno de los descubrimientos más emocionantes de los últimos años fue un maletín, que contenía noventa y siete fotografías y papeles diversos, que había pertenecido a Juan Negrín, primer ministro de la República española. La mayor parte de las fotografías eran de Capa, aunque algunas eran de Taro o de Chim (David Seymour), amigo de ambos. Algunas de las fotografías más intensas de la colección son copias únicas de imágenes cuyos negativos se perdieron a comienzos de la década de 1940. Evidentemente, Capa, que era amigo de Negrín, le entregó las noventa y siete copias al primer ministro, el cual se las llevó a su exilio en Francia. Cuando estalló la Segunda Guerra Mundial y, por consiguiente, tuvo que huir a Francia de incógnito, le entregó el maletín al cónsul sueco en Vichy para que las pusiera a salvo, ya que Negrín sabía que si le aprehendían con una prueba así de su anterior puesto, estaría en grave peligro. Finalmente, el maletín se envió a Estocolmo y lo depositaron en los archivos del ministro de Asuntos Exteriores sueco. A finales de la década de 1970, un empleado del ministro descubrió el maletín, lo abrió y comprendió que debía devolverse al Gobierno español. El embajador sueco lo envió a Madrid en marzo de 1979. El Ministerio de Asuntos Exteriores español editó un catálogo con reproducciones de las noventa y siete fotografías, que ahora forman parte de la colección del Archivo de la Guerra Civil, situado en Salamanca. Este archivo posee pruebas positivas o microfilms de unas dieciocho mil fotografías más de la Guerra Civil española, entre las cuales probablemente habrá alguna de Capa. Los archivos del Partido Comunista Español en Madrid también contiene miles de fotografías de la Guerra Civil, entre las que sin duda se encuentra alguna de Capa.

En lo referente al número de imágenes de la Guerra Civil de Capa desconocidas anteriormente, los cuadernos redescubiertos durante la década de 1980 en los Archivos Nacionales de París son incluso más importantes que la colección de Negrín. Los ocho cuadernos contienen aproximadamente dos mil quinientos contactos de la película de 35 mm de Capa, muchas de las cuales están cortadas en fotogramas individuales, pegadas a las páginas e identificadas por temas. Hay un gran número de fotografías de gran calidad de las que no existen negativos. Con el reciente descubrimiento de técnicas de escáner por láser, estos diminutos contactos se pueden utilizar como si fueran negativos para hacer ampliaciones de gran calidad, con las que sin duda aumentaremos nuestro conocimiento del reportaje que realizó Capa en la Guerra Civil española.

Parece ser que el departamento del Ministerio de Interior francés encargado de investigar a los ciudadanos extranjeros confiscó estos cuadernos del estudio de Capa en París durante el otoño de 1939, poco después del estallido de la Segunda Guerra Mundial. Como europeo del este que había publicado en periódicos de orientación izquierdista, Capa despertó sospechas automáticamente. Afortunadamente, en octubre de 1939 pudo abandonar Francia para dirigirse a Nueva York. En 1952, los cuadernos de Capa estaban incluidos en un traslado masivo del Ministerio de Interior a los Archivos Nacionales. Y permanecieron allí, inadvertidos, hasta que un investigador tropezó con ellos más de treinta años después. Algunas de estas páginas se reproducen en este catálogo.

Barcelona, agosto, 1936